Andrew Fuller was a model pastor with the mind ( There is a great deal we can learn from this faithfu. do that in an engaging and inspiring manner. Brewster has spent time with Fuller in the study, the pulpit, and the pastorate. He knows this man. This book will lead you to appreciate more fully a wonderful Baptist minister who has so much to teach those who serve the Church of the Lord Jesus in the 21st century.

Daniel L. Akin, president
Southeastern Baptist Theological Seminary

Brewster has done the church a favor with his worthy introduction to the life and thought of one of its greats, Andrew Fuller. *Andrew Fuller: Model Pastor and Theologian* offers the reader both a model and a method for doing the work of ministry in a manner that is theologically-informed and still imminently practical. In an era when so many pastors, and those in their flocks, fail to connect heart to head, orthodoxy to orthopraxy, Fuller and Brewster remind us that it's not only possible, it's necessary. May God raise up another generation of pastor-theologians who, like Fuller, take their theology to heart.

Peter Beck
Assistant Professor of Religion
Charleston Southern University

Andrew Fuller, typically overshadowed by his contemporary William Carey, the great missionary pioneer of the 19th century, remains mostly an unfamiliar figure among Baptists today. Paul Brewster skillfully shines a bright light on Fuller's contributions to our Baptist heritage. Brewster demonstrates convincingly how Fuller is a good model for pastors during theologically charged times. Fuller avoided the theological extremes of his day and possessed an unwavering commitment to Scripture and the centrality of the gospel for ministry. Those of us who shepherd the flock can benefit greatly from such an example.

Daryl Cornett, senior pastor
First Baptist Church, Hazard, Kentucky

Andrew Fuller is one of the most influential pastor-theologians in Baptist history. In this excellent study, Paul Brewster does a fine job of demonstrating Fuller's theological approach to ministry and its relevance for our own day. Fuller's dual commitments to God's sovereignty in salvation and the preaching of the gospel to all people provide an approach that many Southern Baptists (and others) will find helpful as we continue to debate the resurgence of Calvinism among contemporary believers. Brewster's work makes an important contribution and I hope it gains a wide readership among pastors and scholars alike.

Nathan A. Finn
Assistant Professor of Church History and Baptist Studies
Southeastern Baptist Theological Seminary

Future historians of the Baptist heritage will likely recognize Andrew Fuller as the most significant theologian produced by the movement during its first four hundred years. Long relegated to the realm of affectionate obscurity, Fuller is making a comeback these days. This fine study of his life and thought is evidence of a "Fuller renaissance" which I am happy to cheer on.

Timothy George, Founding Dean, Beeson Divinity School of Samford University
General Editor of the Reformation Commentary on Scripture

Andrew Fuller is the quintessential pastor-theologian, an excellent model from which contemporary pastors could learn much. His defense of evangelical Calvinism also has great potential for aiding Baptist discussions of soteriology today as it did 200 years ago. Paul Brewster himself is an exemplary pastor-theologian, with more than twenty years experience as a pastor and many years devoted to theological study and reflection on Andrew Fuller. I am happy that the fruits of his study are being made available and heartily commend his work to Baptist pastors, theologians, and church leaders.

John S. Hammett
Professor of Systematic Theology
Associate Dean of Theological Studies
Southeastern Baptist Theological Studies

Andrew Fuller saved Baptist theology from both the winter-chill of hyper-Calvinism and the winter-chill of liberalism. He was a missional theologian before anyone ever thought of such terminology. In Paul Brewster's book you'll get a glimpse at Fuller, the man and the mission. Read it, and pray that God would raise up a new generation of Andrew Fullers.

Russell D. Moore
Dean, School of Theology
Senior Vice President for Academic Administration
Professor of Christian Theology and Ethics
The Southern Baptist Theological Seminary

Good theology is always pastoral, and effective pastoral ministry is always theological. Andrew Fuller is an exemplary pastor-theologian, and Paul Brewster does an exemplary job of introducing his life, theology, and ministry to us. Read this book and your ministry and your theology will be better for it.

David Nelson
Southeastern Baptist Theological Seminary

In any age, but particularly in this increasingly secularized environment, churches need pastor-theologians. Paul Brewster holds before us Andrew Fuller as a worthy model of how a pastor may challenge his theological and philosophical culture and change the trajectory of thought. Brewster's work is saturated with knowledge of the primary sources from which he draws and demonstrates his own conclusions about Fuller. Fully aware of a massive amount of other works on Fuller, he negotiates his originally-developed position with a respectful interplay with these secondary sources. He articulates Fuller's value as a theologian, an apologist, a practitioner of Christian ministry emphasizing preaching and evangelism, and as denominational servant. He investigates Fuller's relevance as a pathmaker for contemporary denominational tensions on Calvinism per se and Calvinism vis a vis Great Commission interests. I heartily recommend this serious work to provoke theological reflection, encourage theologically grounded evangelism, give a model of serious pastoral ministry, and inform responsible evaluation of our present opportunities.

Tom J. Nettles
Professor of Historical Theology
The Southern Baptist Theological Seminary

Paul Brewster's analysis of the life and theology of Andrew Fuller is both insightful and engaging. In particular, the author properly explains Fuller's contributions within the context of English Baptist history during the late eighteenth and early nineteenth centuries. Brewster likewise demonstrates the intimate connections between Fuller's roles as pastor, mission board secretary, and theologian. Most important, the book astutely addresses the significance of Fuller's thought for discussions today about the relationship of Calvinism and Baptist identity.

James A. Patterson, Ph.D.
University Professor and Associate Dean
Union University

Baptist pastors owe a debt of gratitude to Paul Brewster for giving a highly readable, theologically practical study of an important, if often overlooked Baptist of the 19th century. Andrew Fuller is not generally known among us as a theologically-driven pastor though he should be. From his intramural writings aimed at British Baptists to his wider conversations among the English hyper-Calvinists, Fuller demonstrates that a life given to serious theological reflection can be of great blessing to the Church. May Fuller serve as a model for young men embarking on vocation of service in the church. Every pastor is called to be a theologian!

Jeff Straub
Associate Professor of Historical and Systematic Theology
Central Baptist Theological Seminary

# Andrew Fuller

# Andrew Fuller

## MODEL PASTOR-THEOLOGIAN

## PAUL BREWSTER

**STUDIES IN BAPTIST LIFE AND THOUGHT**

MICHAEL A. G. HAYKIN, SERIES EDITOR

NASHVILLE, TENNESSEE

Andrew Fuller:
Model Pastor and Theologian

ISBN: 978-0-8054-4982-2

Published by B&H Publishing Group
Nashville, Tennessee

Dewey Decimal Classification: B
Subject Heading: FULLER, ANDREW \ PASTORAL THEOLOGY \
CHRISTIAN MINISTRY

Printed in the United States of America

2  3  4  5  6  7  8  9  10  11  12 • 20 19 18 17 16

VP

*To my wife Debbie and our four children:*

*Being your husband and father is
the highest privilege and sweetest responsibility
I have known on earth*

# Contents

List of Abbreviations   xiii
Preface   xv

*Chapter 1*
Introduction: The Decline of Doctrine in Baptist Churches   1

*Chapter 2*
The Theological Method of Andrew Fuller   37

*Chapter 3*
The Soteriology of Andrew Fuller   65

*Chapter 4*
From Doctrine to Practice   109

*Chapter 5*
Conclusion: Andrew Fuller as a Pastor-Theologian   159

*Appendix 1*
Andrew Fuller's Confession of Faith   181

*Appendix 2*
Fuller's Theological Dictionary Entry on Calvinism   189

Bibliography   193
Name Index   203
Subject Index   205

# Abbreviations

| | |
|---|---|
| *BHH* | *The Baptist History and Heritage* |
| BMS | Baptist Missionary Society |
| *BQ* | *The Baptist Quarterly* |
| *FJ* | *The Founders Journal* |
| *JHI* | *Journal of the History of Ideas* |
| *JTS* | *Journal of Theological Studies* |
| NASB | New American Standard Bible |
| SBC | Southern Baptist Convention |
| SBHT | Studies in Baptist History and Thought |

# Preface

I t is fascinating to observe that major theologians frequently experience a period, or even several periods, of obscurity subsequent to the initial reception of their thought. The work of the remarkable American theologian Jonathan Edwards, for example, experienced such a period from the late nineteenth century till his "rediscovery" by Joseph Haroutunian and Perry Miller in the middle of the twentieth century. Since then, research, theses, and monographs on Edwards have skyrocketed. And although Andrew Fuller cannot be considered to be as important a theologian as Edwards,[1] the study of his thinking is also currently undergoing a small renaissance.

Such a recovery of his thought is extremely welcome for a number of reasons. In the recent upsurge of interest in Calvinism and its theological perspective, there is the real danger of so stressing the sovereignty of God that the genuine moral agency of men and women is lost. Fuller's battle royal against the unbiblical theology and piety of hyper-Calvinism can serve as' a much-needed corrective for this misguided emphasis. Equally, Fuller's vital involvement in the "Great Commission Resurgence" of his day provides extremely helpful guidelines for ours on how to sustain a missionary mind-set in both the pulpit and the pew.

Finally—and this is where this new volume by Paul Brewster is so helpful—Fuller is the very model of a pastor-theologian. His life and ministry well display what was once the traditional—and I would argue, the biblical—understanding of the pastor as a shepherd of souls, man of prayer, and theological guide. Fuller himself was a man of deep piety, significant friendships—many in his day and after could echo the words of his very close friend William Carey, "I loved him"—and, in time, vast theological erudition. In the words of

---

[1] Joseph Belcher, the editor of the final edition of Fuller's collected works, believed that Fuller's works would "go down to posterity side by side with the immortal works of the elder president Edwards [i.e., Jonathan Edwards Sr.]" ("Preface to the Complete American Edition," in A. Fuller, *The Complete Works of the Rev. Andrew Fuller* [Philadelphia: American Baptist Publication Society, 1845; repr. Harrisonburg, VA: Sprinkle, 1988], 1:viii).

John Newton, though Fuller "had not the advantage of a college, or an academy, or even of a grammar school" and "when he first began to preach he was not only *unlearned,* but quite *illiterate*," by devotion to Christ, divine grace, and dint of hard study, he became one of the most noteworthy theologians of the "long" eighteenth century.[2]

Paul Brewster, both a pastor and academic theologian, is well equipped to show us how Fuller fulfilled this role of pastor-theologian in his own day and how he can function as a model for ours. I fully admit to being biased when it comes to Fuller, but this is a tremendous study that deserves close attention by anyone aspiring to the office of pastor. I judge it to be one of the most important works on Baptist history published in 2010.

Michael A. G. Haykin
Dundas, Ontario
June 17, 2010

---

[2] J. Newton, Letter to H. More, 1794, in W. Roberts, *Memoirs of the Life and Correspondence of Mrs. Hannah More*, 3rd ed. (London: R. B. Seeley & W. Burnside, 1835), 2:408.

# Chapter 1

# Introduction

## The Decline of Doctrine
## in Baptist Churches

I n the last 200 years, Baptist churches have undergone a theological sea change. At the turn of the nineteenth century, theology dominated church life. Sermons were packed with doctrinal content, and theological debates between representatives of rival denominations were eagerly followed by laity and clergy alike. It was axiomatic that the spiritual health and vitality of a church was inseparably linked to the theological soundness of its pastor. A popular English Baptist periodical, *The Baptist Annual Register*, even devoted space to printing a detailed theological dictionary in serial form to foster theological literacy among its readership, many of whom were laity.[1] But about a century later, the celebrated evangelist Billy Sunday (1862–1935) found he could increase his stature in the eyes of most congregations when he declared, "I don't know any more about theology than a jackrabbit does about ping pong, but I'm on the way to glory."[2]

Little has changed since Sunday's quip. If anything, the theological and doctrinal emphasis in Baptist ministry has continued to fade. The prevailing attitude in many Baptist circles seems to be that theology is an indifferent matter. Only a handful of pastors, and far less of the laity, are theologically engaged. Church health is seen much more as a function of using good management and methodology than as a hard-won prize integrally linked to sound theological preaching and teaching. The center of theological discussion has migrated away from churches and taken residence in seminaries. With that

---

[1] J. Rippon, *The Baptist Annual Register* 3 (1798–1801): 461–63, 500–502, 664–66, etc.

[2] W. T. Ellis, *"Billy" Sunday: The Man and His Message* (Philadelphia: Universal Book & Bible House, 1914), 147.

shift has come a corresponding change in the pastoral role. For the most part, "pastor" and "theologian" are now seen as separate callings.[3]

This state of affairs ought to be a cause for concern among Baptists. Past generations certainly were right to argue that theology and church health are inextricably linked. It is no accident that the Pauline Epistles speak first of doctrinal underpinnings and then move on to explore the outworkings of these truths in the daily life of Christians who compose the churches. When it came to advising a novice in the ministry, this same apostle stressed the role of doctrine: "Till I come, give attendance to reading, to exhortation, to doctrine" (1 Tim 4:13). Doctrine and practice are hardwired together throughout the New Testament.

It would seem that many contemporary churches have all but ignored this biblical precedent. David Wells is no doubt correct when he argues that "the evangelical Church has cheerfully plunged into astounding theological illiteracy."[4] Baptists are no exception to this observation. For example, the call to ministry in a Baptist church usually involves a great deal of interaction between the possible candidates and a pastor search committee. Speaking as one who has been involved in that process on several occasions, it is amazing how these exchanges have little to do with doctrinal or theological matters. Typically committees want to know much about a potential pastor's family, his leadership style, his experience as a counselor, and his plans for growing the church. If doctrine is even discussed at all, it is usually a few questions related

---

[3]A trend back toward a more theologically based ministry is on the rise in certain circles, including the Southern Baptist Convention. In 1997, the presidents of the six seminaries supported by that denomination signed a covenant with the churches that support them. This document plainly identifies the first-order task of these schools as "the theological formation of ministers." See "One Faith, One Task, One Sacred Trust: A Covenant Between Our Seminaries and Our Churches." Accessed June 6, 2006. Online: http://www.sbts.edu/ Mohler/FidelitasRead.php?article=fidel014. Nevertheless, S. W. Lemke, the provost at New Orleans Baptist Theological Seminary, admits that this goal has not necessarily taken full root. Lemke ("The Future of Southern Baptists as Evangelicals," unpublished paper presented to the Maintaining Baptists Distinctives Conference at Mid-America Baptist Theological Seminary, Cordova, TN, April 2005. Accessed July 24, 2006. Online: http://www.nobts.edu/Faculty/ItoR/LemkeSW/Personal/SBCfuture.pdf) recently wrote, "I have seen seminary students over the past decade making a significant move away from an interest in doctrinal matters. Theological issues which were matters of lengthy discussions in the past, such as soteriology, pneumatology, and eschatology no longer incite great student interest."

[4]D. F. Wells, *No Place for Truth, or Whatever Happened to Evangelical Theology?* (Grand Rapids: Eerdmans, 1993), 4.

to the potential candidate's views of Scripture, the gift of tongues, and eternal security.[5]

One reason for the decline of doctrine among Baptists is pragmatic. A great many Baptist leaders are cognizant that a period of decline has set in among their churches. Over the last 30 years, that has resulted in a tremendous focus on seeking to help churches grow again. An intuitive perception is that doctrinal specificity tends to make growing the church more difficult. Some think that the less said about doctrine, the less offense is given and the more people will be comfortable gathering under one umbrella.[6]

Although this mind-set is still at work, a new threat to doctrinally driven ministry has also surfaced in certain segments of the Emerging Church movement. Drawing from a chastened postmodern epistemology, some emergent leaders think that the church needs to focus on the transformation of people, not theological pronouncement. For example, one well-known emergent leader has recently stated, "Along the line of the post-evangelical, the emerging movement is suspicious of *systematic theology*."[7] McKnight goes on to clarify that theology per se is not the problem for emergents. It is theological and doctrinal certainty they fear. But when theology is seen to be "flux-like" (McKnight's

---

[5]For example, I once received a pastoral candidate questionnaire from a search committee that gave evidence of careful thought and preparation. But of some 50 questions, less than 10 percent had anything to do with doctrinal issues. Even more distressing, the focus of the questions that could be classed as doctrinal was in the direction of exploring the candidate's views on alien immersion and closed communion—hardly issues of cardinal doctrinal importance.

[6]Though speaking more generally of evangelicals and not specifically of Baptists, T. H. Rainer (*Giant Awakenings: Making the Most of 9 Surprising Trends That Can Benefit Your Church* [Nashville: B&H, 1995], 42) commented on this antidoctrinal trend: "Unfortunately, some church leaders heard the [church growth] movement's plea for application and methodology but failed to see the theological moorings to which these methodologies were anchored. As a consequence, these churches implemented programs, marketing plans, and new preaching styles without considering the theological foundation for their practices. They became completely 'user friendly' but 'biblically silent' in their efforts to engender growth." More positively, Rainer believes that there is evidence of a renewed commitment to theology among evangelical groups.

[7]S. McKnight, "What Is the Emerging Church?" unpublished paper presented at the Fall Contemporary Issues Conference, Westminster Theological Seminary, Philadelphia, PA, October 26, 2006 (emphasis in original). The full text of McKnight's address is available online at http://www.foolishsage.com/wpcontent/uploads/McKnight%20-%20What%20is%20the%20Emerging%20Church.pdf (accessed March 30, 2007). In contrast to this, other segments of the emerging movement show a significant commitment to doctrinal certainty and confidence.

phrase), it is much to be doubted that doctrinal exposition and theologically driven ministry can be maintained.

For whatever reasons, be they pragmatic or epistemological, churches have to a very large extent already made a shift away from doctrine-driven ministry. Sermon series on the attributes of God have given way to those that teach Christians how to handle stress and have a happy marriage. But surely downplaying theology has not enhanced the work of the church in proclamation. Wells has strongly challenged this modern innovation:

> We now have less biblical fidelity, less interest in truth, less seriousness, less depth, and less capacity to speak the Word of God to our generation in a way that offers an alternative to what it already thinks. The older orthodoxy was driven by a passion for truth, and that was why it could express itself only in theological terms. The newer evangelicalism is not driven by the same passion for truth, and that is why it is often empty of theological interest."[8]

Past generations of Baptists also assumed that congregational health traces back directly to the influences of pastors. For all the changes in worship services and styles that have occurred across nearly 400 years of Baptist history, the pastor's sermon remains the focal event in the vast majority of these churches. During those moments in the pulpit, pastors set the theological tone for their congregations. James Petigru Boyce (1827–88), a towering figure in American Baptist theological education, recognized the vital connection between the theological soundness of pastors and the congregations they serve and influence. Speaking of pastors who were not well grounded in theology, Boyce said, "It is needless to say of these that the churches do not grow under their ministry; that, not having partaken strong meat, they cannot impart it."[9]

Given that theology and church health are inseparable and that the primary theological influence in the church comes from the pastor, it is apparent that pastor-theologians are much needed today. But how will such men be formed for the Baptist ministry today? In the years before institutions for theological education were common in Baptist life, pastors almost invariably entered the

---

[8] Wells, *No Place for Truth*, 12.

[9] J. P. Boyce, "Three Changes in Theological Institutions," in *James Petigru Boyce: Selected Writings*, ed. T. George (Nashville: Broadman, 1989), 41.

ministry through an informal system of apprenticeship.[10] Older men took on assistants in local church ministry and served as models of pastoral work. They also were involved in the theological formation of these men through programs of directed reading. Once these novitiates were deemed ready to serve on their own, they were presented as candidates to churches seeking pastors. Not infrequently, these apprentices would step into the role of the senior minister at their mentor's death.

A few signs indicate that some contemporary Baptists recognize that the loss of such mentoring relationships has had a negative effect on the development of church leaders. Several mentoring efforts are on the rise again in isolated sections of Baptist life. For example, Capitol Hill Baptist Church, Washington, D.C., has instituted an intern program designed to expose young men entering the ministry to the pastoral and theological work of their own church leaders.[11] Another example of the growing awareness that something is lost in pastoral preparation when mentoring is absent is found in a recent paper by L. T. Strong, a professor at New Orleans Baptist Theological Seminary. Strong argued that the present Southern Baptist system of seminary training fails to provide adequate pastoral mentoring.[12] It is clear, however, that much more needs to be done to set good models of theologically based ministry before young ministers. Though not equivalent to a hands-on opportunity of

---

[10] Sometimes these apprenticeships did assume a more formal cast. For example, John Sutcliff (1752–1814) conducted a seminary out of his home. See M. A. G. Haykin, *One Heart and One Soul: John Sutcliff of Olney, His Friends and His Times* (Durham, UK: Evangelical Press, 1994), 251–54.

[11] Under the able leadership of pastor Mark Dever, this church has become a steady voice advocating pastoral and theological renewal among Southern Baptists. Nine Marks Ministries (http://www.9marks.org), which was birthed through the ministry of this church, carries on the work of mentoring through weekend conferences and site-based residential internships.

[12] L. T. Strong III, "Mentoring in a Seminary Community," paper presented at the Ola Farmer Lenaz Faculty Lectures, New Orleans Baptist Theological Seminary, New Orleans, LA, May 20, 1999. Accessed January 1, 2007. Online: http://www.baptistcenter.com/Church-Resources.html. Strong notes that integrating meaningful mentoring into large institutions such as those that characterize the six Southern Baptist seminaries will not be easily achieved. Another fine expression of theologically based mentoring is an organization called "Mentoring Men for the Master." The founder of this ministry is a veteran Southern Baptist pastor and educator, Bill Bennett. See their Web site for much helpful material related to mentoring: http://www.mentoringmenforthemaster.org. Cf. E. L. Smither, *Augustine as Mentor: A Model for Preparing Spiritual Leaders* (Nashville: B&H, 2008).

mentorship, studying some of the great pastor-theologians of previous generations may be the next-best substitute.[13]

## WHY ANDREW FULLER?

This book argues that British Baptist pastor Andrew Fuller (1754–1815) is a
model pastor-theologian as demonstrated in his theological method, his leadership during a critical soteriological controversy, and his manner of relating
doctrine and practice. As men can benefit from a personal mentoring relationship with older pastors, so too can they benefit from the study of some worthy
examples of past Baptist leaders.

At the time of his death in 1815, Fuller was the most prominent Baptist
theologian on either side of the Atlantic. His life was the subject of several
popular memoirs.[14] His many scattered publications were gathered and issued
in a considerable number of collected editions.[15] New releases of his writings
were still being issued as late as the eve of the American Civil War.[16] The next
hundred years saw comparatively little academic interest in Fuller. In 1963,
E. F. Clipsham wrote a four-part article on Fuller that appeared in *The Baptist
Quarterly*.[17] Since that time, there has been a growing awareness of the importance of Fuller and a corresponding increase in academic output related to his

---

[13]For a list of potential model pastor-theologians, see T. Ascol, "The Pastor as Theologian," *FJ*
(Winter 2001): 10; cf. T. George, "Southern Baptist Theology: Whence and Whither?" *FJ* 19/20
(1995): 29–30.

[14]J. Ryland Jr., *The Work of Faith, the Labour of Love, and the Patience of Hope, Illustrated;
in the Life and Death of the Rev. Andrew Fuller* (London: Button and Son, 1816); J. W. Morris,
*Memoirs of the Life and Writings of the Rev. Andrew Fuller, Late Pastor of the Baptist Church
in Kettering, and Secretary to the Baptist Missionary Society* (High Wycombe: n.p., 1816). Both
went through multiple editions and were printed in England and the United States.

[15]The first of these "complete" editions appeared as early as 1818. As time passed, many
additional works by Fuller, especially periodical pieces, were added to frequently updated editions. The standard American edition became *The Complete Works of the Rev. Andrew Fuller with
a Memoir of His Life by Andrew Gunton Fuller*, 3 vols., ed. J. Belcher (Philadelphia: American
Baptist Publication Society, 1845; repr., Harrisonburg, VA: Sprinkle, 1988).

[16]J. Belcher, ed., *The Last Remains of the Rev. Andrew Fuller: Sermons, Essays, Letters, and
Other Miscellaneous Papers, Not Included in His Published Works* (Philadelphia: American Baptist Publication Society, 1856).

[17]E. F. Clipsham, "Andrew Fuller and Fullerism: A Study in Evangelical Calvinism," *BQ* 20
(1963–64): 99–114, 146–54, 214–25, 268–76.

life and ministry.[18] The bulk of scholarly attention has been directed to Fuller's defense of evangelical Calvinism and his involvement with the Baptist Missionary Society.[19] This book hopes to contribute to the ongoing rediscovery of Fuller's significance by exploring ways in which he can be viewed as a worthwhile model of a Baptist pastor-theologian. Several things about the life and ministry of Fuller help qualify him as this kind of model.

First, Fuller's work has endured the test of time. His numerous published works were widely read during his lifetime to the profit of many. For decades after his death, his collected works were frequently reissued. When the most common American edition of these anthologies was reprinted after over a century of being out of print, it sold out quickly.[20] Demand for Fuller's works remains so high that a major new edition of his complete works is presently being prepared for the press.[21] Dated though they must be in many points, the esteem in which Fuller's writings are held gives evidence of his enduring usefulness as a model pastor-theologian.

Second, Fuller approached the work of theology with a balanced theological method. The fact that his method highlighted the authority of biblical revelation brings an element of timelessness to many of Fuller's theological conclusions.

---

[18]Nevertheless, as late as 2002, the modern resurgence of interest in Fuller notwithstanding, D. W. Bebbington ("Introduction," in *The Gospel in the World: International Baptist Studies*, ed. D. W. Bebbington, SBHT [Carlisle, UK; Waynesboro, GA: Paternoster, 2002], 1:6) could characterize him as an "outstanding but largely neglected theologian."

[19]For example, see R. Hayden's 1991 Ph.D. thesis for the University of Keele, recently released in book form: *Continuity and Change: Evangelical Calvinism among Eighteenth-Century Baptist Ministers Trained at Bristol Academy, 1690–1791* (Milton under Wynchwood, Chipping Norton, Oxfordshire, UK: Nigel Lynn Publishing for the Baptist Historical Society, 2006); cf. D. L. Young, "The Place of Andrew Fuller in the Developing Modern Missions Movement" (Ph.D. dissertation, Southwestern Baptist Theological Seminary, 1981). Young's dissertation overstates the role of Fuller by failing to understand the extent to which evangelical Calvinism was widespread in his day. Hayden's work corrects this.

[20]This is the three-volume edition reprinted by Sprinkle in 1988 (see note 15). This reprint is hard to find on the used book market, and if it can be found, it usually sells for around $100.

[21]Known as "The Works of Andrew Fuller Project," this effort is going forward under the general editorship of M. A. G. Haykin, professor of Church History and Biblical Spirituality at the Southern Baptist Theological Seminary, Louisville, Kentucky. When completed, this will be the first critical edition of Fuller's works to be published and will include many previously unpublished materials, especially his diary and correspondence. The work will span 15 volumes (including an index) and is hoped to be completed within the following decade.

Third, Fuller instinctively practiced what R. Albert Mohler Jr. has recently labeled "theological triage."[22] That is to say, he responded to the various theological issues of his day by devoting his greatest attention to matters of primary importance. Fuller entered into the ministry at a crucial time in the history of British Particular Baptists. As a young preacher, he quickly grasped that his denomination was deeply divided in its soteriological convictions and practices. He devoted his life to advocating what he became convinced were theological conclusions that stood at the very heart of Christianity. His leadership in the soteriological debates of the eighteenth century was a significant factor in the outcome of denominational events, both in England and America. In his conduct throughout these debates, Fuller modeled the need to prioritize doctrinal discussions according to areas of relative importance and the needs of the times.

Finally, Fuller was a pastor-theologian. Although he was the leading Baptist theological writer of his day, he never served as a professor of theology. Instead, he devoted his entire ministry to the local church, including 33 years as the pastor of Kettering Baptist Church.[23] By virtue of his position of active ministry in the local church, Fuller provides an example of how pastors can relate doctrine to practice. He was not content to contribute to theological debate in print only. Fuller also showed how the theological conclusions he had arrived at could be applied to local church ministry. If the stereotypical picture of a theologian is a reclusive scholar who delights in debating esoteric questions, Fuller provides a powerful counterbalancing example.

## A BIOGRAPHICAL SKETCH OF ANDREW FULLER

Two full-length biographies of Fuller were written in the period immediately after his death.[24] Additional efforts to keep his memory alive were undertaken

---

[22]R. A. Mohler Jr., "The Call for Theological Triage and Christian Maturity," *The Tie* 74 (2006): 2–3.

[23]The church has maintained a continuous ministry to date in Kettering, Northamptonshire, England. It has since been renamed "Fuller Baptist Church," an honor that it is hard to imagine would meet with Fuller's approval. The church maintains a Web site with several pictures of the buildings, which date from Fuller's day. See http://www.fullerbaptist.org.uk.

[24]See note 14. Of the two, Ryland's is the hardest to find but the most valuable.

through the years, especially by family members.[25] Though not a biography, the best book-length introduction to Fuller's life that is readily available today is by Peter Morden.[26] The main contours of Fuller's life are sketched below.[27]

## Fuller's Birth and Early Life

Fuller was born February 6, 1754, in a simple farmhouse at Wicken, Cambridgeshire. Once mostly marshland, the county had been largely drained and converted to farming purposes by Fuller's day. Still, life on the fens was particularly hazardous, requiring constant vigilance from ever-encroaching waters. Common lore had it that the rigors of life on the "fenlands" produced an especially independent and tenacious breed of Englishmen.[28]

His father, Robert Fuller Sr., maintained some small ancestral lands but was compelled to make a living by leasing and working dairy farms. Andrew was the youngest of three sons born to Robert and his wife Philippa. None of the boys received anything beyond the most rudimentary education. Andrew, however, was naturally gifted with a sharp mind. Looking back on his early

---

[25] His son, A. G. Fuller, wrote a memoir of his father's life that was included with several editions of Fuller's collected works (*Complete Works*, 1:1–116). In addition, very late in his life, the same author wrote a freestanding biography: *Andrew Fuller* (London: Hodder & Stoughton, 1882). Additionally, Gunton Fuller's son, T. E. Fuller, produced yet another biography: *A Memoir of the Life and Writings of Andrew Fuller: By His Grandson, Thomas Ekins Fuller* (London: J. Heaton & Son, 1863). The only other full-length biographical work is by G. Laws, *Andrew Fuller: Pastor, Theologian, Ropeholder* (London: Carey Press, 1942). Naturally, all of these have long since gone out of print.

[26] Originally prepared as a dissertation for the University of Wales in 2000, it was quickly published: P. J. Morden, *Offering Christ to the World: Andrew Fuller (1754–1815) and the Revival of Eighteenth-Century Particular Baptist Life*, SBHT 8 (Carlisle, UK; Waynesboro, GA: Paternoster, 2003). Morden's work argues that Fuller perfectly fits the widely accepted description of an evangelical offered by D. W. Bebbington; namely, evangelicals have four core concerns: biblicism, crucicentrism, conversionism, and activism. See D. W. Bebbington, *Evangelicalism in Modern Britain: A History from the 1730s to the 1980s* (n.p.: Unwin Hyman, 1989; repr., London: Routledge, 2004). For a short introduction to Fuller, see the fine chapter by P. R. Roberts, "Andrew Fuller," in *Theologians of the Baptist Tradition*, rev. ed., ed. T. George and D. S. Dockery (Nashville: B&H, 2001), 34–51.

[27] For the milieu of British Particular Baptist life in Fuller's day, see O. C. Robison, "The Particular Baptists in England: 1760–1820" (D.Phil. diss., Regent's Park College, Oxford, 1986); and R. W. Oliver, *History of the English Calvinistic Baptists 1771–1892: From John Gill to C. H. Spurgeon* (Edinburgh, Scotland; Carlisle, PA: Banner of Truth, 2006).

[28] Laws has drawn attention to the formative effects of the fens on Fuller (*Andrew Fuller: Pastor, Theologian, Ropeholder*, 9–16).

educational experiences, Fuller reports that the townspeople of Soham generally believed he was "more learned than my master."[29] In such a setting, there was no point in Fuller tarrying long in school. While still young, he was pressed into the demanding work of maintaining the farm. The discipline and work ethic instilled by the unrelenting burdens of a dairy farm remained a part of Fuller's character long after he was called to Baptist ministry.

Both of Fuller's parents were descended from non-Conformist stock. Of the two, Fuller's mother was the primary spiritual influence.[30] She was the granddaughter of one of the founding members of the Particular Baptist Church in Soham, a village near Wicken. Andrew's family moved to this village when he was a boy of six, and the whole family became regular attendees at the maternal grandmother's old church, sitting under the pulpit ministry of Pastor John Eve (d. 1782). Eve held the pastorate at this church for almost 20 years.[31] Theologically, Pastor Eve was committed to High Calvinism.[32] As Fuller remembered his ministry, Eve "had little or nothing to say to the unconverted. I, therefore, never considered myself as any way concerned in what I heard

---

[29] Fuller, *Complete Works*, 1:12. Though Fuller denied that this was the case, he did allow that the opinion worked to his favor as a young pastor. People came to hear him all the more readily because of their esteem for his supposed intellect.

[30] Indeed, Fuller's father may have died in an unconverted state, even though he attended the Baptist church along with his family. Fuller's diary laments the lost state of his father: "Much affected today for my dear father, who I fear will die. Oh his immortal soul! How can I bear to bury him unconverted!" (*Diary*, January 26, 1781). The original resides at the library of the Bristol Baptist College, Bristol, England. I have accessed Fuller's diary through M. M. McMullen, ed., *The Diary of Andrew Fuller*, in *The Complete Works of Andrew Fuller*, M. A. G. Haykin, ed. (forthcoming). Since the version used is a prepublication proof without firm pagination, subsequent references are cited as Fuller, *Diary*, date.

[31] Haykin, *One Heart and One Soul*, 19.

[32] The terms "High Calvinism" and "hyper-Calvinism" are used interchangeably in this study, as was Fuller's practice. G. F. Nuttall ("Northamptonshire and *The Modern Question*: A Turning-Point in Eighteenth-Century Dissent," *JTS* 16 [1965]: 101, n. 4) has argued that the term "High Calvinism" should be preferred, and his point that one speaks of "High Churchmen," not "hyper-Churchmen," is valid. He is mistaken, however, to argue that "hyper-Calvinism" is anachronistic to the eighteenth-century debate; Fuller used both terms. A more complete discussion of High Calvinism is offered in the chapters that follow. For now, the reader should keep in mind that High Calvinists like Pastor Eve were very hesitant to do anything that might encroach on the sovereignty of God's electing work in salvation. Believing that non-Christians had no power to perform any spiritual duty, they tended toward extreme hesitancy in encouraging the lost to come to faith in Christ. Only when certain "warrants" were present that indicated regeneration had already occurred did they invite men to faith in Christ.

from the pulpit."[33] However deficient it may have been evangelistically, Eve's ministry did sow the Word of God into the hearts and minds of Fuller and his brothers with good effect. Fuller's older brothers became prominent deacons at Baptist churches in the towns where they eventually settled. In time, Fuller would be called to the pastorate of his home church at Soham.

### The Conversion of Fuller

The events surrounding Fuller's conversion are vital to a clear understanding of his subsequent life and ministry. Fuller came to believe that he had been unnecessarily held back from salvation by the faulty theological assumptions that permeated the church of his upbringing. He dedicated much of his ministry to working to overturn the High Calvinistic system then in vogue in many British Particular Baptist churches. The story of Fuller's conversion can largely be told in his own words, thanks to the preservation of a series of lengthy letters he wrote on that topic.

Fuller recounts that the sins of his childhood included "lying, cursing, and swearing."[34] He matured into a powerfully built man over six feet tall. This strong build helped him to excel in wrestling.[35] His success in this popular pastime opened the door to spending free time with "other wicked young people," by which means his "progress in the way of death became greatly accelerated."[36] Petty gambling, acts of daring, and adolescent pranks worked together to deaden Fuller's conscience. Though he sat regularly under the preaching of Pastor Eve, there was little visible effect. Fuller describes why: "The preaching upon which I attended was not adapted to awaken my

---

[33] A. Fuller to C. Stuart, 1798, "The Letters of Andrew Fuller—Copied from Various Sources, by Miss Joyce A. Booth, Gathered by the Rev. Ernest A. Payne," scanned from the original by N. Wheeler, January 13, 2005. The original is at the Angus Library, Regent's Park College, Oxford. Unless noted otherwise, future citations from Fuller's correspondence are from this same collection of letters. Another collection of Fuller's letters is included in the archives of the BMS. Archival materials from 1792 to 1914 were scanned to 90 rolls of microfilm by a cooperative effort between the BMS and the Historical Commission of the Southern Baptist Convention. Roll 21 of this collection contains a wide assortment of letters to and from Fuller that are rarely cited in the literature by researchers.

[34] A. Fuller to C. Stuart, 1798.

[35] H. L. McBeth, *The Baptist Heritage: Four Centuries of Baptist Witness* (Nashville: Broadman, 1987), 181.

[36] A. Fuller to C. Stuart, 1798.

conscience, as the minister had seldom anything to say except to believers, and what believing was I neither knew nor was I greatly concerned to know."[37]

In spite of Pastor Eve's shortcomings as an evangelist, the Word he preached became an effective tool when wielded by the Holy Spirit. Fuller records that at about age 14, he began to have episodic bouts of deep conviction. For example, he recalled,

> One winter evening, I remember going with a number of other boys to a smith's shop, to warm ourselves by his fire. Presently they began to sing vain songs. This appeared to me so much like reveling, that I felt something within me which would not suffer me to join them, and while I sat silent in rather an unpleasant muse, those words sunk into my mind like a dagger, "What doest thou here, Elijah?" I immediately left the company, yet shocking to reflect upon, I walked away murmuring in my heart against God, that I could not be left alone, and suffered to take my pleasure like other young people.[38]

For the first time in his life, the onset of these seasons of conviction caused Fuller "to have much serious thought about futurity."[39] Following a path familiar to almost all English Dissenters, Fuller began to read some of the classic treatises of evangelical Christianity. Among the titles he mentioned are John Bunyan's (1628–88) *Grace Abounding to the Chief of Sinners* and the ubiquitous *Pilgrim's Progress*. He also derived benefit from the work of a Scottish author, Ralph Erskine (1685–1752); he particularly mentions being "almost overcome with weeping" at reading his *A Gospel Catechism for Young Christians; or, Christ All in All in Our Complete Redemption.*[40]

Armed now with more direct information on the necessity of a personal conversion, Fuller struggled for several years with whether or not he had come to faith. Scenes like the following happened to the conscientious young Fuller more than once:

---

[37] Ibid.
[38] Ibid.
[39] Ibid.
[40] Ibid.

I was at times the subject of such convictions and affections, that I really thought myself converted; and lived under that delusion a long time. The ground on which I rested that opinion was as follows: — One morning, I think about the year 1767, as I was walking alone, I began to think seriously what would become of my poor soul, and was deeply affected in thinking of my condition. I felt myself the slave of sin, and that it had such power over me that it was vain for me to think of extracting myself from its thraldom. Till now, I did not know but that I could repent at any time; but now I perceived that my heart was wicked, and that it was not in me to turn to God, or to break off my sins by righteousness. I saw that if God would forgive me all the past, and offer me the kingdom of heaven, on condition of giving up wicked pursuits, I should not accept it. This conviction was accompanied with great depression of heart. I walked sorrowfully along, repeating these words: Iniquity will be my ruin! Iniquity will be my ruin! While poring over my unhappy case, those words of the Apostle suddenly occurred to my mind, "Sin shall not have dominion over you, for ye are not under the law, but under grace." Now the suggestion of a text of scripture to the mind, especially if it came with power, was generally considered by the religious people with whom I occasionally associated, as a promise coming immediately from God. I therefore so understood it, and thought that God had thus revealed to me that I was in a state of salvation, and that therefore iniquity should not, as I had feared, be my ruin. The effect was, I was overcome with joy and transport. I shed, I suppose, thousands of tears as I walked along, and seemed to feel myself, as it were, in a new world. . . . But strange as it may appear, though my face that morning was, I believe, swoln [*sic*] with weeping, yet before night all was gone and forgotten, and I returned to my former vices with as eager a gust as ever.[41]

Fuller assumed that he must be essentially passive in conversion. Following the hyper-Calvinistic teaching of the Soham Baptist Church, he devoted his spiritual energy to seeking evidence that God had moved upon his soul in regeneration. In the parlance of the day, he was seeking a "warrant" to believe.

---

[41] Ibid.

At this point, his mind was blinded to the possibility that he could throw himself on the mercy of God as a sinner.

Though this process was repeated several times during his early teen years, Fuller never exercised personal faith in Christ and was never converted. As he said, "I have great reason to think that the great deep of my heart's depravity had not yet been broken up, and that all my religion was without any abiding principle."[42] Each repeated failure to find spiritual peace led to increasing despair in Fuller's life. He poignantly describes the dilemma he felt:

> Indeed, I knew not what to do! I durst not promise amendment; for I saw such promises were self-deception. To hope for forgiveness in the course that I was in was the height of presumption; and to think of Christ, after having so basely abused his grace, seemed too much. So I had no refuge. At one moment, I thought of giving myself up to despair. "I may," said I within myself, "even return, and take my fill of sin; I can be but lost." This thought made me shudder at myself. My heart revolted. "What!," thought I, "give up Christ, and hope, and heaven!" Those lines of Ralph Erskine's then occurred to my mind:
>
> > *But say, if all the gusts*
> > *And grains of love be spent,*
> > *Say, Farewell Christ, and welcome lusts—*
> > *Stop, stop; I melt, I faint!*
>
> I could not bear the thought of plunging myself into endless ruin.[43]

Though he had gone down these spiritual blind alleys "perhaps ten times over," one cold November morning in 1769, he finally found the Savior:

> I was like a man drowning, looking every way for help, or, rather, catching for something by which he might save his life. I tried to find whether there were any hope in the divine mercy, any in the Saviour of sinners; but felt repulsed by the thought of mercy having been so basely abused

---

[42] Ibid.

[43] Ibid. Fuller's citation is from *The Believer Wading through Depths of Desertion and Corruption* by Ralph Erskine, *The Sermons and Other Practical Works of the Late Reverend Ralph Erskine, A. M.* (London: William Tegg, 1865), 7:246.

already. In this state of mind, as I was moving slowly on, I thought of the resolution of Job, "Though he slay me, yet will I trust in him." I paused and repeated the words over and over. Each repetition seemed to kindle a ray of hope, mixed with determination, if I might, to cast my perishing soul upon the Lord Jesus Christ for salvation, to be both pardoned and purified; for I felt that I needed the one as much as the other.

I was not then aware that any poor sinner had a warrant to believe in Christ for the salvation of his soul; but supposed there must be some kind of qualification to entitle him to it. Yet I was aware that I had no qualifications. On a review of my resolution at that time, it seems to resemble that of Esther, who went into the king's presence contrary to law and at the hazard of her life. Like her, I seemed reduced to extremities, impelled by dire necessity to run all hazards, even though I should perish in the attempt. Yet it was not altogether from a dread of wrath that I fled to this refuge; for I well remember that I felt something attracting in the Saviour. "I must—I will—yes—I will trust my soul, my sinful, lost soul in his hands. If I perish, I perish!" However it was, I was determined to cast myself upon Christ, thinking, peradventure, he would save my soul; and if not, I could be but lost. In this way I continued above an hour, weeping and supplicating mercy for the Saviour's sake. My soul has it still in remembrance and is humbled in me! And as the eye of the mind was more and more fixed upon him, my guilt and fears were gradually and insensibly removed.[44]

Fuller's extended struggle to find peace in Christ was a formative influence in the life of the pastor-theologian. He clarified the role of hyper-Calvinism in sidetracking him spiritually:

I now found rest for my troubled soul; and I reckon that I should have found it sooner, if I had not entertained the notion of my having no warrant to come to Christ without some previous qualification. This notion was a bar that kept me back for a time; though, through divine drawings, I was enabled to overleap it. . . . And if, at that time, I had known that any poor sinner might warrantably have trusted in him for salvation, I

---

[44]Ibid.

believe I should have done so and have found rest to my soul sooner than I did. I mention this because it may be the case with others, who may be kept in darkness and despondency by erroneous views of the gospel much longer than I was.[45]

In many ways, Fuller's life work can be seen as a labor to correct these "erroneous views of the gospel."[46]

### Early Steps of Discipleship and the Call to Ministry

Although Fuller's family was connected with the Particular Baptist Church at Soham, his home congregation very rarely had occasion to practice their namesake ordinance. Not long after his own conversion, Fuller had the opportunity to observe a baptismal service. Though he was 16 at the time, it was the first time he had ever seen believer's baptism practiced. The service had a profound impact on the young man. He came away from it convinced "that this was the primitive way of baptizing, and that every Christian was bound to attend to this institution of our blessed Lord."[47] Accordingly, Pastor Eve baptized Fuller the following month, April 1770.

At the time, English Dissenters constituted a minority among British Christians. Baptists, in turn, formed but a small branch within the dissenting family. So it was not surprising that Fuller quickly encountered ridicule and persecution. Writing in the last year of his life, he reminisced,

> Within a few days or two after I had been baptized, as I was riding through the fields, I met a company of young men. One of them, especially on my having passed them, called after me, in very abusive language, and cursed me for having been "dipped." My heart instantly rose in the way of resentment: but, though the fire burned, I held my peace; for before I uttered a word, I was checked with this passage, which occurred to my mind: — "In the world ye *shall* have tribulation." I wept, and entreated the Lord to pardon me; feeling quite willing to bear the

---

[45] Ibid.

[46] Ibid.

[47] A. Fuller to unidentified friend on January 8, 1815 (cited in Ryland, *Work of Faith*, 16).

*The stream in Soham where Fuller was baptized. Photo © Michael Haykin.*

ridicule of the wicked, and to go even through great tribulation, if at last I might but enter the kingdom.[48]

In this and other spiritual victories, Fuller found confirmation of his conversion.

One habit that Fuller established very early in his Christian life, and never abandoned, was the wholesome practice of forming spiritual friendships.[49] At the time Fuller was baptized, Pastor Eve also baptized a man of around 40 years of age. This older man, Joseph Diver, became Fuller's first spiritual confidant. Diver was a reclusive man, who was much given to Bible reading and theological reflection. He also was an earnest Christian. Fuller felt their relationship recollected the biblical friendship of David and Jonathan and counted

---

[48] Ibid. (cited in Ryland, *Work of Faith*, 17).

[49] Haykin (*The Armies of the Lamb: The Spirituality of Andrew Fuller* [Dundas, Ontario: Joshua Press, 2001], 42–46) has noted this area of Fuller's life as one of the identifying characteristics of his spirituality.

the years he spent with Diver as "one of the greatest blessings in my life."[50] In the months following their baptism, the older man served as both instructor and mentor to his younger protégé. Fuller recalled the summer after his baptism as one of the happiest seasons of his life.

Significant as these pleasant interactions with his friend were in forming Fuller's mind for theological debate and discussion, they pale beside the influence of events that clouded Fuller's life in the fall of 1770. The moral failure of one of the members of the Soham Baptist Church became the occasion for severe theological conflict between Pastor Eve and the congregation. Things eventually came to such an impasse that the pastor resigned and left the tiny church nearly bereft of leadership. In a foreshadowing of what was to await him in later life, the young Fuller was at the center of the controversy. He describes the circumstances surrounding these unpleasant events in some detail:

> The case was this:—One of the members having been guilty of drinking to excess, I was one of the first who knew of it. I immediately went and talked to him, as well as I could, on the evil of his conduct. His answer was, he could not keep himself; and that, though I bore so hard on him, I was not my own keeper. At this I felt indignant, considering it as a base excuse. I therefore told him, that he *could* keep himself from sins such as these, and that his way of talking was merely to excuse what was inexcusable. I knew not what else to say at the time; yet the idea of arrogating to be my own keeper seemed too much.[51]

Fuller took his confusion to his pastor. First, Pastor Eve praised his young convert for his behavior toward the offending brother. Second, he tried to give a theological rationale for why Fuller had been right in demanding the brother hold himself accountable for his sinful actions. The essence of Eve's opinion was that men were indeed powerless "to do things spiritually good; but, as to outward acts, we had power both to obey the will of God, and to disobey it."[52] Unwittingly, Fuller—and perhaps Pastor Eve as well—had stumbled into the heart of the controversy that surrounded hyper-Calvinism.

---

[50]Ryland, *Work of Faith*, 18.
[51]Ibid.
[52]Ibid.

The case for discipline against the offending member was noncontroversial. He was unanimously removed from the membership of Soham Baptist Church. But Fuller wrote,

> [T]he abstract question, of *the power of sinful men to do the will of God, and to keep themselves from sin*, was taken up by some of the leading members of the church, amongst whom was my friend Joseph Diver. They readily excused me, as being a babe in religion; but thought the pastor ought to have known better, and to have been able to answer the offender without betraying the truth.[53]

Eve's crime, as his hyper-Calvinist congregation saw it, was that he had betrayed the key principle of that theological system. He had allowed too much power for sinful man to carry out the will of God. Under a swirl of controversy, Eve resigned.[54]

Fuller was swayed by the arguments of both sides in the controversy. He vacillated between camps for a time but eventually came down on the side of the majority, which also included the influential Diver. Less important than his position in this particular theological scuffle was the impact these events had on the young theologue. He has left an excellent assessment of that impact:

> I never look back upon these contentions, but with strong feelings. They were to me the wormwood and gall of my youth: my soul hath them still in remembrance, and is humbled in me. But though, during these unpleasant disputes, there were many hard thoughts and hard words on almost all hands, yet they were, ultimately, the means of leading my mind into those views of divine truth which have since appeared in the principal part of my writings. They excited me to read and think and pray, with more earnestness than I should have done without them: and, if I have judged or written to any advantage since, it was in consequence

---

[53] Ibid.

[54] It is ironic that, at the time, Eve considered himself a High Calvinist also. His answer to Fuller was careful to distinguish between human ability to do things spiritually good (which Eve denied belonged to the lost) and the ability to obey outward moral demands. The distinction was perhaps too fine for most of the congregation.

of what I then learned by bitter experience, and in the midst of many tears and temptations. God's way is in the deep.[55]

Though he recognized the peculiar dangers inherent in theological dispute, Fuller also saw that the cause of truth could be defended and advanced only when pastors were willing to "earnestly contend for the faith" (Jude 3).

In the providence of God, these theological wranglings also were the means by which Fuller came to recognize a call to the ministry. The fortunes of the congregation at Soham sank to such low ebb that securing a pastor from the outside seemed out of the question. With the removal of Pastor Eve, leadership of the tiny church fell to the laity. Fuller's friend, Diver, was ordained as a deacon and began to take the lead in the weekly worship services. Fuller was active in the church but never engaged in anything beyond public prayers. A series of events soon converged to change that.

About a year after his pastor's resignation, Fuller was riding to a nearby village on business. Along the way, he reports that "my mind fell into a train of affecting thoughts, from that passage of Scripture, 'Weeping may endure for a night; but joy cometh in the morning.'"[56] Though he had no thoughts of entering the ministry at the time, Fuller remembered, "I then felt as though I could preach from it; and, indeed, I did preach, in a manner, as I rode along."[57] That same evening—a Saturday—Fuller rode out to pick up his mother on her return from a trip to London, where she had gone to visit relatives. She announced to him that one of his uncles had agreed to take on Fuller as an apprentice in his trade, on very favorable terms. Though he had previously hoped for such an opportunity, Fuller reports that on that particular evening, his "heart revolted at the proposal."[58]

The following Sunday morning revealed that these circumstances were working toward God's purposes. On his way to worship, Fuller was met by a fellow church member, who came bringing a message from Diver. He informed Fuller that his friend had been slightly injured in an accident and would not be able to lead the service. He added that Diver expressed the wish that "he hopes

[55] Ryland, *Work of Faith*, 20–21.
[56] Ibid., 22.
[57] Ibid., 22–23.
[58] Ibid., 23.

the Lord will be with *you*."[59] Fuller saw the connection between the need of the hour and the thoughts he had had the day before. He delivered his first sermon on Ps 30:5 and spoke "for about a half an hour, with considerable freedom."[60] A further attempt in the coming weeks was not so successful, and for more than a year afterward Fuller refused all opportunities to preach.

But early in 1773, when Diver was again incapacitated, Fuller relented to the pleas of the congregation and delivered another message. This time he both saw and felt evidence of the Lord's favor. He spoke with freedom, the people were much impressed, and several young persons were converted as a consequence of the sermon. The effect on the congregation was so great that Soham Baptist Church recognized that God had raised up a pastor from within their midst. Although he was only 19, Fuller began to speak regularly on Sundays, alternating mornings and evenings with Diver. This arrangement continued for another year until the church formally extended Fuller a call to ministry in January 1774. At that transition point, Fuller reports, "From that time, I exercised from the pulpit."[61] As was customary at the time, his formal ordination was delayed until a suitable trial period had elapsed. Finally, on May 3, 1775, Soham Baptist Church ordained Fuller to the gospel ministry.

### The Formative Years in the Soham Pastorate

Fuller's influence on the theological world largely stemmed from his work as a pastor-theologian at his second and final pastorate in Kettering. But the years in his first pastorate at Soham were crucial to Fuller's theological development. These influences can be summarized under three subjects: family responsibilities, doctrinal clarification and change, and lifelong friendships and denominational relationships.

### Family Responsibilities

The young pastor of Soham Baptist Church took a bride from his own congregation, Miss Sarah Gardiner. They were married in December 1776. Though deeply affectionate toward each other, their life together was characterized by a succession of heartaches. Sarah Fuller gave birth to 11 children before

---

[59] Ibid.
[60] Ibid., 24.
[61] Ibid., 25.

eventually dying of complications from childbirth. Of those children, only two survived into adulthood. One daughter, Sally, died at age six. Her illness and death were particularly grieving to the parents. The rest died in early infancy.

In addition to living constantly under the shadow of death, the Fullers also experienced extreme poverty. The church at Soham was never able to provide adequately for the support of their growing family. Fuller attempted to supplement his salary through several ventures, including shopkeeping and holding school in the home. None of these efforts was successful, and so they were soon abandoned.

The hardship in the young couple's life seems to have taken a deep emotional toll on Sarah. During her last years, she suffered from debilitating bouts of mental illness and required near constant supervision. During her final few months, the situation progressed far enough that she lost all touch with reality and was unable to recognize her husband or children. She died in August 1792.

But as has often been the case, the hardships of life were the fire by which God made Fuller more malleable to His purposes. In his diary, Fuller frequently expressed the belief that God was at work through difficulty. Fuller came to see that the poverty against which he often chafed during the Soham years was actually a gift from God to render him more dependent on the Almighty. For example, he wrote in his diary, "Dejected, through worldly and church concerns; but had some relief, tonight, in casting all my care upon the Lord, hoping that he careth for me. The Lord undertake for me! O thou that managest worlds unknown, without one disappointment, take my case into thy hand, and fit me for thy pleasure. If poverty must be my portion, add thereto contentment."[62] A few months later he added the insight that his poverty was really a disguised blessing: "Had some view, to-night, of the hardships of poverty. What mercies do I enjoy; yet how ungrateful I am! What a world of self-sufficiency is there in our hearts!"[63]

### Doctrinal Clarification and Change

The years at Soham Baptist Church were also a period of doctrinal development for Fuller. Though the seven years he spent at such an out-of-the-way

---

[62] Fuller, *Diary*, July 21, 1780.
[63] Fuller, *Diary*, October 30, 1780.

place were an economic challenge to Fuller, the retired setting came with an inestimably valuable fringe benefit. His son, Andrew Gunton Fuller, described this intangible:

> It would, perhaps, be impossible to over-estimate the value to himself of Mr. Fuller's experience at Soham. His pastoral and pulpit duties occupying but a portion of his time, and there being in so small a town but few demands upon him outside his own church, he had frequent opportunities for reading and study. Having been denied the benefits of an academical training, and being conscious of the value of a classical education, he made considerable progress in the study of the Greek language, and, aided by his friend, Dr. Ryland, gained a sufficient mastery over Hebrew to enable him to refer to the original of the Old Testament Scriptures. In addition to this he read, and not only read but also digested, a whole library of theology, and during these seven years became established in those great truths with which his name is associated. His opinions, though constantly being developed, were never afterwards materially changed. Had he been at first called to a wider sphere of work in which his time would have been fully occupied in the discharge of public duties, it would have been impossible for him to lay so good a foundation as that upon which his mental character was subsequently built.[64]

In spite of the difficulties that he believed hyper-Calvinism had placed in the way of his coming to faith in Christ, Fuller conducted his own early ministry in a similar vein. The earliest systematic theology that the young pastor studied was John Gill's (1697–1771) *A Body of Divinity.*[65] Though Gill can be read either to support or to oppose High Calvinism, at this point in his life Fuller sifted Gill's work through the filter of John Brine (1703–65).[66] Brine

---

[64] A. G. Fuller, *Andrew Fuller*, 50–51.

[65] J. Gill, *A Body of Doctrinal Divinity: or, A System of Evangelical Truths, Deduced from the Scriptures*, 2 vols. (London: n.p., 1769). This book was Gill's magnum opus. It was originally printed by subscription but came out in numerous editions thereafter. It was the standard Baptist systematic theology of Fuller's day and well beyond.

[66] For the view that Gill was a hyper-Calvinist, see C. Daniel, "Hyper-Calvinism and John Gill" (Ph.D. diss., Edinburgh University, 1983). For the contrary position, see T. J. Nettles, *By His Grace and For His Glory: A Historical, Theological, and Practical Study of the Doctrines of Grace in Baptist Life*, rev. ed. (Lake Charles, LA: Cor Meum Tibi, 2002).

was an unabashed High Calvinist who vigorously advocated his views as the sine qua non of orthodoxy in Particular Baptist life. Thus, Fuller's early efforts in the study of this subject tended to confirm his pastoral ministry in the same mold he had learned from Pastor Eve. As he reflected back on the influence of hyper-Calvinism, Fuller wrote, "The effect of these views was, that I had very little to say to the unconverted, indeed nothing in a way of exhortation to things spiritually good or certainly connected with salvation."[67]

Fuller did not fall exactly into lockstep with the High Calvinists who then were favored by many Particular Baptists. At about the same time he was reading Gill and Brine, he was also studying the works of John Bunyan and the English Puritans, especially John Owen (1616–83). He realized that Bunyan and the Puritans had a very different flavor from Gill: "I perceived, however, that the system of Bunyan was not the same with his [Gill's]; for that, while he maintained the doctrines of election and predestination, he nevertheless held with the free offer of salvation to sinners without distinction."[68] At the time, Fuller records that he dismissed Bunyan as a "great and good man" though "not so *clear* in his views of the doctrines of the gospel as the writers who succeeded him."[69] Still, a seed of doubt about the validity of High Calvinism had been planted.

Fuller was not the first to notice that the Calvinism then popular among Particular Baptists was deviating in significant doctrinal respects from its Puritan seedbed. The issue of the appropriateness of gospel appeals to the lost to come to Christ had been long under debate among English Dissenters by the time Fuller became a pastor. One of the many to address the point was an Independent Minister, Abraham Taylor (fl. 1727–40), in a pamphlet titled *The Modern Question Concerning Repentance and Faith* (1742).[70] A few months after his ordination, Fuller made a trip to London. As he searched the

---

[67] Fuller, *Complete Works*, 1:15.

[68] Ibid.

[69] Ibid.

[70] For information on this tract, see Nuttall, "Northamptonshire and *The Modern Question*," 101–2. G. L. Priest ("Andrew Fuller, Hyper-Calvinism, and the 'Modern Question,'" in *At the Pure Fountain of Thy Word*, ed. Michael A. G. Haykin, Studies in Baptist History and Thought 6 [Carlisle, UK; Waynesboro, GA: Paternoster, 2004], 47) mistakenly gives the date of publication as 1735 and incorrectly identifies Taylor as a Particular Baptist. Possibly he followed A. P. F. Sell (*The Great Debate: Calvinism, Arminianism, and Salvation* [Eugene, OR: Wipf & Stock, 1998], 79), who also erroneously dates it to 1735.

secondhand booksellers' wares, he discovered Taylor's booklet. He immediately recognized that it related directly to the issue that had resulted in such grief to the Soham Church some years before; only Taylor took the opposite side of the question from Fuller and his parishioners. Reading *The Modern Question* added fuel to the spark of doubt that Bunyan had ignited. Fuller remembered his reaction to this book:

> I was but little impressed by his reasonings till he came to the addresses of John the Baptist, Christ, and the apostles, which he proved to be delivered to the ungodly, and to mean spiritual repentance and faith, inasmuch as they were connected with the remission of sins. This set me fast. I read and examined the Scripture passages, and the more I read and thought, the more I doubted the justice of my former views.[71]

Fuller's personality was not given to sudden change, and especially not in matters of theology. He continued to study and read all that he could find that related to the intersection of divine sovereignty and human responsibility. As time passed, he became increasingly convinced that hyper-Calvinism was untenable in the light of Scripture. For understandable reasons, however, he was slow to implement these changes in his pastoral work. His diary reveals the conflict that his changing theological convictions caused the young pastor:

> I found my soul drawn out in love to poor souls while reading Millar's account of Eliot's labors among the North American Indians, and their effect on those poor barbarous savages. I found also a suspicion that we shackle ourselves too much in our addresses; that we have bewildered and lost ourselves by taking the decrees of God as rules of action. Surely Peter and Paul never felt such scruples in their addresses as we do. They addressed their hearers as *men*—fallen men; as we should warn and admonish persons who were blind and on the brink of some dreadful precipice. Their work seemed plain before them. Oh that mine might be so before me![72]

---

[71] Fuller, *Complete Works*, 1:15.

[72] Fuller, *Diary*, August 30, 1780. John Eliot (1604–90) was a well-known Puritan missionary to the Indians of North America. He is sometimes given the sobriquet "apostle to the Indians."

Soon after Fuller revealed these thoughts in his diary, the path of duty became clear to him. His son reports that in consequence, "his strain of preaching . . . underwent a change of a most important and valuable character."[73] Predictably, and exactly as Fuller had feared, some in his congregation took exception to their pastor's new direction. A later biographer summarizes the resulting conflict:

> The troubles were theological. Fuller had been moving: many of his people had not. The old hyper-Calvinism still held them. Fuller had followed what he found for himself in the Scriptures. He had dared to preach as John the Baptist preached, and as the Master Himself preached, and as the Apostles preached, inviting and beseeching sinners to believe and live.[74]

If some of Fuller's congregation were offended by their pastor's theological shift, the lost in his community responded favorably to a more fervent appeal. Soon the Baptist Church at Soham began to attract more hearers than could comfortably fit in their tiny building. Fuller came up with a plan whereby they could expand the size of their building, but it was rejected by his people. This choice appears to have been a major factor in Fuller's decision to accept the call of the Baptist Church at Kettering.[75]

*Fuller's Lifelong Friendships and the Northamptonshire Baptist Association*
When Fuller was called to the ministry, the patriarch of Baptist pastors in the Midlands was Robert Hall Sr. (1728–91) of Arnsby. This respected gentleman

---

[73] Fuller, *Complete Works*, 1:18.

[74] Laws, *Andrew Fuller: Pastor, Theologian, Ropeholder*, 34.

[75] Fuller's years-long struggle in discerning the will of God in accepting the call of the congregation is well known. Many researchers tend to focus on the role that financial pressures played in this decision. Though finances were a real consideration, the event that seemed to tilt him finally to accept Kettering's call was the Soham congregation's steady refusal to expand their church in order to accommodate the hearers desiring to attend. Fuller lamented to his friend John Sutcliff, "I of late try'd to get our people to purchase a strong convenient dwelling-house which might have been brought [bought?] and fitted up for less, I think, than £100, but the design is dropped for want of unanimity." Fuller determined to leave Soham very soon after this disappointment. A. Fuller to J. Sutcliff, March 13, 1781.

favored Fuller by coming 70 miles to attend his ordination.[76] Later, when Fuller and other younger pastors began to agitate for a return to an older, evangelical Calvinism, Hall lent the weight of his reputation to this theological course correction.[77] Perhaps the most far-reaching consequence of Hall's interest in the obscure new pastor at Soham was that he introduced Fuller to the fellowship of the Northamptonshire Baptist Association.[78]

Hall's influence was quickly felt. The month following Fuller's ordination, the new pastor led the congregation at Soham to petition for admission to the Northamptonshire Baptist Association, which was readily granted. From that time forward, Fuller's life and ministry were inextricably linked with this body of churches. Of the several ways that this connection influenced Fuller, none was more significant than the friendships he formed with fellow pastors in that association.

Fuller recounts the significance of a few of these friendships:

In 1776, I became acquainted with Mr. Sutcliff, who had lately come to Olney; and soon after with Mr. John Ryland [Jr.], then of Northampton. In them I found familiar and faithful brethren; and who, partly by reflection, and partly by reading the writings of Edwards, Bellamy, Brainerd, &c. had begun to doubt of the system of False Calvinism, to which they had been inclined when they first entered on the ministry, or rather to be decided against it.[79]

---

[76] At that time, distant travel was quite uncommon. An anonymous writer described the difficulties the traveler faced: "Those were the days in which men made their wills, and left affectionate messages, before they ventured far from home." Anonymous, "Andrew Fuller: A Story of Religious Life Sixty Years Ago," in *Men Who Were Earnest: The Springs of their Action and Influence* (London: Gall & Inglis, n.d.), 298.

[77] Hall contributed to the debate about High Calvinism in two key ways. First, he recommended to Fuller that he explore Jonathan Edwards's treatise, *Inquiry into the Modern Prevailing Notions Respecting That Freedom of the Will Which Is Supposed to Be Essential to Moral Agency* (1754). As will be demonstrated in chapter 3, Fuller adopted many of Edwards's views wholesale. Second, Hall delivered an important annual sermon to the Northamptonshire Baptist Association in 1779 that was later expanded and published as *Help to Zion's Travellers* (London: The Book Society, 1781). This book was a stirring call to reject High Calvinism. Thus, Hall was a powerful ally in the association for the defense of evangelical Calvinism.

[78] This association had just been formed in 1764. In spite of its name, it included churches in four counties.

[79] Ryland, *Work of Faith*, 28. In later years, other men were added to his circle of intimates, including William Carey and Samuel Pearce.

Both of these men had been trained at the Bristol Baptist Academy. Morden correctly observed that this made their connection with Fuller all the more noteworthy, since that college "had largely remained committed to an older Calvinism, more expansive and less dependant on High Calvinist theology."[80] Additionally, Ryland was an accomplished linguist who helped Fuller gain a working knowledge of the biblical languages. In short, Fuller's friendships were important because they were "spiritual friendships."[81]

These friendships continued unabated throughout his life. If anything, when Fuller moved to Kettering, the importance of these friendships grew all the more since he was now centrally located. Even Ryland's eventual move to faraway Bristol to assume leadership of the Bristol Baptist Academy and Broadmead Baptist Church failed to hamper his friendship with Fuller. They kept up a constant correspondence for over 20 years. When Sutcliff died in 1814, Fuller preached his funeral; it was Ryland's sad duty to conduct services at Fuller's death a year later. As Ryland prepared his biography on Fuller, he had in his possession 330 letters addressed to him by his friend from which to draw information.[82]

### The Productive Years at Kettering

The story of Fuller's call to leave Soham for the larger and more influential pastorate at Kettering is best told in Ryland's biography. He famously summarized the conscientious manner in which his friend sought to know God's will in the matter by suggesting, "Men who fear not God would risk the welfare of a nation with fewer searchings of heart than it cost him to determine whether he should leave a little Dissenting church, scarcely containing forty members besides himself and his wife."[83] Finally convinced that the path of duty lay with Kettering, Fuller yielded to their repeated calls and became the pastor of

---

[80]Morden, *Offering Christ to the World*, 39. For a detailed study of the evangelical Calvinism then current at Bristol, see Hayden, *Continuity and Change*.

[81]Haykin, *Armies of the Lamb*, 42.

[82]Ryland, *Work of Faith*, viii. Of Fuller's letters to Sutcliff, though not as carefully preserved, nearly 130 are extant.

[83]Ibid., 36. Church membership numbers from this era can be deceptive to modern hearers. Membership was taken so seriously that far more attended Baptist churches than ever actually joined. For example, Fuller's second pastorate at Kettering had a membership of only 174 but an average attendance of over 1,000 at Fuller's death. See Laws, *Andrew Fuller: Pastor, Theologian, Ropeholder*, 44.

*Fuller Baptist Church, Kettering, where Fuller pastored. Photo © Michael Haykin.*

Kettering Baptist Church in October 1782. Fuller served this congregation for over 33 years. From this town, hardly an influential locale, he became the most prominent Particular Baptist theologian of his era.

### The Bishopric

At the suggestion of Robert Hall Sr., the congregation at Kettering pursued Fuller for over three years. They knew exactly who they were getting for a pastor. If the church at Soham had been put off by Fuller's embrace of evangelical Calvinism, his new congregation found Fuller all the more appealing because of it. Instead of opposing efforts to find a larger place of worship, the Kettering Church remodeled and expanded several times during his ministry as need demanded it. Fuller's years at Kettering were marked by the release of innumerable publications and thousands of miles traveled on behalf of the Baptist

Missionary Society, of which he was the founding secretary. To their everlasting credit, his new congregation supported their pastor in this wider ministry to an unusual degree. One of Fuller's early biographers said of the Kettering years that Fuller "had a bishopric, without any of its titles or emoluments; and the care of all the churches, within the immediate circle of his acquaintance, came upon him daily. In their formation, in the ordination of their pastors, and in every case of difficulty, his assistance was required, and in these important services, he excelled."[84]

### A Leading Theologian among Particular Baptists

Fuller had used the more cloistered years of his ministry at Soham to become a sound theologian. As a part of negotiating the call to Kettering, Fuller presented that congregation with a personal statement of faith. This detailed confession of faith contained 20 articles and filled six tightly packed pages in Ryland's biography.[85]

Fuller's theology was clearly Calvinistic, in keeping with his Particular Baptist heritage. It was, however, Calvinism with safeguards in place to prevent the excesses that had been troubling some Particular Baptist congregations. For example, Fuller explicitly denied double predestination:

> I believe the doctrine of eternal personal election and predestination. *However*, I believe, that, though in the choice of the elect God had no motive out of himself, yet it was not so in punishing the rest. What has been usually, but perhaps improperly, called *the decree of reprobation*, I consider as nothing more than *the divine determination to punish sin, in certain cases, in the person of the sinner.*[86]

In other words, election was personal, but reprobation was impersonal. That helped safeguard the responsibility to preach the gospel to all people and also prevented sinners from shifting the responsibility for their evil behavior onto the decree of God.

---

[84] J. W. Morris, *Memoirs of the Life and Writings of the Rev. Andrew Fuller*, 2nd. ed., corrected and enlarged (London: Wightman & Cramp, 1826), 92.

[85] Ryland, *Work of Faith*, 54–59. This confession of faith is reproduced in appendix 1 of this book.

[86] Ibid., 56.

Fuller also embraced the traditional Calvinistic position of a limited atonement: "The Son of God appeared, took our nature, obeyed the law, and endured the curse, and hereby made full and proper atonement for the sins of his own elect."[87] At the same time, he clarified in the very next article that this view of the atonement did not necessarily need to dampen enthusiasm for preaching the gospel indiscriminately:

> I believe, that such is the excellence of this way of salvation, that every one who hears, or has opportunity to hear it proclaimed in the gospel, is bound to repent of his sin, believe, approve, and embrace it with all his heart; to consider himself as he really is, a vile, lost sinner; to reject all pretensions to life in any other way; and to cast himself upon Christ, that he may be saved in this way of God's devising. This I think to be true faith, which whoever have, I believe, will certainly be saved.[88]

Lest there be any misunderstanding, Fuller's confession of faith included an entire article dedicated to responding to the "Modern Question." He clearly expressed in synopsis form the essence of what he would later expand and publish as *The Gospel Worthy of All Acceptation*:[89]

> I believe, it is the duty of every minister of Christ plainly and faithfully to preach the gospel to all who will hear it; and, as I believe the inability of men to spiritual things to be wholly of the *moral*, and therefore, of the

---

[87] Ibid. Fuller commonly spoke of this point of Calvinism under the rubric "particular redemption." He did use the word "limited" but usually linked it with the word "extent." This described more clearly in what way he felt the atonement was limited. See his article on Calvinism (prepared for a religious dictionary) in appendix 2 of this book. It is also found in Belcher, *The Last Remains of the Rev. Andrew Fuller*, 218–22. Compare that to his repeated use of the "limited extent" language in *A Reply to the Observations of Philanthropos* [Dan Taylor], Fuller, *Complete Works*, 2:488–511.

[88] Ryland, *Work of Faith*, 57.

[89] A. Fuller, *The Gospel of Christ Worthy of All Acceptation: or the Obligations of Men Fully to Credit, and Cordially to Approve, Whatever God Makes Known. Wherein Is Considered the Nature of Faith in Christ, and the Duty of Those Where the Gospel Comes in That Matter* (Northampton: T. Dicey & Co., n.d. [other sources indicate it appeared in 1785]). The book was reissued in a significantly revised second edition in 1801. It bore the clearer title *The Gospel Worthy of All Acceptation: or, The Duty of Sinners to Believe in Jesus Christ* (Clipstone: J. W. Morris, 1801). The significance of this influential book is discussed in chapter 3.

*criminal* kind—and that it is their duty to love the Lord Jesus Christ, and trust in him for salvation, though they do not; I, therefore, believe free and solemn addresses, invitations, calls and warnings to them, to be not only *consistent*, but directly *adapted*, as means, in the hand of the Spirit of God, to bring them to Christ. I consider it as a part of my duty, which I could not omit without being guilty of the blood of souls.[90]

The Baptist Church at Kettering knew what they were getting theologically in their pastor. What would have surprised them—and Fuller himself—was the extent to which their new pastor's theology would influence the entire denomination. From an unlikely village in Northamptonshire, Fuller emerged as one of the leading theological writers of the day. His first book, *The Gospel Worthy of All Acceptation*, was a theological bombshell. Though it was far from original in its sentiments, it was a more systematic, biblical, and theologically informed attempt to justify the evangelical Calvinism that was already gaining ground than had ever been attempted. It also served as a call to arms for opponents all across the theological spectrum.

From one side, the High Calvinists claimed Fuller had abandoned Calvinism and with it the true gospel. From the other, Arminians like the General Baptist leader Daniel Taylor (1738–1816) argued that Fuller was trying to use halfway measures when only a clean break would do.[91] He urged Fuller to repudiate Calvinism altogether. The result was that Fuller was obliged to continue to write theology to overturn opponents and to reassure friends. He summed up what came to be the settled condition of his life in a letter to a friend:

I sometimes say Woe is me, for I am born to be a man of strife! Here are Arminians, Socinians, & final Restitutionists always provoking me to write. I seem like a sort of pugilist, who having made a little noise in the world draws upon himself every one that fancies he can master him. In truth, I am obliged to overlook many things in periodical publications; and content myself without having the last word in controversies. Sometimes my heart sick[en]s with contention: and yet I cannot forbear

---

[90] Ryland, *Work of Faith*, 58.

[91] For a recent study of the General Baptists, see F. Rinaldi, *"The Tribe of Dan": A Study of the New Connexion of General Baptists*, SBHT 10 (Carlisle, UK; Waynesboro, GA: Paternoster, 2006).

contending, and earnestly too, for I hope the faith once delivered to the saints.[92]

From the release of *The Gospel Worthy of All Acceptation* in 1785 until his death in 1815, Fuller was one of the most prolific theological writers of his day. Books, sermons, tracts, and essays of all kinds flowed steadily from his pen. Many works were well received and reissued in numerous editions, both English and American. Additionally, Fuller's pieces were much sought after by leading religious periodicals such as *The Evangelical Magazine* and *The Biblical Magazine*.[93] One of Fuller's direct theological descendants, Charles Haddon Spurgeon (1834–92), looked back on Fuller's ministry and declared him "the greatest theologian" of his time.[94]

### Secretary to the Baptist Missionary Society

Though he excelled as a pastor and theologian, Fuller is most often remembered today in conjunction with his role as the founding secretary to the Baptist Missionary Society (BMS).[95] From its formation in 1792 until his death, Fuller was the glue that held the fledgling missionary enterprise together. During his lifetime, the BMS remained "in every respect a child of the [Northamptonshire Baptist] Association."[96] His successful fund raising and administration work in England were the perfect and necessary complement to William Carey's (1761–1834) indefatigable labors in India. Fuller and Carey's deliberations on the possibilities of sending missionaries resulted in one of the indelible

---

[92]A. Fuller to W. Carey, April 18, 1799. Fuller frequently lamented the fact that he often had to play the role of the controversialist. This aspect of his ministry became so identified with Fuller that when the earliest students of the Southern Baptist Theological Seminary in Louisville, Kentucky, formed a debating society, they named it "The Andrew Fuller Society." The Boyce Centennial Library at the Southern Baptist Theological Seminary still contains the minute books of this organization, which was active from 1859 to 1876 (except for a hiatus during the American Civil War).

[93]Ryland calculated that Fuller published at least 167 articles in six periodicals (listed in *Work of Faith*, 132–35).

[94]Cited by M. A. G. Haykin, "Andrew Fuller," in *Biographical Dictionary of Evangelicals*, ed. T. Larsen (Leicester, England; Downers Grove, IL: IVP, 2003), 244.

[95]The BMS was formed in 1792 at the home of one of Fuller's church members. Its original name was "The Particular Baptist Society for Propagating the Gospel Amongst the Heathen."

[96]B. Stanley, *The History of the Baptist Missionary Society: 1792–1992* (Edinburgh: T&T Clark, 1992), 14.

images of the early missionary undertaking. Fuller remembered laying plans for an expedition to reach the lost of the world: "Our undertaking to India really appeared to me, on its commencement, to be somewhat like a few men, who were deliberating about the importance of penetrating into a deep mine, which had never before been explored. We had no one to guide us; and while we were deliberating, Carey, as it were, said, 'Well, I will go down if *you* will hold the rope.'"[97]

Whereas Carey and his associates were obliged to devise a missionary strategy from scratch on the field, Fuller did the same at home with regard to a strategy to recruit, fund, resupply, and otherwise support those who were being sent out. In his capacity as secretary, he crisscrossed England, Scotland, Ireland, and Wales. He taught and preached the cause of missions from Dissenting pulpits of every description. His contagious enthusiasm for the cause was no small factor in the rapid rise of missionary societies in nearly all the major English denominations. When he was not traveling, he was writing, spending upwards of 12 hours a day handling correspondence and other matters pertaining to the work of the society. When he died at the age of 61, many who knew Fuller best agreed with Ryland's opinion that he "probably fell a victim" to the heavy burden of holding the rope for the missionaries.[98]

### Fuller's Death

Though his health had rarely been good, Fuller became seriously ill in the fall of 1814. By the following spring, he knew he was dying. Unable to write on his own, he dictated a letter to his old friend John Ryland. Even in physical weakness, his apologetic fervor remained unabated. He offered one final defense of the evangelical Calvinism of which he had become a principal spokesman:

> We have some, who have been giving out, of late, that "if Sutcliff, and some others, had preached more of Christ, and less of Jonathan Edwards, they would have been more useful." If those who talk thus, preached Christ half as much as Jonathan Edwards did, and were half as useful as he was, their usefulness would be double what it is. It is very singular, that the Mission to the East should have originated with men

---

[97] Fuller, *Complete Works*, 1:68.
[98] Ryland, *Work of Faith*, x.

of these principles; and without pretending to be a prophet, I may say, if ever it falls into the hands of men who talk in this strain, it will soon come to nothing.[99]

With regard to his pending death, Fuller confided to Ryland:

We have enjoyed much together, which I hope will prove an earnest of greater enjoyment in another world. We have also wrought in the Lord's vineyard, and he has given us to reap together in his vintage. I expect this is nearly over; but I trust we shall meet and part no more. I have very little hope of recovery; but I am satisfied to drink of the cup which my Heavenly Father giveth me to drink. . . . I know whom I have believed, and that he is able to keep that which I have committed to him against that day. I am a poor guilty creature; but Christ is an almighty Saviour. I have preached and written much against the *abuse* of the doctrine of grace; but that doctrine is all my salvation and all my desire. I have no other hope, than from salvation by mere sovereign, efficacious grace, through the atonement of my Lord and Saviour. With this hope, I can go into eternity with composure.[100]

On a Sunday, May 7, 1815, Fuller listened to his congregation worshiping in the sanctuary that adjoined the manse. He expressed his regret that he lacked the strength to join them. Although his young associate pastor preached from the text of Ps 23:4, Fuller experienced the reality that his protégé was attempting to describe and walked through the valley of the shadow of death into the presence of the Savior.[101]

---

[99] Ibid., 332.
[100] Ibid.
[101] Ibid., 336.

# Chapter 2

# The Theological Method
# of Andrew Fuller

## INTRODUCTION

**D**espite the fact that Andrew Fuller was essentially a self-taught theologian, his writings were highly valued during his lifetime and beyond. One measure of his influence can be seen by noting that both the College of New Jersey (later Princeton) and Yale awarded honorary Doctor of Divinity (D.D.) degrees to Fuller. He declined both degrees on the grounds that he had not achieved "those literary qualifications which would justify the assumption of academic honours" and that he disapproved of distinctions among brother ministers.[1] Nonetheless, that they were granted speaks volumes about the esteem in which Fuller's theological writings were held in his day. The passage of time has done little to alter that opinion. One of Britain's leading Baptist historians, A. C. Underwood, judged that Fuller was "the soundest and most creatively useful theologian" ever to arise from the Baptist ranks.[2] An American historian echoes that sentiment, venturing the opinion that Fuller "became perhaps the greatest theologian English Baptists ever produced."[3]

Behind such accolades lay a well-grounded theology. This chapter explores the theological method in Fuller's writings. Like Shaker furniture, Fuller's theological method is plain and sturdy. What it lacks in ornamentation is more

---

[1]Laws, *Andrew Fuller: Pastor, Theologian, Ropeholder*, 96. Roberts ("Andrew Fuller," 37) mistakenly reported that Fuller accepted the Yale degree, although he refused to use the title. Fuller's polite and appreciative letter to Yale's president, Timothy Dwight, in which he refused the Yale degree, is contained in Haykin (*Armies of the Lamb*, 199–201). The extent to which Fuller was opposed to the use of academic titles by pastors is made even clearer by his son, A. G. Fuller (A. Fuller to W. Ward, n.d., cited in *Andrew Fuller*, 204), who reports that Fuller said of such titles, "Now to me they are odious. Every one of them half robs me of a Christian brother."

[2]A. C. Underwood, *A History of the English Baptists* (London: Kingsgate, 1947), 166.

[3]McBeth, *The Baptist Heritage*, 182.

ANDREW FULLER.

*Early nineteenth-century line drawing of Fuller that appeared in his collected works.*

than compensated for in strength and durability. As a theologian who was first and foremost a busy pastor, Fuller provides a model for reaching theological conclusions that is well suited for adoption by those who labor in churches.

## FULLER'S THEOLOGICAL METHOD

Given Fuller's powerful impact on his denomination, an investigation into his theological approach is amply warranted. This investigation is greatly facilitated by the fact that he reflected on the nature of the theological task at a number of points in both his published and unpublished writings.

### The Importance of a System

The Puritan culture that gave birth to English Particular Baptists was characterized by a love of theology that was, to put it mildly, "systematic and methodical."[4] But Fuller thought he detected a change in mind-set that had come in with the Enlightenment. He commented, "Systematic divinity, or the studying of truth in a systematic form, has been of late years much decried. It has become almost general to consider it as the mark of a contracted mind, and the grand obstruction to free inquiry."[5] Fighting this trend, Fuller maintained that theology must be approached in a systematic fashion:

> God, in all his works, has proceeded on a system; there is a beautiful connexion and harmony in every thing which he has wrought. . . . Now if God proceeds on system, it may be expected that the Scriptures, being a transcript of his mind, should contain a system; and if we would study them to purpose, it must be so as to discover what the system is.[6]

Anticipating the objection of critics who might argue that the Bible's presentation of doctrine is not systematic, Fuller used analogies to help explain why God revealed "divine truth . . . rather incidentally than systematically:"[7]

> It is not very difficult to discern the wisdom of God in introducing truth in such a manner. If every species of plants and flowers were to grow together, instead of the whole being scattered over the earth, the effect would be very different, and much for the worse; and if all truth relating to one subject were to be found in only one book, chapter, or epistle, we should probably understand much less than we do. There are some Divine truths which are less pleasant than others. Even good men have their partialities, or favourite principles, which would induce them to read those parts of Scripture which favoured them, to the neglect of others. But truth being scattered throughout the Scriptures, we are thereby necessitated, if we read at all, to read the whole mind of God; and thus it is that we gradually and insensibly imbibe it, and become assimilated to the same image. The conduct of God in this matter resembles that of a

---

[4] J. I. Packer, *The Redemption and Restoration of Man in the Thought of Richard Baxter: A Study in Puritan Theology*, SBHT (Carlisle, UK: Paternoster, 2003), 43.

[5] Fuller, *Complete Works*, 1:164.

[6] Ibid., 1:165.

[7] Ibid., 1:537.

wise physician, who, in prescribing for a child, directs that its medicines be mixed up with its necessary food.[8]

According to Fuller, the task of the theologian is to recreate the system of truth that God has revealed in His Word. But a theological system is not lifted verbatim from the pages of Holy Writ. Instead, as with nature, God's system of sacred truth is "scattered in lovely variety."[9] The theologian must be observant in order to "perceive unity, order, arrangement, and fulness [*sic*] of design" as he studies the Bible.[10]

### A System, Not a Straightjacket

Fuller recognized that all theological systems were not equally helpful. Some were so riddled with error as to be counterproductive to the quest for sound doctrine: "If we imbibe a *false* system, indeed, there is no doubt but it will prove injurious; if it be true in part, but very *defective*, it may impede our progress in Divine knowledge."[11] For that reason, any theological system should be adhered to with a sense of humility and with a desire to constantly compare it to the Scriptures.

All things considered, Fuller believed that the systematic study of theology tended to illuminate, not obscure, God's revelation:

That view of things, whether we have any of us fully attained it or not, which admits the most natural meaning to be put upon every part of God's word, is the right system of religious truth. And he whose belief consists of a number of positions arranged in such a connexion as to constitute a consistent whole, but who from a sense of his imperfections, and a remembrance of past errors, holds himself ready to add or retrench, as evidence shall require, is in a far more advantageous track for the attainment of truth, and a real enlargement of mind, than he who thinks without a system.[12]

---

[8] Ibid., 1:539–40.

[9] Ibid., 1:165.

[10] Ibid.

[11] Ibid., 1:164

[12] Ibid., 1:164–65. Fuller's statement that a theologian must always be ready "to add or retrench as evidence shall require" is noteworthy. It shows that the complexities of hermeneutics were not lost on theologians of past generations. What Fuller says blends very well with the model of a

Fuller recognized that even the most carefully constructed theological system was bound to contain imperfection and needed to be constantly subject to revision. When truth from the Scriptures was discovered that did not fit the system, it was a sign the system needed to be corrected.

### *The Role of a Theological System in the Discovery of Truth*

In reaching theological conclusions, Fuller believed that consistency with God's written revelation was a vital checkpoint on one's grasp of truth: "The best criterion of a good system is its agreement with the Holy Scriptures."[13] He also believed that internal consistency could serve as a guide in the pursuit of theological truth. For Fuller, a system was a harmonious way of fitting the Scriptures together to create what John Gill had called *A Body of Doctrinal Divinity*.[14] Each part needed to fit with the rest to create a workable whole. Fuller understood that approaching the study of divine truth from a holistic framework would be an aid to the theologian because the need for coherence in the system would serve as a flag for error. No doubt, Fuller came to this understanding in part from lessons drawn from his own experiences.

At the time Fuller began his theological study, the two leading spokesmen for High Calvinism among English Particular Baptists were John Gill and John Brine. Though they ministered in London, both men were natives of Northamptonshire.[15] They left their stamp on the theology that was preached in the church of Fuller's youth:

> With respect to the system of doctrine which I had been used to hearing from my youth, it was in the high Calvinistic, or rather hyper Calvinistic, strain, admitting nothing spiritually good to be the duty of the

---

hermeneutical spiral that has been popularized in recent times. See G. R. Osborne, *The Hermeneutical Spiral: A Comprehensive Introduction to Biblical Interpretation* (Downers Grove, IL: IVP, 1991).

[13] Fuller, *Complete Works*, 1:164.

[14] Gill's work was the standard systematic theology for Baptists at the time. It was one of the first theological works Fuller read (see chapter 1, note 65).

[15] Nuttall ("Northamptonshire and *The Modern Question*") traced the extensive connections of both men to this county and indeed to the specific group of Dissenters that, in time, became Kettering Baptist Church. He advanced the thesis that part of the surprising impact of Fuller's attack on High Calvinism can be attributed to the fact that it emanated from what had formerly been a High Calvinist stronghold.

unregenerate, and nothing to be addressed to them by way of exhortation, excepting what related to external obedience. Outward services might be required, such as attendance upon the means of grace; and abstinence from gross evils might be enforced; but nothing was said to them from the pulpit in the way of warning them to flee from the wrath to come, or inviting them to apply to Christ for salvation.[16]

In the early days of his ministry, Fuller read Gill and Brine firsthand and stayed in near lockstep with their system of High Calvinism. As he confessed later, "The effect of these views was, that I had very little to say to the unconverted, indeed nothing in a way of exhortation to things spiritually good, or certainly connected with salvation."[17]

But as Fuller began to read more widely, he took up the works of the seventeenth-century open-membership Baptist John Bunyan.[18] He was struck that Gill and Bunyan did not agree:

I perceived, however, that the system of Bunyan was not the same with his [Gill's]; for that, while he maintained the doctrines of election and predestination, he nevertheless held with the free offer of salvation to sinners without distinction. These were things which I could not reconcile, and therefore supposed that Bunyan, though a great and good man, was not so *clear* in his views of the doctrines of the gospel as the writers who succeeded him. I found, indeed, the same things in all the old writers of the sixteenth and seventeenth centuries that came my way. They all dealt, as Bunyan did, in free invitations to sinners to come to Christ and be saved; the consistency of which with personal election I could not understand.[19]

Fuller began to feel the pressure created by two competing Calvinistic perspectives. At this point, he seemed to feel that High Calvinism was more internally consistent. On the other hand, the free addresses to the lost that

---

[16]Fuller, *Complete Works*, 1:12.

[17]Ibid., 1:15.

[18]For a discussion of John Bunyan's status as a Baptist, see J. D. Ban, "Was John Bunyan a Baptist: A Case-Study in Historiography," *BQ* 30 (1984): 367–76.

[19]Fuller, *Complete Works*, 1:15.

had characterized Bunyan and the previous generation of Puritan theologians seemed to square best with the pattern of Scripture.

Two further theological discoveries converged to convince Fuller he had found a more excellent way: a nuanced form of Calvinism that he believed was both consistent with itself and with the Bible. The first discovery was Abraham Taylor's tract *The Modern Question*.[20] In the pamphlet, Taylor set out to prove that repentance and faith were the duty of all sinners who heard the gospel. The High Calvinism prevailing in British Particular Baptist churches of the day had it that the nonelect had neither the power nor the duty to repent and believe. The upshot of this was that ministers called on hearers to repent and believe the gospel only when a warrant was present, that is, evidence of regeneration. Fuller remarks that Taylor's argumentation in *The Modern Question* did little to convince him "til he came to the addresses of John the Baptist, Christ, and the apostles, which he proved to be delivered to the ungodly, and to mean spiritual repentance and faith, inasmuch as they were connected with the remission of sins. This set me fast."[21] The litany of New Testament texts Taylor produced convinced Fuller that his High Calvinist system was out of sync with the Scriptures.

The second theological key for Fuller was the insight he gained into the nature of the fallen human will from reading Jonathan Edwards's *Inquiry into the Modern Prevailing Notions Respecting that Freedom of the Will Which Is Supposed to be Essential to Moral Agency* (1754). Edwards argued for a distinction between natural and moral inability. Viewed from the perspective of their natural abilities, men had freewill, both before and after the fall. But Edwards went on to say that man's greater problem was that, after the fall, he was morally unable to turn to God. That is to say, man had natural ability but moral inability. Fuller accepted this distinction and thus found a way to maintain all the essential sovereignty of God in his Calvinism while at the same time freeing himself to appeal fervently and freely to lost men to come to Christ. Fuller himself describes the impact of Edwards on his thinking:

I had read and considered, as well as I could, Mr. Jonathan Edwards's *Enquiry into the Freedom of the Will*, with some other performances

---

[20] See chapter 1. Taylor was a London Congregationalist and tutor at a Dissenting academy. He and Gill had sparred over several theological points.

[21] Fuller, *Complete Works*, 1:15.

on the distinction of *natural and moral ability, and inability*. I always found great pleasure in this distinction, as it appeared to me to carry with it its own evidence, was clearly and fully contained in the Scriptures, and calculated to disburden the Calvinistic system of a number of calumnies with which its enemies have loaded it, as well as to afford clear and honourable conceptions of the divine government.[22]

The theological system that Fuller put forth in *The Gospel Worthy of All Acceptation* sought both to be internally consistent and faithful to the Scriptures. The theological hurdle for High Calvinists was the issue of how, in the light of particular redemption, one could address *any* fallen, helpless sinner and invite him to repent and believe. If men were powerless to obey the gospel call, these general addresses would seem to be insincere. Edward's dichotomous view of the human will showed that free invitations to the lost were consistent with Calvinism because there was indeed a point of addressability even in fallen men: their natural ability. As Fuller expressed it in the subtitle to *The Gospel Worthy of All Acceptation,* it was *The Duty of Sinners to Believe in Jesus Christ*. Fuller so helped popularize this moderate or evangelical Calvinism among Particular Baptists that it became the new orthodoxy.[23] The desire for systematic coherence was one factor that especially drove Fuller to modify the Calvinism then popular among Particular Baptists.

*A Conservative Innovator*

Another point worthy of mention is Fuller's essentially conservative stance toward the theological system he began with. He insisted throughout his life that he was still a "strict" Calvinist. What he objected to was "false" Calvinism. For example, in responding to a pair of High Calvinists who had castigated him in a letter, Fuller defended his belief in particular redemption:

I very much doubt whether your views of particular redemption be those which are given in the New Testament. It would seem by your manner of writing as if some sinners, were they ever willing to come to Christ for life, could not be saved, for want of a sufficiency in the death of Christ

---

[22] Fuller, *The Gospel Worthy of All Acceptation*, 1st ed., v.
[23] His critics derisively labeled this theological system "Fullerism."

to save them. But no such particular redemption as this is taught in the Scriptures. . . . Neither did Calvin nor the Calvinists in the 16th century entertain any such notion as if there were any want of sufficiency in the sacrifice of Christ even for the whole world, were the whole world to believe in him. . . . I believe in particular redemption, but as it is stated in *The Gospel Worthy of All Acceptation.*[24]

E. F. Clipsham noted that Fuller's careful and limited approach to theological change was one of the factors that accounted for his impact:

Along with the spirit of revolt, and the element of newness in "Fuller-ism" was an essential conservatism. His incurable conservatism, in fact, was one of Fuller's greatest assets in his struggle with hyper-Calvinism. He was able to show men who looked above all for "soundness" of doctrine, and whose dread of Arminianism was almost pathological, that what he was proclaiming was no new doctrine but the faith of the fathers.[25]

### The Priority of Scripture

As has already been seen, Fuller valued an internally consistent system of the-ology. Yet he was always mindful that such consistency could not be purchased at the expense of giving due consideration to the Bible. Throughout his minis-try, Fuller remained a thoroughgoing biblicist.

### The Pitfalls of Traditionalism

Though Fuller consciously desired to be faithful to the Calvinistic Baptist tra-dition, he sought to give pride of place to the Bible, not to his traditions. He understood the necessity of going to the Bible to verify the tradition, instead of using the tradition to mute the voice of Scripture. He counseled reading "the Bible not with a system before your eyes, but as a little child with humility and prayer."[26] In his homespun manner, Fuller explained to a friend the dangers of traditionalism in theological pursuits:

---

[24]Haykin, *Armies of the Lamb,* 216–17.

[25]Clipsham, "Andrew Fuller and Fullerism," 269–70.

[26]Haykin, *Armies of the Lamb*, 217.

My father was a farmer, and in my younger days it was one great boast among the ploughmen that they could plough a strait line *across* the furrows or ridges of a field. I thought I could do this as well as any of them. One day, I saw such a line, which had just been drawn, and I thought, "Now I have it." Accordingly, I laid hold of the plough, and, putting one of the horses into the furrow which had been made, I resolved to keep him walking in it, and thus secure a parallel line. By and by, however, I observed that there were what might be called wriggles in this furrow; and, when I came to *them*, they turned out to be *larger* in mine than in the original. On perceiving this, I threw the plough aside, and determined *never to be an imitator*.[27]

Theologically, this meant the Scriptures alone were the standard by which doctrine should ultimately be judged. Failure to take doctrines back to God's Word was to invite "wriggles" that would magnify themselves in the handing down from one generation to the next.

In the same year he published *The Gospel Worthy of All Acceptation*, Fuller warned the brethren of his Baptist association of the danger of theological imitation: "Another cause of declension, we apprehend, is *making the religion of others our standard, instead of the Word of God.*—The word of God is the only safe rule we have to go by, either in judging what is real religion, or what exertions and services for God are incumbent upon us."[28] Commenting on the dangers of accepting a creedal faith without checking its content against the Scriptures, Fuller noted, "Truth learned only at second-hand will be to us what Saul's armour was to David; we shall be at a loss how to use it in the day of trial."[29]

Fuller commonly expounded his way systematically through a book of the Bible during Sunday morning services.[30] In the preface to the volume of his expositions on Revelation, published in the year Fuller died, the Kettering

---

[27] Fuller, *Complete Works,* 1:111.

[28] Ibid., 3:321.

[29] Ibid., 1:164.

[30] Fuller did not write out his sermons in advance, using instead brief shorthand notes in the pulpit. Though he worked his way through many of the biblical books in the course of his pulpit ministry, his expositions of only two books, Genesis and Revelation, were prepared for publication. Expositions for a third book (Job) were actually readied to print, but they were lost when a fire destroyed the printer's shop. For a list of the biblical books on which Fuller preached a series of expositions, see Ryland, *Work of Faith,* 359.

pastor reveals how he tried to give the voice of Scripture the place of priority in his theological conclusions:

> The method I pursued, was, first to read it [the text of Revelation] carefully over, and, as I went on, to note down what first struck me as the meaning. After reducing these notes into something like a scheme of the prophecy, I examined the best experts I could procure, and, comparing my own first thoughts with theirs, was better able to judge of their justness. Some of them were confirmed, some corrected, and many added to them.[31]

In a letter addressed to a young pastor, attempting to explain how to expound the Scriptures, Fuller repeated much the same advice:

> When I have read a psalm or chapter, which I mean to expound, and have endeavoured to understand it, I have commonly thought it right to consult the best expositors I could obtain, trying and comparing my ideas with theirs. Hereby I have generally obtained some interesting thought which had not occurred to me, and sometimes have seen reason to retract what before appeared to me to be the meaning. But to go first to expositors is to preclude the exercise of your own judgment.[32]

Obviously, Fuller regarded the insight of fellow believers, but what he sought above all was to allow the Scriptures to speak for themselves.

### Fuller's High View of Scripture

Not surprisingly, behind Fuller's desire to privilege the Bible in all matters of theological dispute stood a very high view of Scripture. Commenting on the implications of the phrase "the oracles of God" in Heb 5:12, Fuller wrote, "It is a proper term by which the sacred Scriptures are here denominated, strongly expressive of their Divine inspiration and infallibility; in them God speaks; and to them it becomes us to hearken."[33] These oracles of God must be kept in a unique position by Christians. Fuller's good friend, the scholarly John Ryland

---

[31] Fuller, *Complete Works,* 3:201.
[32] Ibid., 1:714.
[33] Ibid., 1:160.

of Bristol, once sent some American theological books for his friend's use. Though generally sympathetic to the writings of many who immediately followed Jonathan Edwards, Fuller bristled at what he found in one of these volumes:

> I received your parcel, containing several American publications. I have not had time to read them through, though I have looked over some of them. I did not quite like Mr. Bell's mode of appealing to the "unerring oracles of *true philosophy and the word of God.*" God's Word is or is not, a sufficient rule, from whence the man of God may be thoroughly furnished. What is philosophy that it should become an "oracle," by which to try sentiments in divinity?[34]

The era in which Fuller lived brimmed over with challenges to the inspiration and authority of the Bible. Fuller, always ready to take the role of the apologist, responded to many of these attacks on the Scriptures. One of the most influential attacks on Christianity in general, and the Bible in particular, came from the arch-deist Tom Paine (1737–1809). His *Age of Reason* drew rebuttals from some 30 different Christian writers in the first few years following its publication.[35] One of those was Fuller's *The Gospel Its Own Witness* (1799).[36] Paine had argued against the possibility of divine revelation. Sounding remarkably postmodern in his view of the inherent limitations of human language as a vehicle for communicating truth, Paine wrote that "the Word of God cannot exist in any written language. . . . Human language is local and changeable, and is, therefore incapable of being used as the means of unchangeable and

---

[34] Haykin, *Armies of the Lamb,* 139.

[35] Paine's book was published in two parts, 1794 and 1795. For the rebuttals to Paine, see F. K. Prochaska, "Thomas Paine's *The Age of Reason* Revisited," *JHI* 22 (1972): 561–76. For a wide-ranging look at the interchange between Fuller and Paine, see A. P. F. Sell, "*The Gospel Its Own Witness*: Deism, Thomas Paine and Andrew Fuller," in *Enlightenment, Ecumenism, Evangel: Theological Themes and Thinkers, 1550–2000*, ed. A. P. F. Sell, Studies in Christian History and Thought (Carlisle: Paternoster Press, 2005), 111–43.

[36] A. Fuller, *The Gospel Its Own Witness: or The Holy Nature, and Divine Harmony of the Christian Religion, Contrasted with the Immorality and Absurdity of Deism* (Clipstone: J. W. Morris, 1799). M. A. G. Haykin ("'The Oracles of God': Andrew Fuller and the Scriptures," *Churchman* 103 [1989]: 60, 63, 66) noted that Prochaska failed to mention Fuller's work, even though it should be considered the "definitive eighteenth century Baptist response to Deism." Fuller published three editions of this work by 1802, and it remained in print for some 30 years.

universal information."[37] Paine claimed that the only revelation that exists was the witness of nature, what Christians would call general revelation.

With Paine, Fuller affirmed his greatest respect for God's revelation in nature, especially since he found the idea plainly taught in the Bible (e.g., Psalm 19). On the other hand, Fuller stood up for the possibility of divine revelation in Scripture. Having allowed for the reality and beneficial import of general revelation, Fuller asked,

> But does it follow from hence that [special] revelation is unnecessary? Certainly not. It is one thing for nature to afford so much light in matters of right and wrong, as to leave the sinner without excuse; and another to afford him any well-grounded hope of forgiveness, or to answer his difficulties concerning the account which something within him says he must hereafter give of his present conduct. . . . It was, I doubt not, from a close observation of the different efficacy of nature and Scripture, that the writer of the *nineteenth Psalm*, (a Psalm which Mr. Paine pretends to admire,) after having given a just tribute of praise to the former, affirmed the latter, *"The law of Jehovah is perfect, converting the soul."*[38]

At the close of *The Gospel Its Own Witness*, Fuller returned to the theme of the necessity of special revelation:

> When you have ascended to the height of human discovery, there are things, and things of infinite moment too, that are utterly beyond its reach. Revelation is the medium, and the only medium, by which, standing, as it were, "on nature's Alps," we discover things which eye hath not seen, nor ear heard, and of which it never hath entered into the heart of man to conceive.[39]

A further testimony to Fuller's high view of the Scripture is found in the second and third articles of the confession of faith Fuller had provided to the church at Kettering:

---

[37] T. Paine, *The Age of Reason: Being an Investigation of True and Fabulous Theology* (Chicago: Belfords, Clarke & Co., 1897), 25.

[38] Fuller, *Complete Works*, 2:19.

[39] Ibid., 2:97.

II. Yet, considering the present state of mankind, I believe we needed a revelation of the mind of God, to inform us more fully of his and our own character, of his designs towards us, and will concerning us; and such a revelation I believe the Scriptures of the Old and New Testament to be, without excepting any one of its books; and a perfect rule of faith and practice. . . .

III. From this divine volume, I learn many things concerning God, which I could not have learned from the works of nature, and the same things in a more convincing light. Here I learn, especially, the infinitely amiable moral character of God. His holiness, justice, faithfulness, and goodness, are here exhibited in such a light, by his holy law and glorious gospel, as is nowhere else to be seen.[40]

In a word, Fuller believed God's special revelation in the Scriptures was both more complete and more convincing than anything accessible through the light of general revelation.

Though the list of citations could be expanded almost endlessly, one last example of Fuller's reverence for the Scriptures will suffice. Some of Fuller's strongest affirmations regarding the inspiration of the Bible are found in a piece titled "The Veneration of the Scriptures." This work was published in 1793 as one of 15 letters that comprised a work titled *The Calvinistic and Socinian Systems Examined and Compared.*[41] In this letter Fuller argues that true piety always includes "an affectionate attachment to the Holy Scriptures, as the rule of faith and practice."[42] The Socinian writer to whom Fuller was primarily responding—the champion of Unitarianism, Joseph Priestly (1733–1804)—had argued that the Scriptures were merely "faithful records of past transactions" and that they possessed no greater authority than the words of "any other honest and well-informed historian."[43] Thus he elevated human reason as the supreme bar by which all things were to be tried. Fuller defended the premise that the Scriptures were the "rule of faith and practice" because of "the

---

[40] Belcher, *The Last Remains of the Rev. Andrew Fuller*, 209–10.

[41] A. Fuller, *The Calvinistic and Socinian Systems Examined and Compared, as to Their Moral Tendency: in a Series of Letters Addressed to the Friends of Vital and Practical Religion* (Clipstone: J. W. Morris, 1793).

[42] Fuller, *Complete Works*, 2:195.

[43] Ibid., 2:198.

most perfect Divine inspiration."[44] Because of the inspiration that belongs to it alone, the Bible is the only "infallible test of Divine truth, to which all appeals were to be made, and by which every controversy in religious matters was to be decided."[45] Bush and Nettles summed up Fuller's high view of the Bible:

> Fuller believed that the Bible was revelation from God. Its words are inspired so that they are infallible and free from error. Therefore we should venerate them, study them, and submit all our thought and deeds to their authority. Whenever Fuller opposed the heresies of his day, or when he was advising his fellow believers, his appeal was always to the truth of Scripture.[46]

### The Role of Reason in Theological Reflection

A corollary to the priority Fuller insisted must be given to the Scriptures in pursuing theological truth is that reason must also be kept in a subordinate place. Fuller had nothing bad to say about the role of reason per se in pursuing truth:

> We do not suppose faith and *right* reason to be opposites: that be far from us. On the contrary, nothing is more evident than that Christianity is entirely a rational system; and it is its glory that it is so. We should

---

[44]Ibid., 2:197.

[45]Ibid., 2:196.

[46]L. R. Bush and T. J. Nettles, *Baptists and the Bible*, rev. and expanded ed. (Nashville: B&H, 1999), 99–100. Bush and Nettles are right to speak of Fuller's high view of Scripture. In his otherwise excellent chapter on Fuller in *Shapers of Baptist Thought*, J. Tull (*Shapers of Baptist Thought* [Valley Forge, PA: Judson, 1972; repr. Macon, GA: Mercer Press, 1984], 94) sought to characterize Fuller as a biblicist but not a bibliolater. He portrayed Fuller as asking, "What is it that the Scriptures reveal which is of more ultimate authority than the Scriptures themselves?" Tull then reproduced a passage from Fuller's *Letters on Systematic Divinity*, which he claimed shows that Fuller subordinated the Bible to the revelation of God in the cross. In that passage, Fuller wrote, "The only display of the Divine perfections which can be denominated perfect is in the salvation of sinners, through the obedience and death of his beloved Son." Tull set up a false dichotomy and ignored the context of Fuller's statement in order to prove his thesis. Fuller's real point in the citation Tull used was simply that no other single act of God *recorded in Scripture* reveals all the divine attributes as clearly as does the cross. Tull read his own concerns back into Fuller's argument. The passage from Fuller is in *Complete Works*, 1:706. A more accurate portrayal of Fuller's high view of Scripture is found in J. H. Watson, "Baptists and the Bible: As Seen in Three Eminent Baptists," *Foundations* 16 (1973): 237–54, esp. 250. Watson grasped the salient point that Tull obfuscated: namely, Fuller is "concerned to affirm the superiority of the Bible as revelation."

never have been required to give a *reason* for the hope that is in us, if there had been no reason to have been given.[47]

Fuller expressed three main concerns about reason. First, he wished that devotees of reason would remember that human reason was subject to error. Man's reasoning abilities are "shattered and broken by sin, and liable to a thousand variations through blindness and prejudice."[48] Second, because that is so, it follows that "it is wrong and presumptuous to set up *our* reason as a standard competent to decide what is truth and what is error."[49] Reason must retain a subordinate position to the authority of Scripture. Third, reason is limited as to what it can teach. It may capably provide all men need to know in certain fields, but not in spiritual matters. Fuller contrasted reason and revelation in *The Gospel Its Own Witness:*

[The Scriptures] were not given to teach us astronomy, or geography, or civil government, or any science which relates to the present life only; therefore they do not determine upon any system of any of these sciences. These are things upon which reason is competent to judge, sufficiently at least for the purposes of human life, without a revelation from heaven. The great object of revelation is to instruct us in things which pertain to our everlasting peace.[50]

Not only does reason have limits as to what it can help mankind discover, but also its limits come at the most critical point: knowledge of the spiritual realm. Scripture must be given primacy in part because it alone tells man what he most needs to know:

But though nothing in revelation be contrary to right reason, yet there are many things which our reason could never have found out, had they not been made known by the Supreme Intelligence. The plan of redemption by Jesus Christ, in particular, contains a set of truths which the eye had not seen, nor the ear heard, nor had they entered the heart of man to

---

[47] Fuller, *Complete Works*, 1:124.
[48] Ibid.
[49] Ibid., 1:125.
[50] Ibid., 2:88.

conceive, had not God revealed them to us by his Spirit. . . . It staggers our reason to receive it, even now it is told us.[51]

Elsewhere he elaborated on the greater importance of revelation over reason:

> There is an importance in truth, as it relates to philosophy, history, politics, or any other branch of science, inasmuch as it affects the present happiness of mankind; but what is this when compared with that which involves their everlasting salvation? To be furnished with an answer to the question, "What shall I do to be saved?" is of infinitely greater account than to be able to decide whether the Ptolemaic or Copernican system be that of nature. The temporal salvation of a nation, great as it is, and greatly as it interests the minds of men, is nothing when compared with the eternal salvation of a single individual.[52]

## The Role of Experience

To the value of a system and the priority of Scripture over that system can be added a third component in Fuller's theological method: the essential role of Christian experience.

### "Experimental Religion"
In characterizing Fuller as a theologian, Clipsham summarizes his view of experience in true religion:

> Moreover, he insisted, Christianity is not primarily an intellectual system, consisting of propositions about God, man, and the universe, which needs to be proved and defended, but a gospel to be accepted, God's provision for man's deepest needs. Only believers, those who have put the gospel to the test, are competent to judge its worth.[53]

---

[51]Ibid., 1:124.
[52]Ibid., 3:527.
[53]Clipsham, "Andrew Fuller and Fullerism," 273.

One of the clearest expressions of this truth is found in a series dialogues Fuller set up between two imaginary religious conversation partners, Crispus and Gaius. Their third dialogue is titled "The Connexion between Doctrinal, Experimental, and Practical Religion." In this exchange, Fuller seeks to establish that "if God has joined these things together, let no man, whether preacher, or hearer, attempt to put them asunder."[54] Defining what he means by "experimental religion,"[55] Gaius says it is the "proof or trial which we make of Divine things, while passing through the vicissitudes of life. . . . There are many truths taught us in the Divine word, and which we may be said to know by reading; but we do not know them experimentally till we have proved them true by having made the trial."[56] Religious experience, then, works hand in hand with the Scriptures in coming to a right view of doctrine. A pastor-theologian cannot hope to expound fully the doctrines of the Christian religion apart from a fervent and ongoing personal walk with God. It is out of the everyday experiences of lived Christianity that his mind comes to the fullest grasp of the doctrines of the Christian life necessary for him to explain them to others. As Fuller said, "That which we communicate will freeze upon our lips, unless we have first applied it to ourselves; or, to use the language of Scripture, 'tasted, felt, and handled the word of life.'"[57]

For that reason, Fuller's journal is filled with reflections on the presence—or often the absence—of spiritual "exercise." Whether it is a sermon he delivered, a pastoral visit he had made, or time spent in prayer, Fuller weighed all things to see how they were impacting his own soul. Consider some excerpts of his diary from September 1784:

> Returned to Kettering today, little or no exercise of mind. Spoke tonight on *God's statutes being our song in the house of our pilgrimage*. His holy *Word* is the chief source of joy that we have in life, especially his glorious *Gospel*.

> Rode today to Okeham, little exercise by the way. The sight of a drunken man, who was full of religious talk, affecting to me.

---

[54] Fuller, *Complete Works*, 2:654.
[55] This was Fuller's characteristic way to refer to religious experience; see ibid., 2:653.
[56] Ibid., 2:652.
[57] Ibid., 1:714.

But a poorish forenoon and afternoon, but much earnestness and love to souls tonight. Preached on *Loving God's salvation!*

Nothing of any remarkable exercise for these two or three days, except some tenderness in prayer. Last Tuesday I found some heart to pray for *God's Holy Spirit* that it might not be taken from us, and on some seasons since then have felt that desire renewed. Very tender tonight on Christ's legacy, *My peace I give unto you.*

But a poor day. It seems almost impossible to get my sluggish soul to action.[58]

Fuller scrutinized his reaction to all kinds of events for evidence of a spiritual exercise or benefit to his own soul. Since he was a hard taskmaster on himself, his diary can sometimes make for gloomy reading, as the excerpts above tend to reveal.[59]

But when he felt his soul being strengthened by the events of life or ministry, Fuller could also experience great joy. For example, "An affecting forenoon, in preaching from Ezekiel 10:13, an equally affecting afternoon from Psalm 125. . . . My heart, how it melts! A good spirit seemed to take place."[60] He often derived great benefit from times around the Lord's Table, as this excerpt shows: "Preached this afternoon on the *dimensions* of the love of Christ. Great delight at the Lord's Supper. Oh to know more of, and live upon, Christ! He must be our daily bread. Sweet pleasure tonight. Can hardly forbear singing as I go about, 'Oh! For this love let rocks and hills / Their lasting silence break.'"[61]

One subset of religious experience that Fuller believed God especially used for good in His servants was the cup of suffering. For example, when his six-year-old daughter Sarah lay on her deathbed, Fuller wrote to his friend John Ryland,

---

[58] Fuller, *Diary*, September 10–18, 1784.

[59] I agree with Morden's assessment that a distinct change in tone is observable in Fuller's diary once he became active in the work of the BMS. See Morden's chapter "Fuller and the Spiritual Life" in *Offering Christ to the World*, 157–79.

[60] Fuller, *Diary*, July 15, 1781.

[61] Ibid., August 31, 1784.

I can easily see, it may be best for us to part. I have been long praying, in I know not what manner, that I might be brought *nearer to God*; find some particular *evils* in my heart subdued; have my mind enlarged in *experimental* knowledge; and my heart more *weaned* from things below, and *set on things above*. Perhaps, by "terrible things in righteousness" God may answer these petitions. O that it may be so indeed![62]

Trials, then, were not so much to be feared but anticipated as one of God's choice means to help His servants come to a fuller experiential knowledge of the truth.

*The Place of Prayer and Scripture Reading in the Life of the Pastor-Theologian*
In a pietistic vein, Fuller insisted on a proper spiritual frame of mind to understand the Scriptures rightly:

> Moreover, to enter into the true meaning of the Scriptures, it is absolutely necessary that we *drink into the spirit* of the writers. This is the greatest of all accomplishments. I do not mean that you are to expect a spirit of extraordinary inspiration; but that of power, and of love, and of a sound mind. It is impossible to enter into the sentiments of any great writer without a kindred mind. Who but a Pope, or a Cowper, could have translated Homer? and who can explain the oracles of God, but he who, in a measure, drinks into the same spirit? Every Christian knows by experience that, in a spiritual frame of mind, he can understand more of the Scriptures in an hour than he can at other times, with the utmost application, in a week.[63]

And how can that right frame of mind be cultivated? "By conversing with the sacred writers, we shall gradually imbibe their sentiments, and be insensibly assimilated into the same spirit."[64]

The ministers of the Northamptonshire Baptist Association were a close knit group. One of the appealing aspects of Fuller's move to Kettering was that

---

[62]Ryland, *Work of Faith*, 263.
[63]Fuller, *Complete Works*, 1:713.
[64]Ibid., 1:164.

from that central location, he could attend the association's weekly ministers' meeting. At one of these meetings, the conversation revealed the premium Fuller and his friends placed on prayer and Scripture reading in the life of the pastor:

> Today we had a ministers' meeting at Northampton. I preached on being *Of one spirit with Christ* and heard bro. Sutcliff on *Divine Sovereignty* from Rom. 9, and bro. Skinner on Psalm 139 *Search me and try me*. But the best part of the day was, I think, in conversation. A question was put and discussed, to the following purport: *To what causes in ministers may much of their want of success be imputed?* The answer much turned upon the *want* of *personal* religion, particularly the want of close dealing with God in *closet prayer*. Jeremiah 10:21 was here referred to, "Their pastors are become *brutish*, and have not *sought* the Lord; *therefore* they shall not prosper, and their flocks shall be scattered." Another reason assigned was the want of reading and studying the Scriptures more as *Christians*, for the edification of our own souls. We are too apt to study them merely to find out something *to say to others*, without living upon the truth ourselves. If we eat not the book, before we deliver its contents to others, we may expect the Holy Spirit will not much accompany us. If we study the Scriptures as *Christians*, the more we shall feel their importance; but, if otherwise, our familiarity with the word will be like that of soldiers and doctors with death—it will wear away all sense of its importance from our minds. To enforce this sentiment, Proverbs 22:17,18, was referred to, "Apply thine *heart* to knowledge— the words of the wise will be pleasant if thou keep them within thee; they shall withal be *fitted in thy lips*." To this might have been added Psalm 1:2,3.[65]

As Fuller saw it, constant engagement in prayer and immersion in the Word of God was a sine qua non for the pastor-theologian.

---

[65]Fuller, *Diary*, September 30, 1785.

*The "Extravagant Vagaries of Enthusiasm"*

It is important to keep in mind that religious experience was inseparable from the biblical revelation in Fuller's spirituality. He warned against the dangers of unchecked religious experience:

> Revealed truth is represented as a *"form* of doctrine" into which believers are "delivered," Rom. vi 17. As a melted substance, cast into a mould, receives its form from it, and every line in the one corresponds with that of the other; so true religion in the soul accords with true religion in the Scriptures. Without this standard, we shall either model our faith by our preconceived notions of what is fit and reasonable, or be carried away by our feelings, and lose ourselves among the extravagant vagaries of enthusiasm. Our views may seem to us very rational, or our feelings may be singularly ardent; and yet we may be far from being in the right. The question is, Whether they agree line to line with the Divine model?[66]

Thus, whereas Fuller valued religious experience in reaching theological conclusions, he insisted that all subjective experiences be refracted through the objective prism of God's word.

### The Necessity of Accountability

A final component of Fuller's approach to the task of pastoral theology was his understanding of the need for accountability. Freedom of thought was one characteristic of the age of Enlightenment in which Fuller lived. Latitudinarian ideas were by no means confined to the Church of England, but cropped up in all denominations. As a Baptist, Fuller cherished religious liberty. On the other hand, he viewed with concern the abuse of religious freedom.

*The Right and Wrong Use of "Private Judgment"*

In eighteenth-century England, issues pertaining to religious liberty were often discussed under the rubric of the right to "private judgment." Fuller reflected on this topic in an insightful essay titled "An Inquiry into the Right of Private Judgment in Matters of Religion." Properly conceived, private judgment was a blessing of liberty that had been hard won for all English Dissenters,

---

[66]Fuller, *Complete Works*, 1:528.

especially the Baptists. Fuller defined this wholesome type of private judgment as "the right which every individual has to think and to avow his thoughts on those subjects [religious ones], without being liable to any civil inconvenience on that account."[67] Fuller perceived that this liberty was being redefined and turned into license:

> But of late the subject has taken another turn, and men have pleaded not only an exemption from civil penalties on account of their religious principles, in which the very essence of persecution consists, but also that they are not subject to the control of a religious society with which they stand connected for any tenets which they may think proper to avow. The right of private judgment now frequently assumed, is *a right in every individual who may become a member of a Christian church to think and avow his thoughts, be they what they may, without being subject to exclusion or admonition, or the ill opinion of his brethren, on that account.*[68]

This, Fuller concluded, "appears to be highly extravagant, and is what no man can claim is a right."[69] To bolster his argument, he turned again to the pattern of Scripture. He reminded his readers that "not only were those who disbelieved the gospel refused admission to a Christian church, but those who perverted the gospel, or maintained pernicious errors concerning it, were subject to admonition and exclusion."[70] Fuller went on to point out that on no less authority than that of the Lord Jesus Himself, the church at Pergamos was rebuked for "having those *among them* who held the doctrine of Balaam and of the Nicolaitans."[71] Fuller drew the conclusion that "admonishing or excluding from the primitive church those who held pernicious errors was not reckoned to be subversive of the right of private judgment."[72] Thus, Fuller reserved to a church the right to examine and censure the theological positions espoused by its members.

---

[67] Ibid., 3:447.
[68] Ibid.
[69] Ibid.
[70] Ibid.
[71] Ibid.
[72] Ibid., 1:448.

## On the Use of Creeds

In keeping with this, Fuller did not object to the use of creeds or statements of faith.[73] As was fairly typical in that day, he gave the church at Kettering his own personal statement of faith for their perusal as they were considering calling him to be their new pastor.[74] In traveling and preaching on behalf of the Baptist Missionary Society (BMS), an exchange of brief doctrinal statements of faith between himself and host churches was not unheard of.[75] Beyond this, Fuller also wrote an essay that circulated widely, "On Creeds and Subscriptions."[76] Fuller certainly recognized many potential dangers and abuses in handling creeds. But when used correctly, Fuller believed creedal statements had great value and should be used by Baptists. With simple logic he reasoned, "That an individual has a right so to judge, and form his connexions with those whose views are most congenial with his own, will not be disputed; but if so, why have not a society the same right?"[77]

Fuller offered four observations related to the use of confessions of faith. First, he suggested that where the word of God was silent, churches and Christian organizations should follow suit. Otherwise, they ran the risk of "substituting for doctrines the commandments of men, and making void the law of God by his traditions."[78] Second, he recognized that human fallibility meant that creeds must be left open to amendment. Third, because of their provisional nature, creeds were not a valid basis for formulating religious opinions. They were only a secondary source, or an additional witness to the truth. Fuller insisted that "the word of God, and that alone, ought to be the ground of both faith and practice."[79] Fourth, Fuller recognized that not every article of faith that properly delineated a particular religious body was necessarily codified in writing. Whether written or understood, a religious body had a right to expect faithfulness to its articles of belief: "Some societies have no written articles of faith or discipline; but with them, as with others that have, it is always

---

[73] As was then generally the case among English Baptists, Fuller used terms like "creeds," "confessions," or "articles of faith" interchangeably.

[74] Ryland, *Work of Faith*, 54–59. Also found in appendix 1.

[75] Fuller, *Complete Works*, 1:77–78.

[76] See ibid., 3:449–51.

[77] Ibid., 3:450.

[78] Ibid., 3:449.

[79] Ibid., 3:450.

understood that there are certain principles of professed belief of which is deemed necessary to communion."[80]

In concluding his essay, Fuller clearly summed up what has been a widely accepted view of the use of creeds among Baptists of all types: "If the articles of faith be opposed to the authority of Scripture, or substituted in the place of such authority, they become objectionable and injurious; but if they simply express the united judgment of those who voluntarily subscribe them, they are incapable of any such imputation."[81]

## *Baptist Interdependence*

Another important expression of accountability to be observed in Fuller was his commitment to conduct his theological work under the auspices of fellow Baptists.[82] For example, he was committed to a robust associational life. Meetings of the Northamptonshire Baptist Association were held twice a year, with attendance by virtually all ministers a forgone conclusion. In addition, ordinations were treated as significant denominational events and regularly well attended by other pastors. The lengths to which pastors went in order to attend are shocking by modern standards. For example, Fuller wrote that the patriarch of the association when he was ordained, Robert Hall Sr., "Came seventy miles to my ordination, and continued my father and friend till his death."[83] Another expression of associational vitality can be seen in the Northamptonshire Baptists' pursuance of prayer meetings for revival and spiritual awakening, after the model proposed in Jonathan Edwards's famous book, *An Humble Attempt.*[84]

---

[80] Ibid. Fuller was not necessarily advocating that vagueness in confessions is a good thing. Rather, he was pointing out that no succinct creed can possibly cover all possible deviations of faith and practice. A religious society has the right to revisit and clarify its creed as needs arise.

[81] Fuller, *Complete Works*, 3:451.

[82] Though the most celebrated side of Baptist ecclesiology is congregational independence, it is a mistake to discount Baptist interdependence. A. H. Strong (*Systematic Theology: A Compendium*, one-vol. ed. [Old Tappan, NJ: Revell, 1907], 928) explained congregational polity by saying that, among Baptists, "independence is qualified by interdependence."

[83] Fuller, *Complete Works*, 1:15.

[84] The full title was *An Humble Attempt to Promote Explicit Agreement and Visible Union of God's People for the Revival of Religion and Advancement of Christ's Kingdom on Earth* (1747). John Sutcliff, one of Fuller's closest friends, brought this book out in an English edition in 1789. This sparked an ongoing series of prayer meetings in the Northamptonshire Association that many have credited as a key factor in the formation of the BMS in 1792. Fuller encouraged Sutcliff

The meetings of the association were devoted to more than prayer and fellowship. They were the primary forum for addressing the practical and doctrinal concerns of the churches. When a consensus on some particular issue seemed to have been arrived at by the churches of the association, it was common for that view to find expression in published letters designed to be circulated among the fellowship.[85] Fuller carried out his theological work in this atmosphere of cooperation and accountability.

Inseparably entwined with Fuller's commitment to associational life was his habit of forming deep and abiding friendships with fellow Northamptonshire Association pastors. It was through a close network of relationships with fellow pastors that the association made its most profound impact on Fuller. Haykin has pointed out that Fuller's friendships were a major component of his spiritual life precisely because they were "spiritual friendships," not merely social friendships.[86] These pastors regularly prayed together, discussed what they were reading, traded books, critiqued each other's writings prior to publication, and corresponded voluminously. One instance of the esteem these men had for the opinion of their peers was when—at the time Fuller was considering whether to accept the call from the church at Kettering—he submitted the matter to arbitration by a group of nine fellow pastors.

But these spiritual friendships also had theological consequences as well. For example, Fuller originally wrote his most important theological work, *The Gospel Worthy of All Acceptation*, while pastor at Soham. At the time of its composition (1781), he had neither a view toward publishing it nor any prospects to do so if he had desired. It was merely his personal effort to work through pastoral and theological issues that had arisen from his consideration of the "modern question." As Fuller formed close friendships with other pastors after relocating to Kettering, he discovered many were likeminded and shared his manuscript with some of them. They almost insisted that he seek to publish it.

This encouragement was especially significant because Fuller realized the opposition that going public with his theological changes would evoke. He foresaw that he would be placed in a crossfire of criticism, from the

---

in the publication of Edwards's book and was an enthusiastic participant in the resulting prayer meetings.

[85] In the last 23 years of his life, Fuller composed nine of these annual letters.

[86] Haykin, *Armies of the Lamb*, 42.

Arminians on the one side and the defenders of the waning High Calvinism on the other. He confided his fears to his diary: "Many misgivings of heart, about engaging in a defence of what I esteem truth, lest the cause of Christ should be injured through me. Surely, if I did not believe *that* in defence of which I write to be *important* truth, I would hide my head in obscurity all my days."[87] A few days later, he added, "The weight of publishing still lies upon me. I expect I shall have a great share of unhappiness through it. Surely I had much rather go through the world in peace, did I not think that all things considered it was my duty to do as I do."[88] Because of these misgivings, the encouragement he received to publish *The Gospel Worthy of All Acceptation* from his fellow Northamptonshire Association pastors was a decisive factor in taking that step.

## CONCLUSION

Fuller's theological method is well suited to adaptation by pastor-theologians. It recognizes that most pastors begin their ministerial pilgrimage in a recognizable theological framework. Study and mastery of this framework through the discipline of systematic theology is too often neglected. Failure to understand doctrine in an organic and holistic manner, though, will act as a blinder to the detection of theological error.

Fuller also demonstrated a willingness to modify cherished theological positions when they are found to be in conflict with Scripture. There is nothing flighty or unstable in Fuller's theology. But when convinced through careful study that his theology was out of sync with the Word of God, Fuller understood that Scripture must be given the predominant position. In this he faithfully modeled adherence to the important Reformation dictum *sola Scriptura*.

Fuller's pietistic impulse serves as a needed reminder that the church today is little in need of merely academic theologians. As valuable as the right interpretation of Scripture is, it is not enough. What is called for in pastor-theologians is right doctrine imbibed and lived out in the course of ministry.

---

[87] Fuller, *Diary*, August 20, 1784.
[88] Ibid.

Finally, the more isolated a pastor-theologian is, the easier it is for him to fall into error. Although he did not sell cheaply the cherished Baptist distinctive of religious liberty, Fuller's theological method incorporates a strong component of doctrinal accountability to the churches and pastors of his denomination. His views stand as a powerful counteraction to the abuse of Baptist freedom that has become characteristic of this age.

# Chapter 3

# The Soteriology of Andrew Fuller

## INTRODUCTION

T
imothy George recently described Andrew Fuller as "the most influential Baptist theologian between John Bunyan and the present day."[1] If he is correct, Fuller was the most influential Baptist theologian in over 300 years—or almost the entire denominational existence of Baptists.[2] Fuller made his influence felt in many branches of Baptist life: apologetics, pastoral work, missionary impetus, denominational development, and more. But in no area did he have a more profound impact than in the field of soteriology. His best friend and first biographer said, "He never seemed more in his element as when dwelling on the doctrine of the atonement. . . . This doctrine rejoiced his own soul; and this he used to exhibit to others, as of the greatest importance; comprising all the salvation of a needy sinner, and all the desire of a new-born soul."[3]

This chapter explores how Andrew Fuller handled the doctrine of soteriology. His formulation of this doctrine had a profound impact on British Particular Baptists and their theological descendants in America. The chapter is developed along four lines of inquiry. The first one offers a brief examination of the soteriological convictions prevalent among Particular Baptists when Fuller came on the scene. Second, with that background in place, Fuller's

---

[1]Cited on the back-cover endorsement of Morden, *Offering Christ to the World*. W. H. Brackney (*A Genetic History of Baptist Thought: With Special Reference to Baptists in Britain and North America* [Macon, GA: Mercer, 2004], 122) seconds that verdict, claiming that "Fuller was to have the widest transforming influence in the history of the denomination."

[2]Of course, that assumes the correctness of the English Separatist descent theory of Baptist origins.

[3]Ryland, *Work of Faith*, 361.

theological innovations are explained in their proper context.[4] Third, an attempt is made to assess how widely these soteriological changes permeated Baptist life and theology. Finally, the impact of Fuller's doctrinal legacy is evaluated.

## THE SOTERIOLOGICAL CONVICTIONS OF PARTICULAR BAPTISTS PRIOR TO FULLER

The soteriological position of English Particular Baptists in the generation that followed the Act of Toleration (1689) was once thought to be clearly understood. More recent scholarship has cast doubts on the accuracy of the picture handed down by some of the most respected Baptist theologians.

### *The Older Historical Consensus*

The early Baptist historian J. Ivimey (1773–1834) famously characterized the preachers that immediately preceded Fuller's day as preaching from within a "non-invitation, non-application scheme."[5] What Ivimey refers to usually goes under the name of High Calvinism or hyper-Calvinism. In its eighteenth-century Baptist expression, High Calvinism was characterized by an extreme caution in handling the gospel lest anything should be said or done that would infringe on the sovereignty of God in saving souls. Ivimey's curt assessment echoed throughout the nineteenth century until it became almost a maxim in Baptist historiography that High Calvinism "was all but universal among Particular Baptists of the period" and could properly be held accountable "for the spiritual deadness of the churches."[6]

For example, Tull described "the enervating effects of hyper-Calvinism."[7] Underwood vividly spoke of "the winter of hyper-Calvinism."[8] In his choice of imagery, he followed C. H. Spurgeon, who said that High Calvinism "chilled

---

[4] A significant part of Fuller's challenge to High Calvinism had as much to do with practice as doctrine. The present chapter focuses more on Fuller's doctrinal position, whereas chapter 4 focuses on the pastoral methodology that flowed from the doctrine.

[5] J. Ivimey, *A History of the English Baptists* (London: B. J. Holdworth, 1811–30), 3:272, cited in Underwood, *History of the English Baptists*, 134.

[6] Clipsham, "Andrew Fuller and Fullerism," 101.

[7] Tull, *Shapers of Baptist Thought,* 81.

[8] Underwood, *History of the English Baptists*, 160.

many churches to the very soul."[9] McBeth agreed with the consensus position and explained in what sense the Calvinists of the early eighteenth-century Particular Baptists were hyper: "They so exaggerated certain aspects, such as election and predestination, that these came to dominate their entire theology and all else had to be judged in that light. Because they gradually put more stress on the Calvinistic aspects of their faith, and less upon the evangelical, they gradually lost their zeal for evangelism and vital church life."[10] Not surprisingly, as High Calvinistic theology spread among Particular Baptists, their churches declined in both size and number.[11] Fuller himself colorfully described the precarious situation of the denomination at about the time he began to pastor: "Till of late, I conceive, there was such a portion of erroneous *doctrine* and false religion amongst us, that if we had carried matters a little further, we should have been a very dunghill in society."[12]

Historians and theologians have discussed the origins of High Calvinism at length. Inevitably, the blame for the inroads of High Calvinism among the Particular Baptists makes its way back to John Gill. Respected Baptist historian W. T. Whitley expressed the verdict of many when he laid the blame for Baptist High Calvinism at John Gill's feet with stinging criticism: "London Baptists were almost paralysed by Gill's doctrine."[13] Responding to the litany of echoes to Whitley's sentiments, Nettles stated that Gill "has doubtless been judged more harshly and even maliciously than any man of comparable repute in Baptist history."[14]

---

[9]C. H. Spurgeon, *The Metropolitan Tabernacle: Its History and Work* (London: n.p., 1876), 47, cited in R. Brown, *The English Baptists of the Eighteenth Century*, vol. 2 of A History of the English Baptists, ed. B. R. White (London: The Baptist Historical Society, 1986), 76.

[10]McBeth, *The Baptist Heritage*, 172.

[11]Considering primary source material, Morden (*Offering Christ to the World*, 7–10) estimates that the number of Particular Baptist churches in England and Wales declined by at least a third by the middle of the eighteenth century. For a challenge to this standard reading of the evidence, see C. Jarvis, "The Myth of High-Calvinism?" in *Recycling the Past or Researching History?* ed. P. E. Thompson and A. R. Cross, SBHT 11 (Carlisle, UK; Waynesboro, GA: Paternoster, 2005), 231–64.

[12]Fuller, *Complete Works*, 3:478.

[13]W. T. Whitley, *Calvinism and Evangelism in England, Especially in Baptist Circles* (London: Kingsgate, n.d.), 27.

[14]Nettles, *By His Grace*, 84.

### Qualifications to the Historical Consensus

More recent scholarship has challenged the extent to which High Calvinism was normative, the numerical and spiritual decline of the churches, and Gill's culpability for the spreading spiritual malaise.

### Was High Calvinism Really Widespread?

First, the point has been made that Particular Baptists of that era were far too diverse to claim for them anything like a "universal" High Calvinism. Hayden sought to demonstrate that the evangelical Calvinism associated with Fuller was not birthed in a vacuum. He maintained that a vital, evangelistic Calvinism had been the true birthright of Particular Baptists from their seventeenth-century heritage. He further argued that historians have been led astray by focusing too narrowly on the London duo of Brine and Gill:

> [It will be evident that] London Baptists were not at all representative of the far greater number of Baptists in the provinces, and that a true balance can only be made by a proper appreciation of Baptist life in the provinces, where Evangelical Calvinism more than survived. It was a vital factor and a far stronger force than has hitherto been acknowledged by Baptist historians.[15]

The bulk of Hayden's evidence is taken from the ministries of Broadmead Baptist Church in Bristol and the Baptist Academy that grew up with it, imbibing the evangelistic fervor of that famous church.

### Did Baptists Even Decline at All?

Jarvis argued that the notion of numerical and spiritual decline among Particular Baptists in the eighteenth century is nothing but a myth.[16] He summed up his research by stating, "The statistical evidence presented does not lend support to the commonly expressed view that English Baptists in the mid-eighteenth century were in a state of stagnation. . . . In fact, the figures presented

---

[15] Hayden, *Continuity and Change*, xiii.

[16] Jarvis, "The Myth of High-Calvinism?" (esp. p. 249). In my view, Jarvis fails to make his case. High Calvinism was not universal, but it was widespread. It certainly could not be characterized as a "myth."

would tend to suggest the opposite, that English Baptists during this period experienced steady and continuous growth."[17] Although his work is too recent to sufficiently gauge the reception his thesis will receive, I believe it is seriously flawed.[18]

## Was John Gill a Hyper-Calvinist?

Nettles and others have sought in recent years to prove that Gill has been unjustly accused of antinomianism and hyper-Calvinism.[19] These modern champions of Gill have pointed out that all dissenting denominations experienced a severe period of decline following the passage of the Acts of Toleration (1689). Instead of castigating Gill for his lack of evangelistic giftedness and effectiveness, a few voices are now heard suggesting "perhaps, rather than imputing blame upon Gill for the leanness of the times, he should be credited with preserving gospel purity, which eventuated in the efforts to use means for the conversion of the heathen."[20]

## The Consensus: Qualified but Not Set Aside

These corrections to the traditional views of the decline of late eighteenth-century Particular Baptists have considerable merit. The development of theological ideas is hardly linear with clean lines of demarcation. Numerous preachers prior to Fuller held similar doctrinal and methodological approaches to ministry and preaching. Hayden is certainly correct to point out that Fullerism sprang from a well-worked seedbed, of which the Bristol tradition formed the richest portion. And it is surely unfair to fault Gill's ministry for not occurring in a season of unusual divine blessing. The effects of the great Evangelical

---

[17]Ibid., 249.

[18]The primary weakness in his research is the paucity of accurate statistical data from which to draw sound conclusions—a weakness Jarvis acknowledged though he failed to give sufficient weight to it. Additionally, spiritual stagnation and lethargy are almost impossible to measure with the charts and numerical comparisons Jarvis so heavily relies on. Reading his work, one is reminded of the old adage that anything can be proven by the use of statistics.

[19]The first charge is easier to shake than the second. Other than Nettles, T. George ("John Gill," in *Theologians of the Baptist Tradition*, ed. T. George and D. S. Dockery [Nashville: B&H, 2001], 11–33) is probably the most influential scholar to come to Gill's defense. Cf. G. M. Ella (*John Gill and the Cause of God and Truth* [Durham, UK: Go Publications, 1995]), whose scholarship (as noted later) is very uneven, so he must be read with caution.

[20]Nettles, *By His Grace*, 107.

Awakening simply did not come to the Particular Baptists until after Gill's time. Moreover, he cannot be fairly blamed for conducting his ministry in accord with the particular set of gifts that he possessed. Gill's considerable gifts tended toward the exegetical and scholarly, and he used them with great effect to bulwark Particular Baptist churches against the theological threats posed by the encroaching rationalism of the Enlightenment.

On the other hand, contemporary researchers must with caution reject the truly overwhelming witness of men on the scene in the eighteenth century that spiritual deadness was very far progressed among Particular Baptists. Fuller was convinced that High Calvinism had thoroughly permeated the denomination: "If it affects the labours of some of my brethren, I cannot deny but that it may also affect my own. I conceive there is scarcely a minister amongst us whose preaching has not been more or less influenced by the lethargic systems of the age."[21] John Ryland served simultaneously as the pastor to Broadmead Baptist Church and as Principal of the Bristol Baptist Academy—the very heart of where Hayden argued Particular Baptist vitality maintained a stronghold. Nevertheless, even from this vantage point, Ryland agreed completely with Fuller's assessment about the inroads of High Calvinism and its deadening effects on the churches. He began his biography of Fuller by painting a fearsome picture of spiritual decline among Particular Baptists that is in essential agreement with the findings of most Baptist historians.[22] K. Manley offered a good summary of the historiography on this question: "But after all this necessary balance has been drawn in an estimate of Baptist life during the eighteenth century, the common witness was undoubtedly that by about 1760 Particular Baptists in London and in many regions, for whatever reason (and Gill's theology is most commonly cited), evidenced little spiritual vigour."[23]

Evaluating Gill's role in the spread of High Calvinism is, if anything, even more convoluted than assessing decline among Particular Baptists. It is certain that the pervasive influence of John Gill's writings over Particular Baptists

---

[21] Fuller, *Complete Works*, 2:387.

[22] See Ryland, *Work of Faith*, 4–7. To avoid confusion, it should be noted that there is a pagination error in the American edition of Ryland's biography that I used. Chapter 2 begins with what should be page 8 but is mistakenly numbered page 4. In other words, there are two sets of pages labeled 4 through 7. The present reference is to the first set so numbered as found in chapter 1.

[23] K. Manley, *"Redeeming Love Proclaim": John Rippon and the Baptists*, SBHT 12 (Carlisle, UK; Waynesboro, GA: Paternoster, 2004), 2.

at that time of spiritual lethargy is hard to overstate. There is every reason to believe that Fuller's experience in ministerial preparation was typical when he reminisced, "The principal writings with which I was first acquainted were those of Bunyan, Gill, and Brine. I had read pretty much of Gill's *Body of Divinity* and from many parts of it had received considerable instruction."[24] Rightly or wrongly, Gill's own views tended to be lumped together with those of others who might more fairly bear the name of High Calvinists. J. W. Morris addressed all these issues in his biography of Fuller:

> The writings of Hussey, Gill, and Brine, were all in vogue: and such was the veneration in which their names were generally held, that the system of doctrine which they contended for, almost universally prevailed; and *their* works, not the scriptures, became in effect the standard of orthodoxy. It is not affirmed, that there is nothing valuable in the writings of these authors; on the contrary it is readily admitted, that all the leading truths of the gospel are maintained in them. At the same time, it is manifest, that by stretching what are usually called the doctrines of grace, beyond the scripture medium, they introduced a system of *Hyper*-Calvinism, which extended its baleful influence over nearly all the churches, and covered them with a cloud of darkness.[25]

In spite of all the recent efforts to clear Gill of the charge of High Calvinism, Brown is fair when he wrote,

> John Gill and John Brine were men of immense influence. Without doubt, their ministry, extended by voluminous writings, was used to preserve conventional biblical teaching at a time when the acids of rationalism were damaging the churches. Unfortunately, at the same time they diverted the thinking of many Particular Baptist ministers into patterns of occasionally abstruse high Calvinism and caused the good news to be a matter for arid debate rather than confident proclamation.[26]

---

[24]Fuller, *Complete Works*, 1:15.

[25]Morris, *Memoirs of the Life and Writings of the Rev. Andrew Fuller* (1st ed.; London: Wightman & Cramp, 1826), 213–14.

[26]Brown, *The English Baptists of the Eighteenth Century*, 73.

### Gospel Offers to the Unconverted

The first point to observe about the soteriological climate that prevailed in mid-eighteenth-century Particular Baptist circles is that there was a real reluctance to address the lost in terms of open invitations to come to faith in Christ. The principle of making no gospel offers to the unconverted stood at the heart of High Calvinism. As foreign as it sounds today, pastors were hesitant to address the unconverted with strong invitations to repent and trust Christ for salvation.[27] In 1781, R. Hall Sr. of Arnsby effectively summarized this position:

> From the moral inability which the oracles of truth ascribe to man in his fallen state, these divines were induced to divide moral and religious duties into two classes, natural and spiritual; comprehending under the latter, those which required spiritual or supernatural assistance to their performance; and under the former, those which demand no such assistance. Agreeable to this distinction, they conceived it to be the duty of all men to abstain from the outward acts of sin, to read the scriptures, to frequent the worship of God, and to attend, with serious assiduity, to the means of grace; but they supposed that repentance, faith in Christ, and the exercise of genuine internal devotion, were obligatory only on the regenerate. Hence their ministry consisted almost entirely of an exhibition of the mysteries of the gospel, with few or no addresses to the unconverted. They conceived themselves not warranted to urge them to repent and believe the gospel, those being spiritual duties, from whose obligation they were released by the inability contracted by the fall.[28]

In the parlance of the day, the appropriateness of gospel addresses to the unconverted was being discussed by Calvinists in all English dissenting denominations under the heading of "the modern question." By the time of

---

[27] Readers should be careful not to confuse the contemporary practice of extending altar calls with the hyper-Calvinistic reluctance to extend gospel offers to the unconverted. High Calvinists went beyond a fear of altar calls and refused even to offer the gospel as a means of salvation to any lost person unless there was a "warrant" present—meaning, evidence of regeneration.

[28] Hall Sr., *Help to Zion's Travellers*, rev. ed. (n.p.: n.d.), xix, cited in Morris, *Memoirs of the Life and Writings of the Rev. Andrew Fuller*, 214. Morris says he is citing from the preface of "a new edition" of Hall's iconic work. However, he gives no publication data and many versions of that work were printed.

Fuller's ordination to the ministry (1775), that question had been under debate for almost 40 years.[29] Among the Particular Baptists, no less a personage than Brine had answered with a strong and repeated "no" to the question of making indiscriminate gospel offers, and it was generally assumed Gill agreed with his friend.[30] Like most young pastors who cut their theological teeth on Gill, Fuller became convinced that the negative answer to "the modern question" was the correct position. Fuller's early ministry was typical of those who embraced High Calvinist sentiments: "The effect of these views was, that I had very little to say to the unconverted, indeed nothing in a way of exhortation to things spiritually good or certainly connected with salvation."[31]

### Prevailing Particular Baptist Views of the Atonement

Methodologically, the "non-application, non-invitation scheme" was the order of the day for the majority of Particular Baptists in the half-century prior to Fuller's soteriological challenge. Behind that methodology were theological underpinnings having to do with both the extent and nature of the atonement. Views on both of these doctrines were strictly held, and even slight divergence drew quick protests from the defenders of High Calvinistic orthodoxy.

---

[29] Brown, *The English Baptists of the Eighteenth Century,* 73.

[30] Brine issued the tract *A Refutation of the Arminian Principles, delivered in a pamphlet entitled, The Modern Question* in 1743 and a similar publication in 1753 (see Brown, *The English Baptists of the Eighteenth Century*, 74). Although it is generally assumed that Gill and Brine were of the same opinion on the "modern question," Fuller learned to make a distinction between them. In 1787, he wrote that "Mr. Brine is the only [Baptist] writer of eminence who has expressly defended the sentiment. Dr. Gill took no active part in the controversy. It is allowed that the negative side of the question was his avowed sentiment, and this appears to be implied in the general tenor of his writings. At the same time it cannot be denied, that when engaged in other controversies, he frequently argued in a manner favorable for our side." Fuller went on to include nearly a dozen citations taken from Gill's *The Cause of God and Truth* to prove his point (see Fuller, *Complete Works*, 2:422). Evidence of this kind strengthens Nettles's contention that Gill may have been unfairly painted with a brush more fitting for Brine or Hussey (see especially Nettles, *By His Grace*, 99–107). At an earlier point in his ministry, Fuller apparently did think that Gill had embraced the "no gospel offer" position. See his letter to Ryland dated March 23, 1783, where he characterizes the no offer position as "Dr. Gill's system." This letter is found in Ryland, *Work of Faith*, 205.

[31] Fuller, *Complete Works*, 1:15.

## The Extent of the Atonement

The question of the extent of the atonement divided Baptists into two great heads from their earliest beginnings. Those favoring universal atonement made up the General Baptists, whereas those favoring limited atonement made up the Particular Baptists. Within Particular Baptist ranks, perhaps nothing was more commonly believed or tenaciously held than the doctrine that article 21 of the *London Confession* (1644) proclaimed, "That Christ Jesus by His death did bring forth salvation and reconciliation only for the elect, which were those which the Father gave Him."[32] The *Second London Confession* (1677, 1689) made no real change to the theology of the earlier document. It did tend to clarify some of the Calvinistic implications of the earlier creed. For example, it added,

> Those whom God hath predestinated unto life, he is pleased, in his appointed, and accepted time, effectually to call by his word, and Spirit, out of that state of sin, and death, in which they are by nature, to grace and salvation by Jesus Christ. . . .
>
> Others not elected, although they may be called by the Ministry of the word, and may have some common operations of the Spirit, yet not being effectually drawn by the Father, they neither will nor can truly come to Christ; and therefore cannot be saved.[33]

Holding to a limited design in the atonement did little to dampen the evangelistic zeal and outlook of the earliest Particular Baptists. Men of this generation were careful to hold the doctrine of limited atonement in its proper sphere, balancing it with God's capacity to regenerate hearers of the gospel. Believing God worked through preaching to save men, early Particular Baptist pastors were evangelistic in theory and practice. As a body, they would have agreed with E. Chillenden's (fl. 1650s) assessment of preaching: The devil will do all in his power "to hinder the propagation of the Gospel by preaching, because he knows by the power thereof, Christs Kingdome is advanced and inlarged."[34]

---

[32]T. George and D. George, eds., *Baptist Confessions, Covenants, and Catechisms*, Library of Baptist Classics (Nashville: B&H, 1999), 11:42.

[33]W. L. Lumpkin, *Baptist Confessions of Faith*, rev. ed. (Valley Forge, PA: Judson, 1969), 264–65.

[34]Quoted in W. H. Brackney, ed., *Baptist Life and Thought: 1600–1980: A Sourcebook* (Valley Forge, PA: Judson, 1983), 55. Chillenden was a member of the parliamentary army and a strong advocate for unlicensed preaching in England.

Their commitment to limited atonement notwithstanding, seventeenth-century Particular Baptists expanded primarily on the basis of aggressive outreach to the unchurched and unconverted. For example, the congregations of London cooperated to send John Miles and Thomas Pounds to Glamorgan as itinerants.[35] These evangelists gathered five new congregations from 1649 to 1650.[36] But following the Glorious Revolution and the long sought-after Toleration Act of 1689, "a cold fog of religious indifference descended upon the nation."[37] As with the Evangelical Revival that would follow, this religious declension cut across denominational lines. The High Calvinism that developed in Particular Baptist churches served to institutionalize spiritual lethargy and inertia. The delicate theological balance between God's sovereignty and man's responsibility in the salvation of souls was upset. The result was that widespread efforts to spread the gospel through aggressive and ambitious preaching became increasingly uncommon as the eighteenth century unfolded.

Particular Baptists' commitment to limited atonement factored into this downturn. Underwood described the line of reasoning that prompted a decline in evangelistic zeal: "If Christ died not for all but only for the elect, it was useless to invite all to repent and believe in Him."[38] Outwardly, no doctrinal changes had been incorporated into Particular Baptist confessions to prompt such methodological changes. McBeth is probably correct to say "the change came not so much in the doctrines as the tone and spirit in which the doctrines were held."[39] As shown below, Fuller used the evangelistic zeal of a generation past to his advantage as he sought to defend himself from charges of introducing dangerous doctrinal innovation.

## The Nature of the Atonement

A second feature of the soteriological consensus of early eighteenth-century Particular Baptists was a view of the atonement in which it "was commonly interpreted as the literal payment of a debt, and in terms of the crudest

---

[35]Glamorgan was a former county in southeast Wales, located along the Bristol Channel.

[36]B. R. White, *The English Baptists of the Seventeenth Century*, rev. ed., vol. 1 of A History of the English Baptists, ed. R. Hayden (Oxford: The Baptist Historical Society, 1996), 77. These men are representative of a much wider village preaching movement among Particular Baptists.

[37]Underwood, *History of the English Baptists*, 117.

[38]Ibid., 134.

[39]McBeth, *The Baptist Heritage,* 172.

substitutionary theory."[40] According to leading theologians of the day, the heart of the atonement was a transaction "of exact numerical equivalence."[41] Put another way, many Calvinistic Baptists thought of the work of the cross in strict economic terms, whereby it could be said that Christ's sufferings represented an exact mathematical compensation for the debt of the elect's sins—and no further. Thus, the work of the cross was sufficient to save only the fixed number of God's elect. Once the elect have claimed their portion, it is as if nothing is left to go around to the rest of the world. Hence, the nonelect were said to have no "interest" in the work of Christ on the cross. Fuller estimated "nine out of ten of the High Calvinists" held such views. He also identified Gill as one important source of this mindset: "No other notion could be collected from Dr. Gill's exposition of Isa. liii. 6, and all he writes upon the subject seems to go upon that principle."[42]

## FULLER'S SOTERIOLOGICAL CHALLENGE TO HIGH CALVINISM

The reaction against this theological milieu came gradually and from different quarters. But Fuller became the leading spokesman for a thoroughgoing critique, even lending his name to the movement, "Fullerism."[43] It is now time to trace his reaction to the prevailing theological status quo.

### Offering Christ to the World

Morden chose to subtitle his recent study of Fuller *Offering Christ to the World*. His choice of phrase is apt because wrestling with the "modern question" is what started Fuller on a path that would lead to theological innovation. By his own admission, Fuller conceived of *The Gospel Worthy of All Acceptation* as an extended response to the "modern question."[44] In opposition to many of his most respected theological forbears, Fuller embraced the affirmative answer to

---

[40] Clipsham, "Andrew Fuller and Fullerism," 104.

[41] Ibid., 112.

[42] Fuller, *Complete Works*, 2:699.

[43] Nuttall ("Northamptonshire and *The Modern Question*," 101) remarked, "The coining of it ['Fullerism'], and its acceptance by friend as well as foe, points to a remarkable achievement." He also pointed out that the term was translated into Welsh, where it is still in use.

[44] A. Fuller to J. Sutcliff, September 27, 1782.

the "modern question"—thus he argued that it was appropriate to extend the offer of salvation to all who would hear, regardless of their spiritual state. No critic has such force as one who has been converted from the very position he now seeks to overturn, and Fuller was able to operate from such a perspective. His son, Andrew Gunton Fuller, lamented to report that his father "durst not for some years address an invitation to the unconverted to come to Jesus."[45] As has already been shown, once Fuller began to ground himself theologically through widespread reading and closer study of the Bible, the young pastor-theologian concluded that his "views did not quadrate with the Scriptures."[46]

As he remembered the processes that led to his change of sentiment, Fuller gave pride of place to the role of the Bible, as presented through Abraham Taylor's pamphlet titled *The Modern Question Concerning Repentance and Faith*.[47] Within a few years of his watershed encounter with this book, Fuller noted that he had written out the "substance of what I afterwards published under the title of *The Gospel Worthy of All Acceptation; or the Obligations of Men cordially to believe whatever God makes known*."[48] His journal entries in the days prior to submitting the manuscript to the printer reflect Fuller's aware-ness that his new views were outside of the prevailing mainstream of Particular Baptist thought: "The weight of publishing still lies upon me. I expect a great share of unhappiness through it. I had certainly much rather go through the world in peace, did I not consider this step as my duty."[49]

Fuller's fears of opposition were not to be disappointed. The publication of *The Gospel Worthy of All Acceptation* triggered an avalanche of responses. In return, he published three separate books devoted to answering his critics.[50]

---

[45] Fuller, *Complete Works*, 1:xvi.

[46] Ibid., 1:17. See chapter 1.

[47] See chapter 1.

[48] Fuller, *Complete Works*, 1:16. Recently, the handwritten manuscript that was the precursor to *The Gospel Worthy of All Acceptation* came up for auction. It was written in Fuller's own hand during 1777 and 1778 and is titled "Thoughts on the Power of Men to do the Will of God." This previously unstudied document now resides at the archives of the Southern Baptist Theological Seminary.

[49] Ibid., 1:42. The entry is dated August 23, 1784.

[50] In the order of their appearance, the three main responses are A. Fuller, *A Defence of a Treatise Entitled "The Gospel of Christ Worthy of All Acceptation": Containing a Reply to Mr. Button's Remarks and the Observations of Philanthropos* (1787), in *The Complete Works of the Rev. Andrew Fuller*, 2:417–511; A. Fuller, *The Reality and Efficacy of Divine Grace, with the Certain Success of Christ's Kingdom, Considered in a Series of Letters: Containing Remarks upon*

What had started out as a simple plea for a restoration of the older Particular Baptist practice of making indiscriminate gospel offers in preaching developed into a much wider challenge to the High Calvinistic system of doctrine as the debate moved forward. Since Fuller's soteriological position has come to be synonymous with evangelical Calvinism, his views can be conveniently summarized by reference to the traditional acrostic TULIP (total depravity, unconditional election, limited atonement, irresistible grace, perseverance of the saints).

### Fuller's View of Total Depravity

The High Calvinists who criticized Fuller usually insisted that he had given up the doctrine of total depravity. In reply, Fuller argued that they had so misconstrued the doctrine as to deprive men of their responsibility before God. Fuller sought to chart a middle course between the extremes of determinism and human autonomy in salvation. What Fuller contended for in his doctrine of total depravity can be understood by considering the topic under two heads: the distinction in natural and moral ability, and the place of regeneration in the order of salvation.

#### The Distinction between Natural and Moral Abilities

As noted above, Fuller freely acknowledged his indebtedness to Jonathan Edwards for his views of human ability.[51] Like Fuller, Edwards was troubled by the way that the traditional Calvinistic understanding of the doctrine of total depravity was being used to eliminate human responsibility. In his famous *Inquiry into the Modern Prevailing Notions respecting the Freedom of the Will which is supposed to be essential to Moral Agency*, Edwards introduced a new wrinkle to Augustinian and Calvinistic understandings of the will.[52] He

---

the Observations of the Rev. Dan. Taylor on Mr. Fuller's Reply to Philanthropos, in *The Complete Works of the Rev. Andrew Fuller*, 2: 512–60; and A. Fuller, *Remarks on Mr. Martin's Publication. Entitled "Thoughts on the Duty of Man Relative to Faith in Jesus Christ,"* in *Five Letters to a Friend* (1789), in *Complete Works*, 2:716–36. Where dates are not given, I have been unable to determine the original publication dates with certainty. However, all of these replies were made within a few years of the release of *The Gospel Worthy of All Acceptation*. In addition, Fuller published innumerable replies in periodical works, often using the pennames of Gaius or Agnostos.

[51] See chapter 2.

[52] M. A. Noll, "Jonathan Edwards," in *Evangelical Dictionary of Theology*, ed. W. A. Elwell, 2nd ed. (Grand Rapids: Baker; Carlisle: Paternoster, 2001).

postulated a distinction in human ability. Both before and after the fall, men possessed a degree of natural ability. Without that, they would be mere automatons, incapable of moral action. On the other hand, the fall had so corrupted human ability that man was no longer able to exercise his will to choose the good apart from divine influence. In keeping with traditional Augustinian theology, Edwards acknowledged that God must move on the human will in order for persons to choose anything spiritually good, especially to exercise saving faith. Fuller embraced these views wholesale.

Those critics of Fuller who claimed that he had ascribed to fallen man the ability to save himself failed to understand the indispensable role he attributed to God in influencing the will.[53] But the fault hardly lay with Fuller. In order to prevent such a misunderstanding, he included the following point in the preface to *The Gospel Worthy of All Acceptation*: "It is no part of the controversy whether unconverted sinners be able to turn to God, and to embrace the gospel; but what kind of ability they lie under with respect to these exercises; whether it consists in the want of natural powers and advantages, or merely in the want of a heart to make right use of them."[54] In the body of the book, Fuller further addressed objections to his dichotomous view of human ability. Anticipating the arguments of his critics, he wrote, "Some have supposed that, in attributing physical or natural power to men, we deny their *natural depravity*."[55] But Fuller insisted that his intent in drawing out a distinction between natural and moral abilities was designed only to "express those faculties which are strictly a part of our nature as men, and which are necessary to our being accountable creatures."[56] In other words, his intent was to take nothing away from the doctrine of total depravity but to guard against fatalism.

---

[53] A contemporary critic illustrates the profundity of this misunderstanding. G. M. Ella (*Law & Gospel in the Theology of Andrew Fuller* [Durham, UK: Go Publications, 1996], 146, 204) misrepresented Fuller as teaching that lost men have their "full moral powers and natural duties intact" and that it is their "duty to use them savingly." Consequently, he turned Fuller into a full-blown Pelagian. He further stated, "The Fullerite gospel is nothing but a humanistic message which is designed to appeal to man's fallen nature and is of no saving value." The depth of Ella's misrepresentation of Fuller is staggering.

[54] Fuller, *Complete Works*, 2:331.

[55] Ibid., 2:378.

[56] Ibid.

*The Place of Regeneration in the Order of Salvation*

Man's moral inability meant that he was still bound to be a debtor to the primacy of God's intervening grace. Again, Fuller was careful to clarify in *The Gospel Worthy of All Acceptation* that man could not make the first move toward God:

> It is sometimes suggested that to attribute to sinners a natural ability of performing things spiritually good is to nourish their self-sufficiency; and that to represent it as only *moral* is to suppose that it is not insuperable, but may after all be overcome by effort of their own. But surely it is not necessary, in order to destroy a spirit of self-sufficiency, to deny that we are men and accountable creatures, which is all that natural ability supposes.[57]

On the contrary, man's moral inability rendered him completely powerless to believe apart from the life-giving work of the Holy Spirit: "It is depravity alone that renders the regenerating influence of the Holy Spirit necessary."[58] Fuller bolstered his conclusions at this point by a citation from Calvin (1509–64):

> The bare and outward declaration of the word of God . . . ought to have largely sufficed to make it to be believed, if our own blindness and stubbornness do not withstand it. But our mind hath such an inclination to vanity that it can never cleave fast to the truth of God, and such a dullness that it is always blind and cannot see the light thereof. Therefore there is nothing available done by the word without the enlightening of the Holy Spirit.[59]

Some of Fuller's critics, especially from the Arminian side, insisted that positioning regeneration prior to faith hopelessly confused the simple gospel. In return, Fuller pointed out that Calvin had long ago dealt with that critique. He cited Calvin's commentary on John 1:13: "It seemeth that the evangelist dealeth *disorderly* in putting regeneration before faith, seeing that it is rather an *effect* of

---

[57] Ibid.

[58] Ibid., 2:380.

[59] J. Calvin, *Institutes of the Christian Religion*, Book III, Chapter 2, in Fuller, *Complete Works*, 2:380.

faith, and therefore to be set after it."[60] Fuller embraced Calvin's reasoning that regeneration was used in different senses in the Bible, sometimes as that which gives rise to faith and sometimes as the new birth that comes by faith. When he spoke of regeneration preceding faith, Fuller intended only the former. In his reply to Daniel Taylor's criticism of *The Gospel Worthy of All Acceptation*, Fuller clarified his views on the precedence of regeneration in the order of salvation:

> The great question between us is this, Whether the Holy Spirit of God is the proper and efficient cause of a sinner's believing in Jesus Christ; or, Whether it be owing to his holy influence, and that alone, that one sinner believes in Christ rather than another. If the first beginning of God's work upon the mind is *by* the word, let it be but granted that it is by the *agency* of the Holy Spirit causing that word to be embraced by one person, as it is not by another, and so as to become effectual, and we are satisfied. If this is but granted, it will amount to the same thing as that which we mean by regeneration preceding our coming to Christ, since the cause always precede the effect.[61]

### Fuller's View of Unconditional Election

Fuller never wavered in his commitment to the doctrine of unconditional election. An article he wrote on Calvinism for a popular theological dictionary summarizes his settled position on unconditional election:

> Calvinists maintain that God hath chosen a certain number of the fallen race of Adam in Christ, before the foundation of the world, unto eternal glory, according to his immutable purpose, and of his free grace and love, without the foresight of faith, good works, or any condition performed by the creature, as the *cause* of their election: and that the rest of mankind he was pleased to pass by, and leave to the due punishment of their sins, to the praise of his vindictive justice.[62]

---

[60] Calvin, no source given but it comes from Calvin's commentary on John 1:13, in Fuller, *Complete Works*, 2:610.

[61] Fuller, *Complete Works*, 2:462–63. Slight changes in punctuation and capitalization have been made from the original form of this citation.

[62] See appendix 2 in this book. See also Belcher, *The Last Remains of the Rev. Andrew Fuller*, 218. According to the editor of this volume, Fuller wrote the article on "Calvinism" that appeared

## Why Election Must Be Unconditional

Election itself was so clearly revealed in Scripture that Fuller thought no honest reader could deny it.[63] But he felt the force of Taylor's argument that universal gospel addresses could perhaps be better supported by holding to a view whereby election was conditioned on the foreseen faith of believers. In his reply to Taylor, Fuller explained in some detail why he felt compelled to maintain that election must be unconditional. First, he listed a litany of texts that taught the doctrine of election.[64] Next, he supposed no one would argue that these texts must "speak only of *a part* of mankind . . . the *chosen* of God."[65] Then Fuller reasoned that this choosing could be based on three possible things: "Either because of their actually being believers, or because it was foreseen that they would believe, or, as we suppose, because God eternally purposed in himself that they should believe and be saved."[66] Fuller concluded that the first possibility was rendered void because election was said to be "from before the foundation of the world" (Eph 1:4) and also because the elect were "given to Christ prior to their believing in him."[67] The second option must be set aside "because then what he had done for us must have been according to something good in us, and not according to his own purpose and grace, given us in Christ Jesus before the world began" (2 Tim 1:9).[68] That left the third option—unconditional election.

---

in Hannah Adams's (1755–1831) dictionary on religions. Fuller also wrote a preface to the third London edition. For the history of this fascinating dictionary, see T. A. Tweed, "Introduction: Hannah Adams's Survey of the Religious Landscape," in H. Adams, *A Dictionary of All Religions and Religious Denominations: Jewish, Heathen, Mahotmetan, Christian, Ancient and Modern* (Boston: Cummings and Hilliard, 1817); facsimile edition, in Classics in Religious Studies, ed. C. A. Raschke (Atlanta, GA: Scholars Press, 1992), 8:vii–xxxiv. Tweed's article is an introductory piece added to the facsimilie edition of Hannah Adams's book.

[63] A change in perspective on the part of many has occurred since Fuller's day. One well-known Southern Baptist leader is convinced that election has nothing to do with God's choice of individuals to salvation. He has defined election as "a divine act of God, a sovereign God, whereby God sets apart all firsts and chooses all seconds to accomplish His purpose" (F. S. Page, *Trouble with the Tulip: A Closer Examination of the Five Points of Calvinism*, 2nd ed. [Canton, GA: Riverstone, 2006], 61.) This definition is distinct from the standard definitions of the word "election" and from any of the standard Baptist confessions of faith.

[64] Fourteen, to be exact. Fuller, *Complete Works*, 2:493.

[65] Ibid.

[66] Ibid.

[67] Ibid.

[68] Ibid.

*Unconditional Election Not Incompatible with the Use of Means*
Fuller recognized that many people felt unconditional election was incompatible with the use of means in preaching and evangelizing. In arriving at this position, he thought they had to set aside the positive example of some of the greatest pastors and theologians in church history. He wrote,

> Neither Augustine nor Calvin, who each in his day defended predestination, and the other doctrines connected with it, ever appear to have thought of denying it to be the duty of every sinner who has heard the gospel to repent and believe in Jesus Christ. Neither did the other Reformers, nor the puritans of the sixteenth century, nor the divines at the synod of Dort, (who opposed Arminius,) nor any of the nonconformists of the seventeenth century, so far as I have any acquaintance with their writings, ever so much as hesitate on the subject. The writings of Calvin himself would now be deemed Arminian by a great number of our opponents.[69]

As Fuller saw it, the denial of universal gospel offers was truly "a modern question." He offered two lines of reasoning why this doctrinal innovation must be rejected. First, Fuller thought that to reach this conclusion was to place reason over revelation. He gave a clear explanation of how to handle two texts of Scripture that appear to differ in meaning:

> If I find two doctrines affirmed or implied in the Scriptures, which, to my feeble understanding, may seem to clash, I ought not to embrace the one and to reject the other because of their supposed inconsistency. . . . Yet in this manner many have acted on both sides: some, taking the general precepts and invitations of Scripture for their standard, have rejected the doctrine of discriminating grace; others, taking the declarations of salvation as being a fruit of electing love for their standard, deny that sinners without distinction are called upon to believe for the salvation of their souls. Hence it is that we hear of *Calvinistic* and *Arminian texts*; as though these leaders had agreed to divide the Scriptures between them. The truth is, there are but two ways for us to take: one is to reject them

---

[69] Ibid., 2:367. Fuller frequently opined that the High Calvinists had gone beyond Calvin himself.

*both*, and the Bible with them, on account of its inconsistencies; the other is to embrace them both, concluding that, as they are both revealed in the Scriptures, they are both true, and both consistent, and that it is owing to the darkness of our understandings that they do not appear so to us.[70]

Second, Fuller thought that it was poor reasoning to conclude that unconditional election implied no use of means could be permitted to bring God's decrees to pass. He argued that "if this mode of reasoning prove any thing, it will prove too much: it will prove that it is not the duty of *some* men to attend the means of grace, or in any way to seek after the salvation of their souls."[71] In other words, if unconditional election were incompatible with the use of means to bring men to salvation, consistency required that it be just as incompatible in the case of the elect as in the case of the nonelect.

*The Unknown Identity of the Elect*

Perhaps the most cogent reason Fuller offered as to why unconditional election was not incompatible with the use of means in bringing the lost to Christ was that the identity of the elect was known only to God. Fuller delighted to use a quotation from one of the leading hyper-Calvinists, John Brine, to bolster his point: "'God's word,' says Mr. Brine, 'and not his secret purpose, is the rule of our conduct.'"[72] Fuller demonstrated that Brine had gone back to that most revered of English Calvinists, John Owen, for the inspiration of this comment. Fuller was content to let Owen state his own position:

"We must exactly distinguish," says Dr. Owen, "between man's duty and God's purpose; there being no connexion between them. The purpose and decree of God is not the rule of our duty. . . . Especially is this to be seen and considered in the duty of the ministers of the gospel; in the dispensing of the word, in exhortations, invitations, precepts, and threatenings committed unto them; all which are perpetual directives

---

[70] Ibid.

[71] Ibid., 2:371 (emphasis added).

[72] J. Brine, *The Certain Efficacy of the Death of Christ Asserted . . . in Answer to a Book Called "The Ruin and Recovery of Mankind"* [Isaac Watts] (London: Aaron Ward, 1743), 151, cited in Fuller, *Complete Works*, 2:373.

of our duty. . . . A minister is not to make inquiry after, nor to trouble himself about, those secrets of the eternal mind of God, viz. whom he purposeth to save, and whom he hath sent Christ to die for in particular; it is enough for them to search his revealed will, and thence take their *directions*, from whence they have their *commissions*. . . . [Ministers] command and invite all to *repent* and *believe*; but they know not in particular on whom God will bestow repentance unto salvation, nor in whom he will effect the work of faith with power."[73]

Fuller was able to deflect much of the force of his critics by demonstrating that the hyper-Calvinists were the real doctrinal interlopers among English Particular Baptists.

### Fuller's View of a Limited Atonement

In *A Defence of a Treatise Entitled 'The Gospel Worthy of All Acceptation,'* Fuller acknowledged, "The extent of Christ's death is well known to have been a matter of great controversy."[74] Fuller was unable to escape that tendency to controversy. His own view of the atonement was the most contentious part of his overall challenge to High Calvinist soteriology.

#### The Atonement: Sufficient for All, Efficient for the Elect

As always, Fuller advocated theologians resolve the controversy surrounding this issue by appealing to arguments that rested "chiefly [upon] the result of reading the sacred Scriptures."[75] Nevertheless, in spite of this disclaimer, Fuller was also quick to point out that his interpretations had a lengthy line of supporters from the Calvinistic tradition. He characterized his theological tradition as follows:

> Calvinists in *general* have considered the particularity of redemption as consisting not in the *degree* of Christ's sufferings, (as though he must have suffered more if more had been finally saved,) or in any *insufficiency* that attended them, but in the sovereign purpose and design of the

---

[73] J. Owen, *The Death of Death*, Book IV, Chapter 1, cited in Fuller, *Complete Works*, 2:373.
[74] Fuller, *Complete Works*, 2:488.
[75] Ibid.

Father and the Son. . . . They suppose the sufferings of Christ, in themselves considered, are of *infinite* value, sufficient to have saved all the
world, and a thousand worlds, if it had pleased God to have constituted
them the price of their redemption, and to have made them effectual to
that end. Further, whatever difficulties there may appear in these subjects, they in general suppose that there is in the death of Christ a sufficient ground for indefinite calls and universal invitations, and that there
is no mockery or insincerity in the Holy One in any of these things.[76]

Once again, Fuller was on firm ground in claiming that precedence was in
favor of his position that universal gospel offers could safely be grounded in
the infinitely sufficient merit of the atonement.

Fuller went on to assert that he stood squarely in this tradition on the extent
of the atonement: "These views of the subject accord with my own."[77] He tried
to clarify his position on the sufficiency of the cross by creating a hypothetical
case: "If we were to suppose, for argument's sake, that all the inhabitants of
the globe should thus return [to Christ as the way of salvation], it is supposed
not one soul need be sent away for want of a sufficiency in Christ's death to
render his pardon and acceptance consistent with the rights of justice."[78] As to
the limitation in the design of Christ's death, Fuller added,

But great and necessary as this mercy is, if nothing more than this had
been done, not one of the human race had ever been saved. It is necessary
to our salvation that a *way* and a *highway* to our God should be opened:
Christ is such a way, and is as free for any sinner to walk in as any highway whatever from one place to another: but, considering the depravity
of human nature, it is equally necessary that some effectual provision
should be made for our *walking* in that way. We conceive that the Lord
Jesus Christ made such a provision by his death, thereby procuring the
certain bestowment of faith, as well as all other spiritual blessings which
follow upon it; that, in regard of all the *sons* who are finally brought to
glory, he was the *Surety* or *Captain* of their salvation; that their salvation

---

[76] Ibid., 2:488–89.
[77] Ibid., 2:489.
[78] Ibid.

was, properly speaking, the end or design of his death. And herein we suppose consists the particularity of redemption.[79]

To prove his point about the antiquity and consistency of this interpretive tradition, Fuller provided a footnote with quotes of similar content drawn from other theologians, including one of his favorite sources—John Owen.[80]

### Fuller on the Nature of the Atonement

According to Fuller, the doctrine of the atonement constitutes "the life-blood of the gospel system."[81] So it is not surprising that he developed his doctrine about the nature of the atonement carefully. It was also an area of theology to which he gave ongoing thought, so that his views of the atonement were not static. Between the first and second editions of *The Gospel Worthy of All Acceptation*, Fuller's views of the atonement changed significantly. In the second edition, Fuller discussed this important doctrine in language that reflected a governmental understanding of the cross; that is, in punishing Christ, God was displaying His justice against sin as a moral governor of the universe. During the interval between the editions, Fuller had read considerably from the New Divinity School of theologians who came to prominence following the death of President Jonathan Edwards. He seized upon their governmental view of the atonement and began using such language himself.

Although the influence of the New Divinity School on Fuller is well known, a second factor is also important.[82] Thomas Paine had raised objections to the atonement in *The Age of Reason* (1794, 1795), his influential defense of deism. A letter Fuller wrote to Carey reveals the pressure Fuller felt from Paine's arguments:

> P. S. Could you answer Paine's objection to the atonement: "If I owe a person money and cannot pay him, and he threatens to put me in prison, another person can take the debt upon himself, and pay it for him. But

---

[79] Ibid.

[80] Ibid.

[81] Ibid., 1:687.

[82] M. A. G. Haykin, "Particular Redemption in the Writings of Andrew Fuller," in *The Gospel in the World: International Baptist Studies*, ed. D. W. Bebbington, SBHT 1 (Carlisle, UK; Waynesboro, GA: Paternoster, 2002), 119–22.

if I have committed a *crime*, every circumstance of the case is changed. Moral justice cannot take the innocent for the guilty, even if the innocent would offer himself. To suppose justice to do this is to destroy the principle of its existence, which is the thing itself. It is then no longer justice. It is indiscriminate revenge." (*Age of Reason*, p. 20. Part I.) I have tried to answer it and have sent my answer to Pearce, Ryland, Sutcliff, & Scott. If I have overturned Paine's, I have overturned the High Calvinistic notion of Redemption, as a draw and credit business. Scott finds sad fault with me. I suppose I must not print it; but must copy it if I can for you. I wish for your thoughts on the objection.[83]

Fuller's answer to Paine was to move away from any representation of the atonement based on commercial justice. For example, his reference to the "draw and credit business" plays upon the fact he had been reviewing the financial matters of the Mission in exactly those terms only a few paragraphs before. Instead, he sought to ground the atonement in God's sense of moral justice.

In spite of his declaration to Carey that he had better not go to print with this view for fear of the reactions, Fuller did so in less than a year. He included a version of the reply sent to Carey for review in his full-length response to Paine's challenge, *The Gospel Its Own Witness* (1799). A few years later, the same basic position would make its way into the revision of *The Gospel Worthy of All Acceptation* (1801). As it turns out, he was right to fear that this theological shift would set him at odds with many in the preceding generation of Particular Baptist pastors. In fact, Fuller's views on the nature of the atonement even served to estrange him from men who had previously been his allies in pressing for a more vibrant evangelistic ministry.

One example of this is found in the debate that developed between Fuller and the London pastor Abraham Booth (1734–1806). An older man with a considerable reputation as a theologian among Particular Baptists, Booth was in some way Fuller's precursor in striving for a return to the more evangelistic Calvinism of the seventeenth century. He wrote *The Reign of Grace* in 1768, after converting from General to Particular Baptist views.[84] The book

---

[83] A. Fuller to W. Carey, August 22, 1798. A few abbreviations in the original have been spelled out completely in the citation for clarity.

[84] A. Booth, *The Reign of Grace: From Its Rise to Its Consummation* (Leeds: Griffith Wright, 1768).

was strongly evangelical and typical of many of the pro-Awakening works of that era. After Fuller came on the scene, Booth at first became an enthusiastic supporter of the younger man. For example, when Secretary Fuller sought collections for the Baptist Missionary Society (BMS), Booth was one of the few London pastors to support the fledgling enterprise. But after Fuller issued the revised version of *The Gospel Worthy of All Acceptation*, Booth became critical of changes in Fuller's understandings of the atonement. The conflict between the two leading Particular Baptist theologians of the day resulted in a series of letters from Fuller to John Ryland, in which Fuller thoroughly explained and defended his views on two key areas of doctrinal controversy: imputation and substitution.

### Fuller on Imputation

R. Oliver maintained that Fuller and Booth largely talked past each other in this debate because neither understood how the other defined his terms.[85] Fuller started out trying to clarify his intent to Ryland by going back to square one. He wrote, "To *impute* signifies, in general, to *charge, reckon,* or *place to account,* according to the different objects to which it is applied. This word, like many others, has a *proper* and a *figurative* meaning."[86] Some, including Booth, apparently assumed that Fuller's use of "figurative" to describe imputation might as well have meant "fictitious." But Fuller clarified that this was not his intent. By figurative imputation he simply meant "charging, reckoning, or placing to the account of persons or things, that which does not properly belong to them, as though it did."[87] As an example, Fuller cited Phlm 1:18: "If he [Onesimus, Philemon's runaway slave whom Paul was returning] hath wronged thee, or oweth thee aught, put that on my account." This is figurative because Onesimus's debts do not properly belong to Paul, even though he is willing to take care of these obligations. By contrast, Fuller defined proper imputation as "charging, reckoning, or placing to the account of persons and things that which properly belongs to them."[88] Here he cited 1 Cor 4:1 as an example: "Let a man so account of us, as the ministers of Christ, and stewards

---

[85] R. W. Oliver, "Andrew Fuller and Abraham Booth," in Haykin, *At the Pure Fountain of Thy Word*, 212.

[86] Fuller, *Complete Works*, 2:702.

[87] Ibid., 2:703.

[88] Ibid., 2:702.

of the mysteries of God." The imputation here is proper because Paul was, in fact, a minister of Christ and had been so entrusted with gospel mysteries.

With that background, Fuller explained,

> It is thus also that I understand the imputation of sin to Christ. He was made sin for us, in the same sense as we are made the righteousness of God in him. He was accounted in the Divine administration as if he were, or had been, the sinner; that those who believe on him might be accounted as if they were, or had been, righteous.[89]

At stake for Fuller in this debate was erecting a barrier against the teachings of certain High Calvinists who leaned toward or openly embraced the views of the ultra-Calvinistic Anglican pastor, Tobias Crisp.[90]

As he had previously done when challenged, Fuller charged that in this instance he was being attacked not for denying Calvinism but for denying false accretions that had collected like barnacles on Calvin's teaching. In another letter to Ryland relative to the dispute with Booth, Fuller went on to write,

> The sentiment which I oppose does not appear to me to be Calvinism, but Crispism. I never met with a single passage in the writings of Calvin on this subject that clashed with my own views; but in Dr. Crisp I have. He considers God, in his charging our sins on Christ, and accounting his righteousness to us, as reckoning things as they are. "Hast thou been an idolater," says he, "a blasphemer, a despiser of God's word, a profaner of his name and ordinances, a thief, a liar, a drunkard? If thou hast part in Christ, all these transgressions of thine become actually the transgression of Christ, and so cease to be thine; and thou ceasest to be a transgressor from that time they were laid upon Christ to the last hour of thy life: so that now thou art not an idolater, a persecutor, a thief, a liar, &c.—thou art not a sinful person. Reckon whatever sin you commit,

---

[89] Ibid., 2:703–4.

[90] Tobias Crisp (1600–1643) may be the best candidate for the title of the Father of High Calvinism. "Crispism," as Fuller called it, was the seedbed for Gill's doctrine of eternal justification (i.e., the view that justification occurs in eternity past and not at the moment of belief in Christ). In a similar way, Crisp's views tended to lead to antinomianism by its woodenly literal readings of such concepts of Christ being "made sin for us" and our "being made the righteousness of God" in him. Gill thought highly of Crisp and recommended his works to others.

whereas you have a part in Christ, you are all that Christ was, and Christ is all that you were."[91]

Fuller is not gratifying a desire for hypothetical and obscure theological debate. The matter had direct consequence for one of the most significant theological aberrations troubling Particular Baptists at that time: antinomianism. Perhaps not so coincidentally, antinomianism generally found its most comfortable home in the same High Calvinist circles that spawned most of Fuller's opposition.

Fuller was convinced that wrong ideas about imputation were behind antinomianism. Writing again to William Carey, he remarked, "antinomianism . . . has made some inroads, and required some exclusions." Fuller further stated that some pastors "have considered our controversies as little more than a strife of words, and have been for keeping in with both sides. They may now see that it affects *things*."[92] The Kettering pastor maintained Crisp's views made believers flippant about sin, since their overly literal notions of imputation tended to absolve them from any sense of responsibility. Fuller believed the perspective on imputation that Crisp and other High Calvinists argued for "undermines all ground for confession or repentance."[93] Still worse, he thought these false notions led people brazenly to demand their salvation from God as a right. Fuller summarized the reasoning behind this view as follows:

> If Christ by imputation became deserving of punishment, we by non-imputation cease to deserve it; and if our demerits be literally transferred to him, his merits must of course be the same to us; and then, instead of approaching God as guilty and unworthy, we might take consequence to ourselves before him, as not only guiltless, but meritorious beings.[94]

Such an idea would always be abhorrent to Fuller's spiritual senses. Fuller's views of any sinner's merits are revealed in a letter he wrote to John Ryland in

---

[91] Fuller, *Complete Works*, 2:713.

[92] A. Fuller to W. Carey, June 7, 1799. William Huntington (1745–1813) was a popular independent preacher who is often associated with antinomianism. The only recent biography is G. M. Ella, *William Huntington, Pastor of Providence* (Darlington: Evangelical Press, 1994). R. Oliver (*History of the English Calvinistic Baptists*, 119, note 34) characterized this work as "regrettably uncritical."

[93] Fuller, *Complete Works*, 2:713.

[94] Ibid., 2:705.

the last week of his life: "I am a poor guilty creature, but Christ is an almighty Saviour. . . . I have no other hope than from salvation by mere sovereign, efficacious grace, through the atonement of my Lord and Saviour. With this hope, I can go into eternity with composure."[95]

### Fuller on Substitution

Booth charged Fuller with denying not only imputation but also the related doctrine of substitution, at least "in the sense in which Calvinists commonly hold and have held them."[96] Fuller devoted his third letter to Ryland to the refutation of this charge. He began by expressing surprise that anyone could doubt his commitment to the doctrine of substitution:

> Whether Christ laid down his life as a substitute for sinners was never a question with me. All my hope rests upon it; and the sum of my delight in preaching the gospel consists in it. If I know anything of myself, I can say of Christ crucified for us, as was said of Jerusalem, "If I forget thee, let my right hand forget; if I do not remember thee, let my tongue cleave to the roof of my mouth!"[97]

Fuller perceived that Booth's concerns narrowed down to one issue: who exactly "were the persons for whom Christ was a substitute . . . the elect only, or mankind in general?"[98] Fuller found it impossible to answer this question without reverting to his previous distinction concerning the sufficiency efficiency of the atonement. He wrote,

> If I speak of it [Christ's death as a substitute for sinners] irrespective of the purpose of the Father and the Son, as to its objects who should be saved by it, merely referring to what it is in itself sufficient for, and declared in the gospel to be adapted to, I should think that I answered the question in a Scriptural way by saying, It was for sinners as sinners; but if I have respect to the purpose of the Father in giving his Son to die,

---

[95] Haykin, *Armies of the Lamb*, 269.
[96] Fuller, *Complete Works*, 2:702.
[97] Ibid., 2:706.
[98] Ibid.

and to the design of Christ in laying down his life, I should answer, It was for the elect only.[99]

In other words, Fuller answered the question, "For whom did Christ die as a substitute?" by saying, in effect, both the whole world and only the elect. He admitted the difficulty of reconciling these answers: "Whether I can perfectly reconcile these statements with each other, or not, I believe they are both taught in the Scriptures; but I acknowledge that I do not at present perceive their inconsistency."[100] In his mind, Fuller avoided a contradiction by maintaining that Christ's death was intended to accomplish different things for these two classes of hearers.

Fuller found it important to say that in some sense Christ died as a substitute for the whole world in order to ground the appropriateness of universal gospel offers. He stated,

I find the apostles and primitive ministers . . . addressing themselves to sinners without distinction, and holding forth the death of Christ as a ground of faith to all men. . . . On this principle the ambassadors of Christ besought sinners to be reconciled to God, "for" (said they) "he hath made Him to be sin for us who knew no sin, that we might be made the righteousness of God in Him."[101]

Fuller also held that this offer was sincere: as many as came to Christ could rest assured that He would accept them.

On the other hand, Fuller insisted on maintaining Christ was a substitute for the elect in a special sense:

If it be a proper definition of substitution of Christ, that he died for, or in the place of others, that they should not die, this, as comprehending the designed end to be answered by his death, is strictly applicable to none but the elect; for whatever ground there is for sinners, as sinners,

---

[99] Ibid., 2:707.
[100] Ibid.
[101] Ibid.

to believe and be saved, it was never the design of Christ to impart faith to any others than those who were given him of the Father.[102]

If Christ's death as a substitute "for sinners as sinners" was the ground for universal offers, then his dying as an effectual substitute only for the elect was the clue as to why some who heard believed and others did not. Gospel offers were effective only when coextensive with the "purpose and discriminating grace of God."[103]

Behind Fuller's insistence on a distinction in the substitutionary nature of Christ's death lay some of the same concerns that motivated his teaching on imputation. Haykin said that, on the death of Christ, Fuller "did not wish to understand its substitutionary nature in strictly commercial terms where Christ suffers the exact amount necessary to pay for the debt of the elect."[104] Fuller argued, "Sin is a debt only in a metaphorical sense; properly speaking, it is a crime, and satisfaction for it requires to be made, not on pecuniary, but on moral principles."[105] In the second edition of *The Gospel Worthy of All Acceptation*, Fuller had distanced himself from a commercial view of Christ's sufferings:

If the atonement of Christ were considered as the literal payment of debt—if the measure of his sufferings were according to the number of those for whom he died, and to the degree of their guilt, in such a manner as that if more had been saved, or if those who are saved had been more guilty, his sorrows must have been proportionately increased—it might, for aught I know, be inconsistent with indefinite invitations. . . .

On the other hand, if the atonement of Christ proceed not on the principal of commercial, but of moral justice, or justice as it relates to crime—if its grand object were to express the Divine displeasure against sin, (Rom. viii. 3,) and so render the exercise of mercy, in all the ways wherein sovereign wisdom should determine to apply it, consistent with righteousness (Rom. iii. 25) . . . no such inconsistency can justly be ascribed to it.[106]

[102] Ibid.
[103] Ibid.
[104] Haykin, "Particular Redemption," 118.
[105] Fuller, *Complete Works*, 2:688.
[106] Ibid, 2:373–74.

Though his opponents would loudly claim that Fuller had denied the substitutionary nature of the atonement, the truth is that he simply added governmental language to his repertoire of speaking and writing about the cross. He in no way abandoned his commitment to the substitutionary nature of Christ's death. Nettles said, "Fuller's use of governmental language did not involve him in the mistakes of the governmentalists; the atonement never became merely symbolic of justice, but maintained its character as an actual act of justice."[107] What one scholar said of Jonathan Edward's use of governmental descriptions of the cross is apparently true of Fuller as well: "These are never at the expense of the satisfaction theory. Rather, they are founded on it."[108]

### Fuller's View of Irresistible Grace and Perseverance of the Saints

Fuller was much more likely to use the term "effectual" than "irresistible" to describe the workings of God's grace on the soul. By whatever terminology, the concept of irresistible grace formed a vital part of Fuller's soteriology. His views of human depravity necessitated that the Holy Spirit be given a primary place in bringing men to faith in Christ.

#### The Spirit's Work Is Both Resistible and Irresistible

One of the rare times Fuller did use the word irresistible in reference to the working of the Holy Spirit was in the course of his replies to Daniel Taylor's criticisms of *The Gospel Worthy of All Acceptation.* Fuller said of the work of the Holy Spirit, "I apprehend he is both resistible and irresistible, in different respects."[109] Three points explain what Fuller meant. First, the Holy Spirit very often works through a variety of means, including Scripture, preaching, acts of providence, and more. Second, it needs no proof to demonstrate that men have frequently resisted even the most powerful instances of the Sprit's activity. Third, it was similarly self-evident that the Holy Spirit did work effectually in the hearts of some. Because of Fuller's view of human depravity, salvation could come in no other way: "From the depravity or perverseness of the

---

[107] Nettles, *By His Grace*, 128.

[108] J. H. Gerstner, *The Rational Biblical Theology of Jonathan Edwards* (Orlando: Ligonier Ministries, 1991–93), 2:436, cited in Oliver, "Andrew Fuller and Abraham Booth," 216. For a very different reading of Fuller on the atonement, see Ella, *Law & Gospel in the Theology of Andrew Fuller*, 89–105.

[109] Fuller, *Complete Works*, 2:518.

human heart arises the necessity of a *special* and *effectual* influence of the Holy Spirit."[110]

Fuller had come to this understanding of the effectual work of the Holy Spirit very early in his struggle with High Calvinism. As he was just beginning to extend general gospel calls while a young pastor at Soham, his journal reveals his view of effectual grace:

> Preached this forenoon on *love to Christ*; and in the afternoon a new year's sermon to the young people, from Psalm 34:11, Come ye children and I will teach you the fear of the Lord! . . . Felt a very tender heart and longing desire for the welfare of the young people. . . . Very tender in reading Mr. Bunyan's *Holy War*; particularly that part where the four captains agree to petition the King for more force. Felt a great satisfaction in my principles concerning preaching to sinners, and a desire to pray, like them, for help from on high, to render the word effectual.[111]

*The Outward Call of the Gospel versus the Inward Call*

Put another way, Fuller made a distinction between the outward call of the gospel, which was to be made as widely as possible through preaching, and the inward call that could only come through the Spirit's agency. Fuller believed it was the certainty that the latter sometimes coincided with preaching that empowered the church's sense of mission.

One of the circular letters Fuller wrote on behalf of the Northamptonshire Baptist Association expressed this perspective. The letter was titled, "The Promise of the Spirit the Grand Encouragement in Promoting the Gospel."[112] The acceptance of Fuller's soteriology was widespread enough by then that he could write, "We take for granted that the spread of the gospel is the great object of your desire. . . . The true churches of Jesus Christ travail in birth for the salvation of men. They are the armies of the Lamb, the grand object of whose existence is to extend the Redeemers's kingdom."[113] Seeing open doors for expanding missionary work abroad and at home, Fuller stressed that "the

---

[110] Ibid.

[111] Fuller, *Diary*, January 2, 1785.

[112] The letter was composed in 1810 and is found in Fuller, *Complete Works*, 3:359–63.

[113] Ibid., 3:359.

time for the promulgation of the gospel is come."[114] Baptists could go forth through open doors in "full dependence on the promise of the Spirit" to accomplish salvation in the lives of the elect.[115]

*Fuller's Views on the Perseverance of the Saints*

Fuller's soteriological challenge to High Calvinism involved no point of disagreement on the doctrine of the perseverance of the saints. For the sake of completeness in this analysis, let it be briefly noted that his views on this point were in full accord with the broader Calvinistic tradition. Fuller believed that all who were truly united to Christ in faith would persevere in that relationship. Nevertheless, he pinned his hopes for the eternal welfare of believers squarely on the work of Christ. Jesus' work on the cross was the basis "for the certain accomplishment of whatever he undertook; as, that all that were given him should come to him, should not be lost, but raised up at the last day, and be presented without spot and blameless. All this I consider as included in the design of the father and the Son, with respect to the application of the atonement."[116]

## THE SOTERIOLOGICAL LEGACY OF FULLER ON BAPTISTS

Fuller left deep and mixed soteriological impacts on his denomination. Because of his extensive involvement with the Modern Missions movement, it is no exaggeration to say Fuller's theological legacy was felt literally to the ends of the earth.

### *Fuller's Impact on British Particular Baptists*

Even in his lifetime, Fuller was able to see the widespread acceptance of the theological views he had championed. In 1793, Fuller compiled a digest of information on the state of religion in his home county, Northamptonshire.[117] Of 21 Baptist congregations then having pastors, Fuller estimated only four

---

[114] Ibid., 3:363.

[115] Ibid.

[116] Fuller, "Three Conversations on Imputation, Substitution, and Particular Redemption," in *Complete Works*, 2:691.

[117] G. F. Nuttall, "The State of Religion in Northamptonshire (1793) by Andrew Fuller," *BQ* 29 (1980): 177–79.

or five "embrace what is called the High Calvinist Scheme, disapproving of unconverted sinners being exhorted to the performance of anything spiritually good."[118] Of the remaining 16 or 17 churches, Fuller reported "seven or eight" were less than 20 years old. And all of these churches Fuller was able to count as theological allies: "But the greater part of the Baptists, while they embibe [*sic*] the Doctrines of grace, consider them as Calvin, and all the Reformers did, as being consistent with the obligations of men to repent from sin and believe in Christ, and therefore make no scruple of exhorting them to these duties."[119]

Northamptonshire had been the home of both John Gill and John Brine and was once considered a point of strength for High Calvinist theology. The relative weakness of High Calvinism at this early date reveals the danger of attributing to Fuller too much credit for the theological changes, as if he worked alone. Even Fuller recognized he stood on other men's shoulders, adding this postscript to the letter:

> Pure religion, it is thought by many has of late years been upon the increase. It were improper to name places, or persons, who are yet living, thus much however, I may say, The labours of *Hervey, Mattock, Doddridge, Ryland* [John Collett], *Grant, Maurice*, and some others, were productive of effects which are still seen with pleasure in different parts of the country.[120]

Part of Fuller's impact can be traced to the timing—or timeliness—of his work on the "modern question." Clipsham identified this as a first-order reason for explaining why Fuller should have become the person so identified with the influence of the admittedly much broader Evangelical Awakening on Particular Baptists. He wrote, "At the very time when Fuller was working out and propagating his doctrine, others including a group of young ministers of outstanding ability and growing influence were thinking along lines similar to his own. . . . In other words, *Fuller provided a theology such as thinking men were seeking*."[121] In a sense, Fuller's most influential book was the straw that broke

---

[118] Ibid., 178.
[119] Ibid.
[120] Ibid.
[121] Clipsham, "Andrew Fuller and Fullerism," 269.

the camel's back: "With the publication of *The Gospel Worthy of All Accepta-tion*, the walls of High Calvinism fell flat."[122]

Given a few more years, the impact of Fuller's theology spread among Par-ticular Baptists until it could be said "Fullerism became the new orthodoxy."[123] For example, in 1797 a group of deacons wrote to the evangelical Baptist pas-tor Joseph Kinghorn (1766–1832) with a request that he help them locate a new pastor. They drew a profile of the type pastor they wanted: a "lively, zealous and affectionate preacher" who was "orthodox." Lest there be any misunderstand-ing, a marginal gloss defined "orthodox" as "of Mr. Fuller's sentiments."[124]

A further measure of Fuller's influence can be seen in the eventual for-mation of the Baptist Union in Britain. The theological modifications Fuller defended to Particular Baptists were necessary precursors to union. R. Brown wrote, "With the increasing acceptance of Andrew Fuller's moderate Calvin-ism, evangelical General Baptists discovered a new confidence within the wider life of Baptist people."[125] Fullerism helped narrow the theological gulf between the Particular Baptists and the New Connexion of General Baptists under the orbit of Dan Taylor's influence. In fact, Fuller himself had person-ally sought to promote a rapprochement in this age-old Baptist division. He preached at Taylor's church in 1806, with the stated goal being "to convince the world that perfect cordiality" was to be had between himself and Taylor.[126] Years after Fuller's death, his theological legacy would provide the means by which the two main trunks of British Baptists were reunited in the Baptist Union (1832). Payne wrote of this merger: "'Fullerism' had provided a bridge between Particular Baptist churches and those of the New Connexion of the General Baptists."[127]

---

[122]Nuttall, "Northamptonshire and *The Modern Question*," 123.

[123]M. R. Watts, *The Dissenters: From the Reformation to the French Revolution* (Oxford: Oxford University Press, 1978), 460.

[124]Morden, *Offering Christ to the World*, 100.

[125]Brown, *The English Baptists of the Eighteenth Century*, 112.

[126]Ibid. It would be erroneous to mistake "cordiality" for absolute doctrinal agreement. Though Dan Taylor and Fuller exchanged theological broadsides through the years, Fuller's son mentioned that his father always cheerfully admitted that Taylor conducted himself with both charity and acu-men. This is much more than could be said for many of his opponents.

[127]E. A. Payne, *The Baptist Union: A Short History* (London: Kingsgate, 1959).

### The Strict Baptist Reaction against Fuller

Not every part of Fuller's legacy tended to consolidate Baptist work. Part of that legacy was the drawing away of the High Calvinist wing of the Baptists into a separate body, the Strict and Particular Baptists. But even those who oppose Fuller's theological legacy agree his influence on Baptist soteriology has been immense. For example, Ella called the year of the first publication of *The Gospel Worthy of All Acceptation* (1785) an "*annus calamitosus*," opining that "1785 was a bad year for truth, sound sense, moral integrity and Gospel theology."[128] Ella's attitude is representative of the strident response a new generation of High Calvinists offered to the juggernaut of Fullerism. Oliver summarized the situation well: "By the time of Andrew Fuller's death in 1815, his views on faith were widely accepted by English Particular Baptists. Nevertheless, the strength of Fullerism should not be exaggerated. The old High Calvinism was not extinct. Gill, Brine and their associates had done their work too thoroughly for their memory and teaching to be forgotten so soon."[129]

The High Calvinists that still lingered around the fringes of Particular Baptist life found new life under the dynamic leadership of men like William Gadsby (1773–1844). Gadsby traveled far and wide with his message, planting churches in over 40 cities. That fact alone illustrates that this second generation of English High Calvinists were considerably different from men like Skepp, Brine, or Gill. The key issue for the first generation had been gospel offers or duty faith, but High Calvinists of Gadsby's type tended to be characterized at least as much by their commitment to antinomianism as they were to the "non-invitation scheme" of preaching.[130] The Strict Baptists developed a separate denominational consciousness only slowly. For a generation, they primarily contented themselves with the outlet provided by a string of magazines devoted to their causes, such as *The Gospel Standard*, *The Gospel Herald*, and the *Earthen Vessel*. Oliver, who has done much work on Strict Baptist origins, concluded, "It seems fair to say that in the 1850s, the Strict Baptists formed

---

[128] Ella, *Law & Gospel in the Theology of Andrew Fuller*, 18.

[129] R. W. Oliver, "The Emergence of a Strict and Particular Baptist Community among the English Calvinistic Baptists, 1770–1850" (D.Phil. thesis, London Bible College, 1986), 148.

[130] The Strict and Particular Baptists had a wide variation in how they dealt with antinomianism. A few were comfortable with the name as a label but most sought to refute it. Nonetheless, it seems accurate to say that a strong tendency toward doctrinal—if not actual—antinomianism was prevalent in this group.

an embryonic denomination, which had come into existence to defend and promote High Calvinism as a system of doctrine, and as the basis of Christian experience."[131]

### Fuller's Impact on American Baptists

The impact of Fuller on American Baptists has been too little investigated and thus never fully assessed. Tull offered this explanation:

> Fuller's influence upon a more vital evangelism among the Baptists of America was certainly real, though of an undetermined extent. The rise of a missionary spirit among American Baptists between the turn of the century and 1859 had developed markedly through the agency of many factors, of which the weight of Fuller's theology was only one consideration. The effect of the Carey mission in India, the work of Adoniram Judson in Burma, of the heroic labors of Luther Rice in America, of the missionary outreach sponsored by the Triennial Convention and by numerous other missionary societies, the intense evangelism of the Separate Baptists—these were all additional factors which must be taken into account.[132]

Though this question is too large and involved to fully investigate here, one line of evidence can be suggested that points to the probability that Fuller's influence was substantial. Some measure of Fuller's impact can be formed from considering what some near-contemporary Baptists thought about their brother's importance.

In 1836, the newly formed Baptist Union sent two of their own to America to assess the state of Baptist work in the United States and bring fraternal greeting to the Triennial Convention. These men, F. A. Cox (1783–1853) and J. Hoby (1788–1871), summarized their experiences and published them in 1836 under the title *The Baptists in America: A Narrative of the Deputation from the Baptist Union in England to the United States and Canada*.[133] In many of

---

[131] Oliver, "The Emergence of a Strict and Particular Baptist Community," 311.

[132] Tull, *Shapers of Baptist Thought*, 99.

[133] F. A. Cox and J. Hoby, *The Baptists in America: A Narrative of the Deputation from the Baptist Union in England to the United Sates and Canada* (New York: Leavitt, Lord and Co., 1836).

the cities and churches they visited, these men reported finding evidence "of a division of the body, in consequence of disagreements relating chiefly to high and low Calvinism."[134] It reminded them of what had happened in England during Fuller's lifetime:

> We left Philadelphia with the impression, that the churches, both Baptist and paedo-baptist, were considerably divided in sentiment, on what is termed high and low Calvinism. They appear to be passing through a process similar to that which agitated the English churches for some years after Mr. Fuller appeared on the field of controversy.[135]

Though Cox and Hoby frequently recorded the presence of such theological debate, they seldom provided enough detail to verify Fuller's role in it. An exception to this is their comment on the overall condition of New England Baptists: "Their theology may be denominated moderate Calvinism, of which a competent opinion may be formed by remarking their high estimation of the works of Andrew Fuller and Robert Hall."[136]

Another witness to Fuller's influence on American Baptists is *Fifty Years among the Baptists* (1860) by D. Benedict (1779–1874).[137] Benedict devoted a ten-page chapter of his work to describe the impact of Fuller's theological initiatives. He noted that "the modern question" was a transatlantic phenomenon: "Our old Baptist divines, especially those of British descent, were generally strong Calvinists, as to their doctrinal creed, and but few of them felt at liberty to call upon sinners in plain terms to repent and believe the gospel, on account of their inability to do so without divine assistance."[138] As to Fuller's influence in America, Benedict summarized,

> Forty years ago [1820] large bodies of our people were in a state of ferment and agitation, in consequence of some modifications of their old Calvinistic creed, as displayed in the writings of the late Andrew Fuller,

---

[134] Ibid., 21.

[135] Ibid., 23.

[136] Ibid., 449.

[137] D. Benedict, *Fifty Years among the Baptists* (New York: Sheldon & Co.; Boston: Gould & Lincoln, 1860).

[138] Ibid., 136.

of Kettering, England. This famous man maintained that the atonement of Christ was general in its nature, but particular in its application, in opposition to our old divines, who held that Christ died for the elect only. He also made a distinction between the natural and moral inability of man.[139]

Benedict's discussion in this chapter revealed that he plainly saw the errors of the High Calvinists. At the same time, he also hinted strongly of his concern that Fullerism had led Baptists too far toward Arminianism. In any event, Benedict was convinced Fullerism had made great inroads among American Baptists. As Fullerism had helped lead to the union of General and Particular Baptists in England, Benedict could see the same process at work in America. He remarked, "On this subject I lately remarked to a Freewill Baptist minister, 'Your side has been coming up, and ours has been going down, till the chasm between the two parties is by no means so great as formerly.'"[140]

A final example is cited to establish Fuller's impact on American Baptists, this one taken from the Georgia Baptist pioneer, Jesse Mercer (1769–1841).[141] As publisher of *The Christian Index*, Mercer was visible and knowledgeable about Baptist affairs in the South.[142] In 1830, Mercer published a series of letters to clarify his views on the atonement and clear himself of the charge of "defection" into Arminianism. The charge had come about because Mercer had declined the invitation to preach a doctrinal sermon on the atonement while visiting a Georgia Baptist association. Instead, he chose to preach a "practical discourse." All of this coincided with a stir among the Baptists in the South over the publication of Cyrus White's *A Scriptural View of the Atonement*, which claimed to be faithful to Fuller but was actually more in keeping with Arminian sentiments. Mercer reported that his refusal to preach on the requested topic was taken as a sign that he agreed with White. And so, to clear himself of Arminian suspicions, Mercer published *Letters Addressed to the*

[139] Ibid., 135.

[140] Ibid., 140.

[141] For an excellent account of this man and his role in Baptist life, see A. L. Chute, *A Piety above the Common Standard: Jesse Mercer and the Defense of Evangelical Calvinism* (Macon, GA: Mercer, 2004).

[142] This periodical had wide readership at the time. It is the oldest, continually published weekly religious periodical in the United States. See Chute, *A Piety above the Common Standard*, vii.

*Rev. Cyrus White; In Reference to His Scriptural View of the Atonement. By His Friend and Fellow Labourer in the Gospel of Christ.*[143]

Mercer's defense is interesting at several points, and not least is the fact that he took some pains to distance himself from Fuller on one point: the commercial nature of the atonement. Mercer wrote,

> I do not mean to contend for the atonement as a commercial transaction; but I mean to oppose the idea of a vague atonement. I must contend with [i.e., against] Fuller that though we cannot view the great work of redemption as a commercial transaction betwixt a debtor and his creditor; yet the satisfaction of justice, in all causes, requires to be *equal* to what the nature of the offence is in reality.[144]

In other words, Mercer was protesting Fuller's fondness for governmental language. He insisted, "The blood of Christ is our redemptive price, and redemption itself is a commercial transaction. I see no reason, therefore, why we should depart from [commercial language and imagery in discussing the atonement]."[145]

Taken as a whole, the booklet reveals Mercer had thoroughly read and understood Fuller. He was able to follow Fuller's sometimes tedious discussions of imputation and substitution with ease. In his reply to White, Mercer cited from nearly a dozen different places in Fuller's collected works.[146] Altogether, nearly half of the book's 46 pages consist of lengthy quotations from Fuller himself. The immersion of Mercer in Fuller's theology and the weight he gave to Fuller in developing his argument against White reveal the considerable impact Fuller had on American Baptists in the early South.[147]

---

[143] J. Mercer, *Letters Addressed to the Rev. Cyrus White; In Reference to His Scriptural View of the Atonement. By His Friend and Fellow Labourer in the Gospel of Christ* (Washington, GA: Printed at the News Office, 1830). The fact that Mercer felt the need to respond to such thin allegations gives some idea of the depth of Calvinistic sentiment in the South.

[144] Ibid., 7.

[145] Ibid., 8.

[146] He used the first collected edition, an imperfect eight-volume set published in 1824.

[147] J. H. Burch's recent study of an early southern American Baptist leader concurs that Fuller's theology was the gold standard in the antebellum South. Burch said (*Adiel Sherwood: Baptist Antebellum Pioneer in Georgia*, Baptists: History, Literature, Theology, Hymns, ed. W. B. Shurden [Macon, GA: Mercer, 2003], 12) of his subject, Adiel Sherwood, that he "promoted the same theological emphases as Fuller."

Historians have tended to agree with the verdict that Fuller's impact was profound. F. Wayland (1796–1865) believed that at the start of the nineteenth century, "Gill's Divinity was a sort of standard" for American Baptists.[148] But he went on to note that "within the last fifty years . . . a change commenced upon the publication of the writings of Fuller, especially his 'Gospel Worthy of all Acceptation,' which, in the northern and eastern States, has become almost universal."[149] The passage of time has done little to change this verdict. Recently, P. Roberts wrote,

> For most of the nineteenth century, evangelical Calvinism would typify the theological position of the vast majority of English and American Baptists, including those who would constitute the Southern Baptist Convention (1845). Andrew Fuller's work, particularly the *Gospel Worthy of All Acceptation*, made perhaps the most notable contribution toward providing a missionary theology and incentive for world evangelism in the midst of a people both Calvinistic and church oriented. . . . Charles Spurgeon and J. P. Boyce would be fervent evangelical Calvinists rather than stricter and more scholastic Calvinists typical of Fuller's predecessors at Kettering and London pastors like John Gill and John Brine.[150]

### Evaluating Fuller's Impact

As a pastor-theologian, concern for faithfulness to the ministerial responsibility of preaching always weighed heavily on Fuller's mind. Toward the end of his life, he summed up the preacher's burden:

> In preparing for the pulpit, it would be well to reflect in some such manner as this:—I am expected to preach, it may be to some hundreds of people, some of whom may have come several miles to hear; and what have I to say to them? Is it for me to sit here studying a text merely to find something to say to fill up the hour? I may do this without imparting

---

[148] F. Wayland, *Notes on the Principles and Practices of Baptist Churches* (New York: Sheldon, Blakeman & Co.; Boston: Gould & Lincoln; Chicago: S. C. Griggs & Co., 1857), 18–19, cited in Nettles, *By His Grace*, 133–34.

[149] Nettles, *By His Grace*, 133–34.

[150] Roberts, "Andrew Fuller," 46.

any useful instruction, without commending myself to any man's conscience, and without winning, or even aiming to win, one soul to Christ. It is possible there may be in the audience a poor miserable creature, labouring under the load of a guilty conscience. If he depart without being told how to obtain rest for his soul, what may be the consequence? Or, it may be, some stranger may be there who has never heard the way of salvation in his life. If he should depart without hearing it now, and should die before another opportunity occurs, how shall I meet him at the bar of God?[151]

The preceding statement on the gravity of preaching was offered as advice to a young minister. It was advice that flowed from a lifetime of pastoral work. His concern for the souls of those who would hear him preach illustrates Fuller's greatest legacy among the Baptists: to support a missionary-oriented theology that helped foster deep concern for the salvation of the lost. Certainly as much as any other person, Fuller's efforts helped to ensure that the results of the Evangelical Awakening would not be confined to Presbyterians or Methodists but would find a welcome home among the Baptists on both sides of the Atlantic. For this role, Baptists owe him a profound debt of thanks.

At the same time, it is appropriate to recognize that by relaxing the Calvinistic standards of the Particular Baptists, Fuller may have helped open the door to methodological changes that have sometimes had a less than beneficial impact on Baptists churches. To use I. H. Murray's distinction, what in Fuller's day could be seen as a healthy embrace of revival degenerated over time into an embrace of revivalism.[152] This tendency was noted as early as 1836 in Cox and Hoby's report on Baptist life in America. Though they believed a genuine reviving work of God was under way among many Baptists, they also reported with obvious disdain on instances when they felt that revivalist methods and preachers had commandeered the work and hence ruined it.[153]

---

[151] Fuller, *Complete Works*, 1:715–16.

[152] I. H. Murray, *Revival and Revivalism: The Making and Marring of American Evangelicalism: 1750–1858* (Edinburgh; Carlisle, PA: Banner of Truth, 1994). By revival, Murray means a sovereign work of God that stirs churches and Christians to new fervor. By revivalism, he means an embrace of an essentially Arminian theology that replaces God's sovereignty with means and methods designed to produce the same effects. He considered Finney's efforts as the quintessential example of revivalism.

[153] For one of several such instances, see Cox and Hoby, *The Baptists in America*, 172. In this account, the writers gave a scathing assessment of revivalism in Vermont, commenting

Although he agreed that the changes Fuller espoused were needed, D. Benedict was well aware of the possibilities for detrimental doctrinal changes to enter Baptist life through the door the English theologian had opened. He perceptively warned in 1860,

> While our creed, like the thirty-nine Articles, remains the same, this moderating still goes on, in theological training, in ministerial functions, and in public sentiment, and to what point of moderation we shall in time descend, it is difficult to foretell.
>
> John Leland, although a Calvinist, was not one of the straitest class. Two grains of Arminianism, with three of Calvinism, he thought, would make a tolerably good compound.
>
> An English statesman once said of his own church, "We have a Calvinistic creed, a Roman ritual, and an Arminian clergy." This in time may apply to us, minus the ritual, in some cases.[154]

The degree to which the rise and spread of Fullerism is responsible for the acceptance of Arminianism in Baptist life is a hotly disputed question.[155] As shown above, writers from the Strict and Particular Baptist camp consider Fuller the chief instigator of this event, and hence a great enemy of the gospel. But this perspective is hardly fair, given the fact that Fuller never disowned Calvinism and never felt the slightest need to modify the old seventeenth-century Calvinistic Baptist confessions of faith. Morden was more on target in evaluating Fuller's role in the rise of Arminianism when he commented,

---

prophetically that the field of work there would likely be ruined for years to come.

[154] Benedict, *Fifty Years among the Baptists*, 144. John Leland (1754–1841) was an influential itinerant Baptist preacher in Virginia for over 60 years.

[155] Speaking particularly of Fuller's impact on the view of the atonement held in Southern Baptist theology, W. W. Richards (*Winds of Doctrine: The Origin and Development of Southern Baptist Theology* [Lanham, MD: University Press of America, 1991], 55) opined, "Probably the most significant single factor in the break-up of Calvinism was the work of Andrew Fuller of England." As has been demonstrated, Fuller was influential in a shift among Baptist Calvinists. But a long train of authorities regard Fuller as genuinely Calvinistic. For example, J. P. Boyce (*Abstract of Systematic Theology* [Cape Coral, FL: Founders Press, 2006], 311–17) classified Fuller's view of the atonement as distinct from the Arminian position of a general atonement. Boyce's reading of Fuller is followed by Nettles (*By His Grace*, 108–30), who presently teaches at the seminary Boyce struggled to establish.

Certainly nineteenth-century Strict Baptists regarded Fuller as their *bête noire*. . . . But the nineteenth-century shift away from what Fuller termed "strict Calvinism" was far more attributable, as Ian Sellers states, to "the tide of nineteenth-century opinion [which] was running against religious particularism of any form." Those who laid the "blame" for the erosion of Calvinistic distinctives amongst the Particular Baptists at Fuller's door were wrong. Rather than abandoning Calvinism and opening the door to Arminianism, Fullerism actually opened the door to expansive gospel ministry by allowing increasing numbers within the Particular Baptist denomination to hold together strict Calvinism and invitational gospel preaching. That he was able to do this so successfully was a large part of his genius as a theologian.[156]

Arminianism certainly did make deep inroads into the heretofore Calvinistic Baptist denominations in the years following Fuller's ministry. For those who view this as a negative development, it is probably best not to blame Fuller too heavily for what came into the denomination for quite some time after he lived and wrote. Instead, the lesson to be learned from this development is the need for a greater measure of willingness to carefully evaluate and weigh doctrinal issues, especially those related to soteriology. In this regard, Fuller provides a model rarely matched since his day.

---

[156]Morden, *Offering Christ to the World*, 101–2. The citation from I. Sellers is from his article, "John Howard Hinton, Theologian," *BQ* 33 (1989): 123.

# Chapter 4

# From Doctrine to Practice

## INTRODUCTION

J udging from Andrew Fuller's extensive literary output, one might conclude he passed life barricaded in his study. In truth, there were seasons when he did spend inordinate amounts of time engaged in literary pursuits.[1] But over and beyond his labors to renew Particular Baptist doctrine through a writing ministry, Fuller was a man of extraordinary action. Ryland characterized his friend's exertions for the kingdom of God:

> Had Mr. Fuller's life been protracted to ever so great a length, he could never have put in execution all the plans he would have laid for attaining his ultimate end; since, as fast as some of his labours had been accomplished, his active mind would have been devising fresh measures for advancing the divine glory, and extending the kingdom of Christ. As it was, he certainly did more for God than most good men could have effected in a life longer by twenty years. And, while others admired his zeal and activity, he kept a constant watch over his own heart, and was perpetually applying to himself the divine interrogation—*Did ye do it unto me?*[2]

The doctrinal conclusions Fuller reached became the mainspring that powered the many facets of his active ministry. This chapter explores how Fuller's soteriological beliefs impacted his daily ministry as a pastor-theologian.

---

[1]But Morris remarked (*Memoirs of the Life and Writings of the Rev. Andrew Fuller*, 357) that even then Fuller did not bury "himself six feet deep in his study." Instead, "he generally sat at his desk, surrounded with the members of his family, in their common sitting-room, where, with astonishing rapidity, he composed his various papers for the press."

[2]Ryland, *Work of Faith*, 361.

This goal is pursued by examining Fuller's work as a local church pastor, as secretary to the Baptist Missionary Society (BMS), and as an apologist.

## FULLER AS A PASTOR

Fuller occupied the office of pastor for over 40 years. Only his unusual stores of energy enabled him to accomplish what he did outside his pastorates and still manage to cover the essential elements of pastoral work.[3] Fuller's embrace of robust views of human responsibility in salvation certainly worked itself out in his conduct as pastor over the years.

### *The Priority of Preaching*

As Fuller saw it, the heart of the ministry for any pastor was his time in the pulpit. The issues that hung in the balance of the pastor's sermon were so weighty that he once remarked, "A pulpit seems an awful place! An opportunity for addressing a company of mortals on their eternal interests. Oh how important! We preach for eternity."[4] The primary application he hoped readers would take from *The Gospel Worthy of All Acceptation* was a reformation in preaching. He concluded the book with a summary of the duty of ministers in dealing with the unconverted. Fuller characterized the lethargic state of most pulpit ministrations at that time: "We have sunk into such a compromising way of dealing with the unconverted as to have well nigh lost the spirit of the primitive preachers; and hence it is that sinners of every description can sit so quietly as they do, year after year, in our places of worship."[5] Like a number of his contemporaries, Fuller sought to model a new approach to preaching for English Particular Baptists.

---

[3]Both of his early biographers, Ryland and Morris, agreed that Fuller's other work sometimes did distract him from the fullest attention to his pastoral duties. Nonetheless, the Kettering Baptist Church very much supported his wider work for the kingdom of God. The bond of affection between church and pastor was genuine and strong.

[4]Fuller, *Diary*, February 5, 1781.

[5]Fuller, *Complete Works*, 2:387.

*Prescribing His Own Cure*

Fuller originally wrote out the sentiments contained in *The Gospel Worthy of All Acceptation* as an exercise in thinking his way clear on the "modern question." In his early ministry, he went through a learning curve in the application of these principles. His diary reveals a dawning realization that his preaching fell short of the New Testament standard. For example, after a day of pastoral visitation, he confided to his diary:

> Surely I do not sufficiently study the cases of the people, in preaching. I find, by conversation today, with one seemingly in dying circumstances, that but little of my preaching has been suited to her case. Visiting the sick and conversing sometimes even with the unconverted part of my hearers, about their souls, and especially with the godly, would have a tendency to make my preaching more experimental.[6]

A month later, another entry reveals that Fuller's realization that his own preaching stood in need of reformation had crystallized:

> I found also a suspicion that we shackle ourselves too much in our addresses; that we have bewildered and lost ourselves by taking the decrees of God as rules of action. Surely Peter and Paul never felt such scruples in their addresses as we do. They addressed their hearers as *men*—fallen men; as we should warn and admonish persons who were blind and on the brink of some dreadful precipice. Their work seemed plain before them. Oh that mine might be so before me![7]

As has been demonstrated above, when he did become bolder and more direct in invitations to the lost, his hyper-Calvinistic congregation at Soham began to grow restive.[8] On the other hand, the church at Kettering was prepared to embrace Fuller's evangelistic Calvinism, in both its formal doctrinal expression and its practical outworkings in the pulpit.

---

[6]Fuller, *Diary*, July 29, 1780. By "experimental," Fuller meant applicable or pointed.

[7]Fuller, *Diary*, August 30, 1780; also cited in chapter 1.

[8]See chapter 1.

## The Matter and Manner of Preaching

Fuller was a much sought-after preacher on all sorts of special occasions. Among the most frequent requests made of him was that he speak at the ordination of younger pastors.[9] He gave addresses on this topic so frequently that he eventually began a work to express his sentiments on the subject: *Thoughts on Preaching, in Letters to a Young Minister*.[10] In one of those letters, he drew attention to what he called the "*matter* and the *manner* of preaching."[11] His thoughts on this theme illustrate the implications of his soteriology on the most conspicuous portion of pastoral work.

As to its matter, Fuller said, "Unless the subject-matter of your preaching be truly evangelical, you had better be any thing than a minister."[12] By that, Fuller clarified that he meant sermons must contain the content of the gospel. He defined the gospel by supplying a list of verses that boiled the apostles' message down to its essence: salvation was accomplished through the sacrificial death of Jesus Christ and was freely available to all who in repentance and faith would call on Jesus' name. Put another way, he encouraged that "every sermon should contain a portion of the doctrine of salvation by the death of Christ."[13] Of course, Fuller recognized that not every sermon would speak directly of the cross. But he did believe that salvation through the cross was the unifying theme of the Bible. Therefore, any biblical subject had some sort of relationship to the cross. In handling any topic, Fuller advocated that "if we would introduce [it] in a truly evangelical manner," it must be to clarify its relationship to the cross.[14]

But it was in the manner of preaching that Fuller's soteriology led him to advocate a radically different path for Particular Baptist pastors than was then common. First, the true gospel preacher must bring a certain focus to his task. Fuller insisted that "in every sermon we should have an errand; and one of such importance that if it be received or complied with it will issue in eternal

---

[9] Nigel Wheeler, a Ph.D. candidate at Queen's University (Belfast, North Ireland) is presently writing a dissertation on Fuller's ordination sermons.

[10] In Fuller, *Complete Works*, 1:712–27. Like many other works, this one lay unfinished at Fuller's death.

[11] Ibid., 1:714.

[12] Ibid.

[13] Ibid., 1:716 (emphasis in original).

[14] Ibid.

salvation."[15] By this Fuller meant that the pastor must clearly keep his goal in preaching in mind. His aim must not be merely "to find something to say, in order to fill up the time."[16] Instead, he must preach with the objective of bringing his hearers to the point of decision. Second, and most controversially, Fuller opined that simply proclaiming the gospel was inadequate. A sermon was not complete until the gospel had been clearly explained and *accompanied* "with earnest calls, and pressing invitations, to sinners to receive it, together with the most solemn warnings and threatenings to unbelievers who shall continue to reject it."[17]

### Fuller's Pulpit Work

The evidence suggests that Fuller embodied the advice he gave younger men. His contemporary biographers agree that he was not the most eloquent or free-spoken man among them. Morris described Fuller's preaching style in almost painful detail:

> As a preacher he soon became popular, without any of the ordinary means of popularity. He had none of that easy elocution, none of that graceful fluency, which melts upon the ear, and captivates the attention of an auditor. His enunciation was laborious and slow; his voice strong and heavy; occasionally plaintive, and capable of an agreeable modulation. He had none of that eloquence which consists in a felicitous selection of terms, or in the harmonious construction of periods; he had a boldness in his manner, a masculine delivery, and great force of expression. His style was often deformed by colloquialisms, and coarse provincials; but in the roughest of his deliveries, "the bones of a giant might be seen." . . .
>
> In entering the pulpit, he studied very little decorum, and often hastened out of it with an appearance of precipitation. . . . Not aware of its awkwardness, in the course of his delivery, he would insensibly place one hand upon his breast, or behind him, and gradually twist off a

---

[15] Ibid., 1:715.
[16] Ibid.
[17] Ibid., 1:717.

button from his coat, which some of his domestics had frequent occasion to replace . . . He was not the exact model of an orator.[18]

But even Morris admitted that in the pulpit, Fuller "seldom failed to acquit
himself without honour and success."[19]

One of Fuller's sons agreed that his father's effectiveness in the pulpit was
not to be traced to "the observance of the rules of oratory."[20] Instead, he thought
it flowed from "strong, nervous utterances of a heart fraught with a deep and
abiding sense of the truth and importance of the message he had to deliver."[21]
That was exactly the quality in preaching that Fuller sought to commend to
younger pastors: passion over oratorical skill.

In his home pulpit, Fuller preached primarily exegetical sermons, working his way through the Bible book by book. He was careful to avoid getting
bogged down or sidetracked by historical incidences of little importance.[22]
Instead, for each text he sought to compare it to the "analogy of faith, pointing
out its application, and deducing its consequences . . . carrying conviction to
the heart."[23] This concurs with Ryland's opinion that when Fuller preached, it
was inevitably for the "good of souls."[24]

Fuller's concern to see souls converted through his pulpit ministry can be
illustrated through several steps he took at Soham and Kettering to increase
his number of auditors. As was mentioned earlier, Fuller was frustrated at the
Soham congregation's lack of willingness to move to a larger facility.[25] Though

---

[18] Morris, *Memoirs of the Life and Writings of the Rev. Andrew Fuller*, 81–82. To be fair, Morris also mentioned that Fuller overcame some of these weaknesses as he gained experience. It
should also be noted that Fuller and Morris came to a falling out over the latter's bankruptcy—or
more specifically, over the fact he refused to accept any fault in it. Previously, they had been close
friends, with Morris serving as Fuller's printer for a time. Ryland implied that Morris was less than
charitable at some points in his memoirs and even that he was exploiting Fuller's death in their
release. On the other hand, Ryland and other contemporaries tended to agree that eloquence was
not Fuller's mainstay.

[19] Ibid., 81.

[20] A. G. Fuller, *Andrew Fuller*, 61.

[21] Ibid. The word "nervous" here is used in the sense of passionate or heartfelt.

[22] His son (A. G. Fuller, *Andrew Fuller*, 85) said that he successfully avoided the error of
spending more time "ascertaining the form and dimensions of an oriental tea-kettle, than in show-
ing to men the way of salvation."

[23] Ibid.

[24] Ryland, *Work of Faith*, 359.

[25] See chapter 1, note 75.

the size of their building remained a limiting factor, Fuller took what measures he could to reach more people. For example, he added an evening service to the Sunday schedule.[26] During his years at Kettering, he led the church to expand their facilities twice, once by remodeling and the other by constructing a new sanctuary altogether.[27]

Fuller also recognized that many people were more receptive to the gospel in their youth than at any other point in life. To that end, he delivered an annual series of sermons aimed at their conversion. These sermons were delivered on the first Sunday of the New Year. They were also frequently printed for distribution. Ryland remembered that in them, Fuller "poured forth all his heart" and "spake as one who was *willing to have imparted to them, not the gospel of God only, but also his own soul, because they were dear* unto him; exhorting and charging every one, as a father doth his children."[28] God blessed his efforts such that these special sermons came to be highlights in the life of the church and community. Fuller said of these times, "The Lord has blessed these annual addresses more than usual. Many of our serious young people date their convictions from those sermons."[29]

In addition to these evangelistic special-event sermons, Fuller engaged in further efforts to lead the youth of his community to salvation. On Friday evenings, he held a series of lectures aimed at those under conviction: "The Friday evening discourses are now, and have been, for nearly a year, much thronged, because they have been mostly addressed to persons under some concern about their salvation."[30] Beyond that, Monday nights were devoted to follow-up with those who had questions. At seasons, the fruit of his evangelistic labors was so abundant as to cause Fuller to curb his usual extensive efforts to travel on behalf of the BMS. Ryland recorded the following thrilling account from Fuller's *Diary*: "There appears to be so much of an earnest inquiry after salvation, among our young people, that I feel it necessary to be absent from them

---

[26]Fuller, *Diary*, October 22, 1780. That meant Fuller preached three messages on the Lord's Day. They were styled the "forenoon" and "afternoon" sermons and the evening "lectures."

[27]The new sanctuary was completed in 1806 and designed to comfortably accommodate 900 people. As many as 1,000 attended at the peak of Fuller's ministry. The crowds were sometimes so immense that the balconies had to be propped for safety's sake. The building is still in use today by Fuller Baptist Church.

[28]Ryland, *Work of Faith*, 359–60.

[29]A. Fuller to W. Ward, December 31, 1803.

[30]Ryland, *Work of Faith*, 238.

as short a time as possible. We have a weekly meeting [on Mondays], in the vestry, for all who choose to come for conversation. Four have been accepted, and wait for baptism."[31]

### Fuller's Efforts at Village Preaching

One hallmark of Fuller's soteriology was that man's responsibility to repent and believe the gospel was restored to the prominence it had held with Particular Baptists a generation earlier. With that came a concomitant responsibility for preachers to take the gospel to all who would hear. When he was being set apart for the pastorate at Kettering, Fuller made plain his view of the gospel ministry: "I believe, it is the duty of every minister of Christ plainly and faithfully to preach the gospel to all who will hear it . . . I consider it as a part of my duty, which I could not omit without being guilty of the blood of souls."[32]

Three factors—the presence of spiritually destitute multitudes in the parishes around their churches, the inspiring success of the Methodist itinerants, and internal theological renewal—converged to result in the rediscovery of village preaching among the Particular Baptists.[33] From the 1790s forward, it was pursued with vigor and organization heretofore never attempted. The preaching responsibilities for settled pastors varied, but Fuller's approach of three sermons each Sunday was common. When a pastor began to seek to extend his ministry, he frequently traveled to a nearby village for the Sunday night sermon. As these efforts met with spiritual success, they were contagious. It was not uncommon to add services on week nights as well. Fuller's passion to reach the lost through preaching can be illustrated by his vigorous pursuit of opportunities for itinerant preaching.

The theological climate at his Soham pastorate was not conducive to itinerant work. On top of this, Fuller was never paid enough at Soham to support his growing family. The young pastor tried to make ends meet with several unsuccessful business ventures. This weekday work, coupled with Soham's

---

[31] Ibid. This entry is dated March 2, 1810, by Ryland. Along with several others that he cited, it is no longer to be found among the extant pages of Fuller's diary.

[32] Belcher, *The Last Remains of the Rev. Andrew Fuller*, 215.

[33] The best book-length treatment of village preaching among Dissenters broadly considered is D. W. Lovegrove, *Established Church, Sectarian People: Itinerancy and the Transformation of English Dissent, 1780–1830* (Cambridge: University Press, 1988). For a more focused look at itinerancy among Baptists, see Lovegrove, "Particular Baptist Itinerant Preachers during the 18th and 19th Centuries," *BQ* 28 (1979): 127–41.

*John Sutcliff, from a nineteenth-century composite of Baptist ministers.*

geographical isolation, added to the obstacles keeping him from much effort in village preaching. Fuller's frustration with this state of things is revealed in a letter he wrote to John Sutcliff, a fellow pastor initially united to him by a common admiration for the writings of Jonathan Edwards:

> Am sorry at your loss of so many by death: but better so than by sin. Religion is very low and things look gloomy with us. We have had two excluded and none added since last June. It is some pain to me that I have no manner of opening for Village Preaching on week days. It is a work I think I should love to be more employed in. I hear you are [preaching] pretty constantly. The Lord succeed your labours in so good a work![34]

From his mention of "week days," it may be that Fuller was engaged in some satellite preaching on Sunday evenings. But if so, his journal from this period of his ministry does not reveal it.

---

[34] A. Fuller to J. Sutcliff, March 13, 1781.

117

In the fall of 1782, Fuller moved to the pastorate of the Baptist church in Kettering. This church was likeminded with him in embracing an evangelical Calvinism that encouraged the use of means in order to win converts. Kettering offered not only a much larger congregation, but it was also a bustling market town. Outlying villages were now scattered within reach of this energetic young pastor. Even in Soham, although virtually unknown, Fuller's ministry had attracted many new hearers. He launched an extensive writing ministry soon after arriving at Kettering, which helped him command still more respect and attention.

Fuller's diary entries from about the time that *The Gospel Worthy of All Acceptation* was published reveal that he was certainly practicing what that book was all about. He was aggressively taking the gospel to as many as would hear him. From April through December 1784, Fuller records that he preached in no less than 33 different villages near Kettering.[35] In several cases, he preached in some villages more than once. A few representative journal entries from this era of his ministry will illustrate the prominent place that village preaching had by then assumed in his pastoral work:

[1786 January] 15.—Preached at home on keeping the Sabbath, from Isa. lviii 13, 14. At night went to Warkton and with more than usual feeling and affection, preached from Luke xiii. 3. On Tuesday preached at Geddington, about blind Bartimeus [*sic*]: next morning rode to Bedford, and to Shefford with brother Sutcliff, where I preached on putting on the Lord Jesus. Felt some pleasure there, in company with some other ministers, in advising the people to moderation in their opposition to a minister who is now a probationer at S——. Heard Mr. Carver at Southhill, and preached at Bedford. Returned home on Friday. I have heard since of the sermon at Bedford, on soul prosperity, being blessed to the conversion of a poor man.[36]

Looking back, his journal reveals that he had been engaged at that torrid pace for some time:

---

[35] A. Fuller, *Diary*, April 17, 1784, through December 16, 1784.
[36] Ryland, *Work of Faith*, 102.

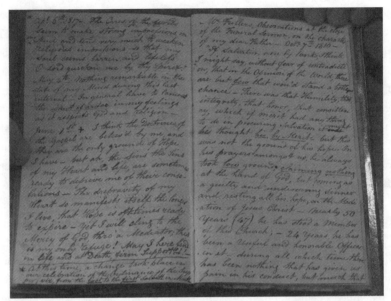

*A portion of Fuller's diary. Photo © Nigel Wheeler.*

Nov. 21, 1785.—For above a fortnight past, I have been chiefly out in journies to Bedford, Arnsby, Bosworth, Eltington, Guilsborough, and Spratton. Preached at each of these places with more or less earnestness. Came home on Friday, and spoke with some tenderness, from "Hold thou me up, and I shall be safe." On Lord's day, I preached on *the evil nature and dangerous tendency of mental departures from God*, from Prov. Xiv. 14. Also, on *soul-prosperity*, from 3 John ii. Had a tender and earnest mind.[37]

Plainly, the desire Fuller expressed to Sutcliff that he be more engaged in village preaching had been met at Kettering.

Two other insights into Fuller's thoughts on preaching and ministry can be illustrated from the extant records of his involvement in village work. First, the fruit that resulted was preserved by means of careful pastoral work. Describing his habits in a letter to his close friend William Carey, Fuller said, "Village preaching is diligently followed up, & I hope with some success."[38] What that

[37] Ibid.

[38] A. Fuller to W. Carey, April 18, 1799.

meant was that the converts gathered through these preaching tours were given discipleship and organized into new churches when possible. For example, in April of 1784, Fuller's journal mentions that he "preached at Winnick." Details are lacking, but he recorded at the time, "O it gives me sweet pleasure to see any appearance of the prosperity of Christ's kingdom."[39] By the fall of that year, he was back in Winnick. His journal entry from October shows that he and his fellow pastors had indeed been diligent in the work: "Rode with Mr. R.[yland] jun. to Winnick, to assist the good people there in forming themselves into a church. Heard him preach, and the people relate their experiences afterwards, more privately."[40]

Second, the mention of Fuller's fellow pastor and dearest friend, John Ryland Jr., exemplifies the cooperative manner in which village preaching was carried out. Ryland also served as pastor nearby, at College Lane Baptist Church in Northampton. Plainly these men, and undoubtedly others from their close-knit Northamptonshire Baptist Association, coordinated their schedules. If the villages could not have preaching every Sunday, at least where the work was promising, they were able to provide it with some regularity. The evangelical Calvinism of which Fuller had become a principal spokesman had gained a firm foothold in the Northamptonshire Baptist Association.

### The Cure of Souls

Like Richard Baxter (1615–91) before him, Fuller realized that a faithful pulpit ministry was greatly enhanced by attention to other aspects of pastoral work.[41] Fuller modeled the use of a wide array of pastoral means in assisting his hearers on the way to conversion.

### Pressing for Decisions
As Fuller often acknowledged, his High Calvinistic fellow pastors generally grasped the salvific doctrines connected with the gospel as well as anyone.

---

[39] Ryland, *Work of Faith*, 84.

[40] Ibid., 89.

[41] J. W. Black has recently published a very helpful work on Baxter (*Reformation Pastors: Richard Baxter and the Ideal of the Reformed Pastor*, Studies in Christian History and Thought, ed. A. P. F. Sell et al. [Carlisle, UK; Waynesboro, GA: Paternoster, 2004], 167–91) in which he pointed out that Baxter modeled the need to wed public preaching to private dealing in the care of souls.

What rendered their ministries so impotent was their reluctance to urge all who heard them to come to faith in Christ. Even after reaching a more evangelical soteriological position, Fuller himself struggled to translate doctrine to practice. A comparison of how he counseled two family members—one early and one late in his ministry—illustrates that Fuller did eventually make this transition.

In January of 1781, Fuller's father, Robert, lay dying. At that time, Fuller had already become convinced that High Calvinism was in error. His diary entries corresponding to his father's last week of life reveal that putting his new evangelical convictions in practice was still hard for Fuller:

> 1781, January 22—Visited my father today, who I fear will die. Found a strong inclination to converse with him concerning his soul, but did not.

> 1781, January 24—Today visited my father again, but he seems to have no thought of death. I found my heart much drawn out tonight to pray for him.

> 1781, January 26—Much affected today for my dear father, who I fear will die. Oh his immortal soul! How can I bear to bury him unconverted! Father, if it be possible, let this cup pass from me! I have had many earnest outgoings of soul for him, and some little conversation with him. "Have you any outgoings of soul, father, to the Lord?"—"Yes, my dear, I have."—"Well, father, the Lord is rich in mercy to all that call upon him: this is a great encouragement."—"Yes, my child, so it is: and I know, if I be saved, it must be by him alone. I have nothing to recommend me to his favor: but my hopes are very small."[42]

There the record ends, except for the sad conclusion to the matter on January 29, "O he is gone! He is gone! Forever gone!"[43] Morden is on target when he assesses this data: "Probably Fuller found it easier to put his new principles into practice in the pulpit than one-to-one, and doubtless his hesitation here was due

---

[42]Fuller, *Diary*, January 22–26, 1781.
[43]Fuller, *Diary*, January 29, 1781.

in some degree to a natural reticence in speaking with his father. But this still falls short of what we might expect from him at this stage in his career."[44]

It is obvious that his failure to press his father more closely on his need for salvation weighed on Fuller's conscience. The very next entry in his diary after the one where he recorded Robert's death reveals the state of Fuller's thinking:

> I think I have never yet entered into the true idea of the work of the ministry. If I had, surely I should be like Aaron, running between the dead and the living. I think I am by the ministry, as I was by my life as a Christian before I read *Edwards on the Affections*. I had never entered into the spirit of a great many important things. Oh for some such penetrating, edifying writer on this subject! Or, rather, that the Holy Spirit would open my eyes, and let me into the things that I have never yet seen![45]

Years later, Fuller had occasion to provide spiritual counsel to another dearly loved relative. This was his eldest son, who had been named Robert in honor of his grandfather. From young adulthood on, Fuller's son was a source of constant concern. He was unstable in work habits and given to rowdiness. His craving for travel and adventure eventually led him to sea as a sailor in the Royal Navy. At Robert's request, Fuller twice purchased his son's freedom from the obligations of duty. But all efforts at reform proved futile. His association with unsavory characters in coastal taverns eventually led to his induction in the Royal Marines, this time through a press gang. After his father had given up nearly all hope for Robert (in fact, he had been misinformed that he was dead), a letter finally came in which the son begged his father's forgiveness. Robert also indicated that he was heading to Lisbon with the fleet and feared he should not return alive.

Fuller answered his son's plea for mercy in December 1808. Fuller assured Robert he still had a place in his father's affections: "You may be assured, that I cherish no animosity against you. On the contrary, I do, from my heart, freely forgive you. But that which I long to see in you, is, repentance towards God,

---

[44]Morden, *Offering Christ to the World*, 105.

[45]Fuller, *Diary*, February 3, 1781.

and faith towards our Lord Jesus Christ; without which, there is no forgiveness from above."[46] This time Fuller was not willing to allow the opportunity to press the need for a decision to pass. He continued,

> My dear son! I am now fifty-five years old, and may soon expect to go the way of all the earth! But before I die, let me teach you the good and the right way. "Hear the instructions of a father." You have had a large portion of God's preserving goodness; or you had, ere now, perished in your sins. Think of this, and give thanks to the Father of mercies, who has hitherto preserved you. Think too, how you have requited him, and be ashamed for all that you have done. Nevertheless, do not despair! Far as you have gone, and low as you are sunk in sin, yet, if *from hence*, you return to God by Jesus Christ, you will find mercy. Jesus Christ came into the world to save sinners, even the chief of sinners. If you had been ever so sober and steady in your behaviour towards men, yet, without repentance towards God and faith in Christ, you could not have been saved: and, if you return to God by him, though your sins be great and aggravated, yet you will find mercy.[47]

Fuller was not privy to know how his son received his admonition. But as Robert had feared, it was to be his last voyage. He died aboard ship off the coast of Lisbon in March 1809.

The Sunday after he received word of Robert's death, Fuller preached what he would have loved to share with his son. His text was, "But what saith it? The word is nigh thee, even in thy mouth, and in thy heart: that is, the word of faith, which we preach; That if thou shalt confess with thy mouth the Lord Jesus, and shalt believe in thine heart that God hath raised him from the dead, thou shalt be saved" (Rom 10:8–9). He made three points in connection with this sermon:

> 1.The doctrine of free justification by the death of Christ is suited to *sinners of all degrees* . . . 2. It is suited to the *helpless condition* of sinners . . . 3. It is suited to sinners *in the last extremity*. It answers to the promised mercy in Deut. iv 29.—*If from thence* thou seek the Lord thy

---

[46] A. Fuller to R. Fuller, December 1801, in Ryland, *Work of Faith*, 288.

[47] Ryland, *Work of Faith*, 288.

God, thou shalt find him. Some are far from home, and have no friend, in their dying moments to speak a word of comfort . . . but this is near![48]

Between the death of his father in 1781 and the death of his son in 1809, Fuller's practice caught up with his doctrine.[49] He now boldly pressed for decisions when he had the opportunity.

### Embracing Every Available Means

Fuller's renewed focus on human responsibility in his soteriology led to his constant advocacy of the fullest possible use of means to help people toward salvation. Whereas the High Calvinists tended to regard such means as meddling with the mysterious sovereignty of God in salvation, Fuller thought their reticence was a cloak for disobeying the simplest of New Testament commands. He rebuked those who were troubled by his practice: "But the *command* of Christ is not to be trifled with. He to who we must shortly give account of the use we have made of every talent committed to us has said, 'Go, teach all nations—preach the gospel to every creature!'"[50]

Whether the unreached were in a foreign land or in unevangelized portions of England, Fuller was convinced that High Calvinistic sentiments stood in the way of the progress of the gospel. Speaking of those Christians who were unwilling to seek to extend Christ's kingdom beyond those presently in churches, he said, "We have long acted as if we thought the rest were to be given up by consent, and left to perish without any means being used for their salvation!"[51] The position of too many was that, "If God means to save any of them, it seems, he must bring them . . . the gospel in some miraculous manner."[52] Or again, "We *pray* for the conversion and salvation of the world, and yet *neglect the ordinary* means by which those ends have been used to be accomplished."[53] All of this inactivity Fuller believed was overturned by

---

[48] Ibid., 289–90.

[49] Fuller's family later received word from Robert's companions on board ship that gave cause to hope that the young man heeded his father's last advice and was saved; see A. G. Fuller, *Andrew Fuller*, 72.

[50] Fuller, *Complete Works*, 1:186. In the original, Fuller's synopsis of the Great Commission is in all capitals.

[51] Ibid., 1:188.

[52] Ibid.

[53] Ibid., 1:148.

simply taking the New Testament at its word: "The command of the Saviour is that we *go*, and preach it to every creature. All that Israel gained was by the dint of the sword."[54]

To this end, Fuller believed that one-on-one work with people was vital to the progress of the gospel. His diary regularly records instances of his willingness to devote time to this vital ministry. For example, "In the spring of this year there appeared a religious concern amongst five or six of our young people. I proposed to meet them once a week at the vestry, to talk and pray with them."[55] The obvious appeal Fuller had with the youth of his church probably can be partly traced to the fact that he took the time to catechize them as smaller children.[56] He had also demonstrated his love for them in other unique ways.

Though Fuller could be gruff and intimidating, yet the tenderness of his heart for the souls of the children in Kettering is touchingly revealed in a plan he concocted to evangelize some of the least among his flock:

> I have been thinking of a plan for disseminating the truth among our little lacemakers. A quantity of white wrapping-paper is used in the sale of small parcels of lace thread; so I will draw up a number of little hymns, the most impressive that I can either find or make, and get them printed on one side of the paper. Then every child that comes for a small quantity of thread, will find it wrapped up in a paper containing a short impressive hymn addressed to its heart.[57]

As this plan reveals, Fuller plainly thought that "preaching" the gospel was a wide-ranging duty that embraced the use of all manner of means.

Fuller also insisted that evangelistic work was not solely the purview of pastors. A circular letter for the Northamptonshire Baptist Association (1806)

---

[54] Ibid., 1:188.

[55] Fuller, *Diary*, 1791 (no other data is given for this entry). That this became a long-term custom can be illustrated by noting that Fuller was continuing the practice as late as 1810; see note 31.

[56] For example, Fuller, *Diary*, November 21, 1784, and February 19, 1786.

[57] A. Fuller to an unnamed friend, cited in Morris, *Memoirs of the Life and Writings of the Rev. Andrew Fuller*, 65.

made Fuller's position clear.[58] Fuller began by pointing out that New Testament churches did not make sharp distinctions between clergy and laity:

> The primitive churches were not mere assemblies of men who agreed to meet together once or twice a week, and to subscribe for the support of an accomplished man who should on those occasions deliver lectures on religion. They were men gathered out of the world by the preaching of the cross, and formed into society for the promotion of Christ's kingdom in their own souls and in the world around them. It was not the concern of the ministers or elders only; the body of the people were interested in all that was done, and, according to their several abilities and stations, took part in it . . . They spoke the truth; but it was in love: they observed discipline; but, like an army of chosen men, it was that they might attack the kingdom of Satan to greater advantage. Happy were it for our churches if we could come to a closer imitation of this model![59]

Therefore, on behalf of the association's pastors, Fuller asked the laity to come to their assistance in the work of the ministry.

As it pertained to evangelism, Fuller saw two broad areas where congregational involvement was essential. First, he thought that "in every church of Christ we may hope to find some persons *inquiring after the way of salvation*."[60] These inquirers needed access to more than just one guide: "But if, when men are inquiring the way to Zion, there be none but the minister to give them information, things must be low indeed . . . For who that has obtained mercy by believing in Jesus should be at a loss to recommend him to another?"[61] Fuller lamented that even among serious Christians, "Some members of churches act as if their whole duty consisted in sending the party [with spiritual interest] to the minister."[62] Describing far too many churches, he concluded, "A church

---

[58]The letter is found in Fuller, *Complete Works*, 3:345–51, and was titled "The Pastor's Address to His Christian Hearers, Entreating Their Assistance in Promoting the Interest of Christ."

[59]Ibid., 3:346.

[60]Ibid., 3:348.

[61]Ibid.

[62]Ibid.

composed of such characters may be opulent and respectable; but they possess nothing inviting or winning to an awakened mind."[63]

Second, Fuller clarified that all Christians had a duty to take the gospel to the "considerable number of people who are *living in their sins*, and in a state of *unconcernedness about salvation*."[64] Instead of holding forth the sovereignty of God as an excuse for passivity in these cases, Fuller advocated aggressive evangelistic activity:

> You are acquainted with many who do not attend the preaching of the word. If, by inviting them to go with you, an individual only should be caught, as we say, in the gospel net, you would save a soul from death. Such examples have frequently occurred. It is an established law in the Divine administration, that men, both in good and evil, should in a very great degree draw and be drawn by each other. The ordinary way in which the knowledge of God is spread in the world is, by every man saying to his neighbor and to his brother, Know the Lord. It is the character of gospel times, that "Many people shall go and say, Come, let us go up to the mountain of the Lord, to the house of the God of Jacob; and he will teach us of his ways, and we will walk in his paths; for out of Zion shall go forth the law, and the word of the Lord from Jerusalem." Add to this, by visiting your neighbors under affliction you would be furnished with many an opportunity of conversing with them to advantage. Men's consciences are commonly awake at such seasons, whatever they have been at others.[65]

The widest use of means by the widest number of Christians resulted in active churches that God would use to pluck sinners "as brands out of the burning!"[66]

---

[63] Ibid. To bolster his reader's confidence in handling seekers, he included a lengthy section with tips on how to guide men to faith in Christ. His advice boiled down to one maxim: "Point them directly to the Saviour."

[64] Ibid., 3:350.

[65] Ibid., 3:351.

[66] Ibid., 3:319.

## *The Vital Place of Divine Assistance in Evangelism*

If Fuller was an innovator at the time in arguing for the fullest use of means in the church's mission to seek out the lost, he nonetheless retained the highest regard for the absolute necessity of divine influences as well. Thus, means and prayer were inseparably wed in Fuller's ministry: "As we must never confide in God to the neglect of means; so we must never engage in the use of means without a sense of dependence on God."[67] His soteriological convictions meant that few elevated the role of prayer in evangelism more than Fuller. Two illustrations highlight how prayer held a vital place in Fuller's efforts to win souls to faith in Christ.

First, consider one of Fuller's well-received circular letters to the Northamptonshire Baptist Association called "The Promise of the Spirit the Grand Encouragement in Promoting the Gospel."[68] Fuller pointed out that the influence of the Holy Spirit in bringing people to faith in Christ was misrepresented by two extremes. On the one hand, some all but denied that the Holy Spirit was necessary in evangelism. They act "as though the Lord had long since forsaken the earth, and men were now to be converted by the mere influence of moral suasion."[69] On the other side stood the hyper-Calvinists, "Who abuse the doctrine, by converting it into an argument for sloth . . . God can convert sinners, say they, when he pleases, and without any exertions or contributions of ours."[70] Fuller replied to this logic by saying, "Yes, he can; and probably he will. Deliverance will arise from other quarters, and they who continue in this spirit will be destroyed!"[71]

The proper Christian response was to use the fullest use of means in seeking the conversion of sinners while praying that God would accompany them with the Holy Spirit's necessary influences:

> If all our help be in God, to him it becomes us to look for success. It was from a prayer-meeting, held in an upper room, that the first Christians descended, and commenced that notable attack on Satan's kingdom in which three thousand fell before them . . . We have seen success enough

---

[67] Ibid., 1:416.
[68] This letter is found in ibid., 3:359–63, and was written in 1810.
[69] Ibid., 3:359.
[70] Ibid., 3:360.
[71] Ibid.

[in the first years of the BMS's work] to encourage us to go forward; and probably, if we had been more sensible of our dependence on the Holy Spirit, and more importunate in our prayers, we should have seen much more.[72]

Prayer, then, was a required complement to the use of means in successful evangelism.

A second illustration of the vital place prayer assumed in Fuller's pastoral work is found in noting that he kept a book to guide his prayers for the souls of those who heard him preach. This book contained a list of "families who attend the meeting" and was found after Fuller's death.[73] On its opening page, Fuller had written about his purpose in keeping such a list: "A review of these may assist me in praying and preaching."[74] Of particular interest is the fact that in this book, Fuller kept a separate list of persons he thought to be under conviction of their need for salvation. Fuller's soteriological convictions committed him to do all in his power to win these people to faith in Christ. At the same time, those same convictions drove him to acknowledge that all his efforts were in vain unless the Spirit of the Lord was at work in their lives as well. Fuller prayed fervently for an outpouring of this divine influence.

## FULLER AND THE BAPTIST MISSIONARY SOCIETY

R. Brown has noted that "once Fullerism began to be accepted, its implications for evangelism were eagerly grasped and applied."[75] Nowhere was this effect more dramatic than in the formation of the BMS. Similarly, no area of his ministry better illustrates the vital link between doctrine and practice than Fuller's involvement with the BMS.

---

[72]Ibid., 3:362.

[73]Ryland, *Work of Faith*, 358.

[74]Ibid., 358.

[75]Brown, *The English Baptists of the Eighteenth Century*, 123.

## Opening the Mine

Fuller famously compared the commencement of efforts to evangelize the world through the BMS to descending a mine shaft by means of a rope.[76] The attempt of such an ambitious project by English Particular Baptists owed no small part to Fuller's influence.[77] Aside from his contributions to the changing theological climate among Particular Baptists, Fuller took an active hand in the chain of events that led to the formation of the BMS.

### Fuller Supports Carey's Dream

When Fuller's *The Gospel Worthy of All Acceptation* was published, William Carey was a young novice just settling into his first pastorate at Moulton. History records that it was Carey who drew the first public inference that the moderate Calvinism then taking root in the English Midlands implied it was the responsibility of Christians to take the gospel into all the world. He did so in 1786 at one of the Northamptonshire Baptist Association's frequent ministers' meetings. Carey was called on to present a topic for discussion at this gathering. He suggested that the ministers present discuss "whether the command given to the apostles to 'teach all nations,' was not obligatory on all succeeding ministers to the end of the world, seeing that the accompanying promise was of equal extent."[78] Although the exact response of the chairperson of the meeting, John Collett Ryland (1723–92), cannot now be ascertained with certainty, the evidence overwhelmingly suggests it was not favorable. The most often-cited version of that answer runs, "Young man, sit down. When God pleases to convert the heathen, He will do it without your aid or mine."[79] According to

---

[76] See chapter 1.

[77] D. Young sought to highlight what he saw as Fuller's neglected role in the formation of the BMS in his doctoral dissertation, "The Place of Andrew Fuller in the Developing Modern Missions Movement." His thesis that Fuller's memory has been eclipsed by the veneration afforded to William Carey is probably overstated. When it comes to Fuller's role in the changing theological climate among Particular Baptists in the eighteenth century, Young certainly overstated the case. He wrote that Fuller "almost single-handedly turned the theological tide from hyper-Calvinism to a moderate Calvinism that demanded vigorous evangelism" (p. 2). Fuller was indeed the point-man for this change, but he would have scoffed at the notion he worked almost alone.

[78] Stanley, *The History of the Baptist Missionary Society*, 6.

[79] Ibid., 6–7. Though John Ryland is thought to have been a faithful biographer for his friend Fuller, he apparently was unable to accept this report about his father's comments. He strenuously denied that the "ill-natured anecdote" ever took place. See Ryland, *Work of Faith*, 99. On

*Painting of William Carey at McMaster Divinity College. Photo by Michael Haykin. Permission to use granted by McMaster Divinity College, Hamilton, ON, Canada.*

Morris, "This was the first time Mr. Carey had mentioned the subject openly, and he was greatly abashed and mortified."[80] Fuller came alongside Carey to encourage the younger minister at this critical juncture. Once the domineering older Ryland had withdrawn, Fuller recommended to Carey that he continue to pursue this line of thought. This was the beginning of a lifetime friendship between the two men that not even Carey's removal to India was able to lessen.

the other hand, J. W. Morris gave compelling firsthand evidence that the comment was made. He especially defended its veracity in the second edition of his *Memoirs of the Life and Writing of the Rev. Andrew Fuller*, 101–2, in note. Others, including Fuller and Carey, corroborated the essence of Morris's account.

[80] Morris, *Memoirs of the Life and Writings of the Rev. Andrew Fuller*, 101–2.

## Fuller and Carey: The Influence Runs Both Ways

Upheld by Fuller's encouragement, Carey continued his investigations into the plausibility of foreign mission work. During the next few years, Fuller's evangelical Calvinism gained a loyal following, especially in the churches of his native Northamptonshire. Soon the leading figures of the Northamptonshire Baptist Association "no longer needed convincing of the theological case for missionary endeavor; what Carey still had to persuade at least some of them was that an immediate initiative on their part was both 'prudent' and 'realistic.'"[81] To this end, Carey believed a tract needed to be written that would clear objections to launching a missionary-sending effort. Recognizing his own limited standing in the association, Carey arranged for a meeting with Fuller, Sutcliff, and John Ryland. He laid out the case why such a book was called for and urged one of them to rise to the task. They all agreed that Carey ought to write it instead. To bolster him in his timidity, they promised to act as an editorial team to review his work. Thus came into being the influential manuscript that was called *An Enquiry into the Obligations of Christians to Use Means for the Conversion of the Heathens.*[82] When Carey presented it for review by his friends, they found nothing worthy of substantive change. They assured Carey it was ready for publication.

Now, instead of tracing Fuller's impact on the production of this invaluable publication, it must be noted that the influence begins to run the other way. Within months of reviewing Carey's manuscript, its impact showed up in Fuller's preaching at another crucial gathering of ministers. In the spring of 1791 Fuller delivered a sermon at the Northamptonshire Baptist Association.[83] The sermon was titled "Instances, Evil, and Tendency of Delay, in the Concerns of Religion."[84] The influence of Carey's book was unmistakable. Fuller echoed Carey in almost his own words:

---

[81] Stanley, *The History of the Baptist Missionary Society*, 11.

[82] W. Carey, *An Enquiry into the Obligations of Christians to Use Means for the Conversion of the Heathens* (Leicester: Ann Ireland, 1792; facsimile edition, London: Baptist Missionary Society, 1942).

[83] At that time, the association held spring and fall meetings.

[84] This sermon is found in Fuller, *Complete Works*, 1:145–51, and was published by the Northamptonshire Baptist Association.

Instead of waiting for the removal of difficulties, we ought, in many cases, to consider them as purposely laid in our way, in order to try the sincerity of our religion. . . .

Let it be considered whether it is not owing to this principle that so few and so feeble efforts have been made for the propagation of the gospel in the world. When the Lord Jesus commissioned his apostles, he commanded them to go and teach "all nations," to preach the gospel to "every creature;" and that notwithstanding any difficulties and opposi- tions that would lie in the way. The apostles executed their commission with assiduity and fidelity; but, since their days, we seem to sit down half contented that the greater part of the world should still remain in ignorance and idolatry. . . . And why is this so? Are the souls of men of less value than heretofore? No. Is Christianity less true or less important than in former ages? This will not be pretended. Are there no opportu- nities for societies, or individuals, in Christian nations, to convey the gospel to the heathen? This cannot be pleaded so long as opportunities are found to trade with them, yea, and (what is a disgrace to the name of Christians) to buy them, and sell them, and treat them with worse than savage barbarity? We have opportunities in abundance: the improve- ment in navigation, and the maritime and commercial turn of this coun- try, furnish us with these; and it deserves to be considered whether this is not a circumstance that renders it a duty peculiarly binding on us.

The truth is, if I am not mistaken, we wait for we know not what.[85]

Morris, who was present for this sermon, records that, "Every heart was penetrated with the subject; and the ministers retired, scarcely able to speak to one another. A scene of such deep solemnity has seldom been witnessed."[86] Still, when Carey pressed for the formation of a missionary-sending society, the task seemed too large for the majority. Instead, he had to settle for a reso- lution that requested he publish his manuscript (the existence of which had

---

[85] Ibid., 1:147.

[86] Morris, *Memoirs of the Life and Writings of the Rev. Andrew Fuller*, 103. This impact is the more profound by noting that the ministers frequently stayed up late into the night at such gatherings for camaraderie and conversation. Fuller himself was especially fond of such late-night meetings.

been noised abroad at the meeting) for the edification of the association on this topic.

At the spring meeting of the association in 1792, Carey delivered his famous sermon, "Expect Great Things—Attempt Great Things."[87] It appeared that no definitive action would be taken yet another time even though the ministers were deeply stirred again. As the annual meeting drew to its close, Carey reportedly grasped Fuller by the hand and pled for his friend to use his influence to seize the moment. So it was that Fuller rose to make the motion: "Resolved, That against the next meeting of ministers at Kettering, a plan should be prepared for the purpose of forming a society for propagating the gospel among the heathen."[88]

The action Carey longed to see finally happened at that meeting, October 1792. Following the formal proceedings of the Northamptonshire Baptist Association, 13 interested ministers retired to the home of one of Fuller's members, Mrs. Beeby Wallis.[89] Following prayer, together they drew up the by-laws of the BMS. They also collected their first mission-offering, which was so meager as to fit in a snuff can. Fuller was elected as the founding secretary to the new society. By the end of the month, Carey's offer to go out among the first group of missionaries had been accepted. The evidence suggests that Fuller's theological insight combined with Carey's single-minded devotion to the cause of international missions to stimulate their denomination to bold action. Though Fuller's soteriological convictions had helped lay part of the foundation, the BMS was a work that had to be constructed from the ground up. Efforts to further the cause of missions would consume Fuller's life from this point forward.

---

[87] Sadly, no copy of Carey's sermon has been preserved. Even the title is uncertain, although the shorter title given previously is almost certainly to be preferred as original over the expanded one, "Expect Great Things from God, Attempt Great Things for God." See A. C. Smith, "The Spirit and the Letter of Carey's Catalytic Watchword," *BQ* 33 (1989–90): 226–37.

[88] Morris, *The Memoirs of the Life and Writings of the Rev. Andrew Fuller*, 104.

[89] The number of attendees is variously reported in the literature. There were actually 12 pastors, one ministerial student, and one deacon. For an excellent account of the society's birth, see S. P. Carey, *William Carey: 1761–1834* (London: Hodder & Stoughton, 1923), 88–94.

## *Holding the Rope*

Fuller's tireless exertions on behalf of the BMS are inexplicable apart from understanding his soteriological convictions. Although he recognized that churches tended to get sidetracked on issues of lesser importance, Fuller warned that "the true churches of Jesus Christ travail in birth for the salvation of men."[90] As the value of new human life compensated the agony and risk of labor, Fuller was content to pour his life into the work of the BMS. An unnamed biographer well stated that Fuller's efforts on behalf of the BMS are nothing more than *The Gospel Worthy of All Acceptation* "put to life . . . what he had written and spoken, he set to the dull music of hard, grinding toil, and *until death* worked out the conception of his earlier years."[91]

### *Securing the Funds Necessary to Sustain the Effort*

Within a year of its founding, the BMS was able to send out its first pair of missionaries; others followed rapidly in the years to come. The costs associated with their transport, supply, and ongoing work were enormous.[92] The bulk of the responsibility for securing these funds rested squarely on Fuller's shoulders. Though frequently torn between his local church responsibilities and the needs of the mission, he explained the thought that was never far from his mind:

> Carey, as it were, said, "Well, I will go down if *you* will hold the rope."
> But before he went down, he, as it seemed to me, took an oath from each
> of us at the mouth of the pit to this effect, that while *we* lived we should
> *never* let go of the rope. You understand me. There was great responsi-
> bility attached to us who began the business."[93]

Carey and his associates had chosen the right man to anchor the mission rope.

Initially organized along the society method, success in procuring sufficient funds depended in no small part on a passionate and articulate spokesman. Add to that the novelty of the very idea of sending missionaries to non-Christian

---

[90]Fuller, *Complete Works*, 3:359.

[91]Anonymous, "Andrew Fuller: A Story of Religious Life Sixty Years Ago," 289.

[92]Nearly £90,000 was donated to the cause of foreign missions during the years of Fuller's secretaryship. See J. B. Myers, ed., *The Centenary Volume of the Baptist Missionary Society, 1792–1892* (London: Baptist Missionary Society, 1892), 27.

[93]A. G. Fuller, "Memoir," in Fuller, *Complete Works*, 1:68.

countries and the stubborn theological objections posed by High Calvinists, and it can be seen that the representative of the BMS needed to be able to answer practical and theological objections as well. As a pastor-theologian, Fuller seemed to have been specially made for the role he stepped into as secretary to the BMS.

Fuller was indefatigable in his fund-raising work. In his quest for like-minded donors, he made five tours of Scotland, one of Ireland, and hundreds of forays all across England.[94] The idea of asking for funds was ever repulsive to Fuller. His son recorded that his usual method was to "'tell the mission tale,' and leave the results [to God].'"[95] Still, only the strongest conviction that this work was incumbent on him as a faithful steward of the gospel could have induced him to engage in any fund raising. His diary records the tension: "I am going out for a month altogether among faces which I have never seen. My spirit revolts at the idea, but duty calls."[96] Again, it can be seen that his doctrine drove his practice.

On the other hand, it would be wrong to leave the impression that Fuller loathed his new responsibilities. Fuller found his greatest sense of satisfaction in the work he did on behalf of the BMS. From September 1792 to July 1794, Fuller recorded no entries in his diary. When he broke his silence, the entries are telling:

> Within the last two years I have experienced perhaps as much peace and calmness of mind as at any former period. I have been enabled to walk more near to God than heretofore . . . Within the last year or two we have formed a Missionary Society, and have been enabled to send out two of our brethren to the East Indies. My heart has been greatly interested in this work. Surely I never felt more genuine love to God and to his cause in my life. I bless God that this work has been a means of reviving

---

[94] Fuller suffered a stroke in January 1793. Many of his travels were conducted while he was in less than perfect health. He frequently lamented in his diary that poor health prevented him from accepting all the requests that poured in for him to come and speak on behalf of the BMS. John Sutcliff was a constant source of help in this work. For a study of Sutcliff, see Haykin, *One Heart and One Soul*.

[95] A. G. Fuller, "Memoir," in Fuller, *Complete Works*, 1:67.

[96] Fuller, *Diary*, October 2, 1799.

my soul. If nothing else comes of it, I and many more have obtained a spiritual advantage.[97]

## The Administrative Load

The fund-raising requirements formed only a portion of the administrative burden that devolved on Fuller. He performed a number of other vital duties in his unpaid capacity as secretary. For example, Fuller was heavily involved in the promotion of the work through various written venues. He discovered early on that information was the lifeblood of mission support. People could not be expected to pray intelligently or give enthusiastically if they were uninformed about the cause of missions. It fell to Secretary Fuller to act as the chief publicist for Carey and his associates. To that end, he wrote numerous status reports on the progress of the BMS that were inserted in many of the leading religious periodicals of the day.[98] The BMS soon found it expedient to begin self-publishing their missionary updates, which were called the *Periodical Accounts*.[99] Though one of Fuller's friends, Samuel Pearce (1766–99), initially served as editor of these periodicals, he died in 1799.[100] Although Fuller had been active in the project even when Pearce was editor, at his death the full responsibility came to rest on Fuller's shoulders.

One snapshot of Fuller's deep involvement in this work will have to suffice. In a letter to John Sutcliff, who probably helped Fuller in the work of the BMS

---

[97]Fuller, *Diary*, July 10, 1794, and July 18, 1794. Fuller also recorded that one reason for the silence in the diary was that he was too busy with mission concerns to write. In fact, for the rest of his life, Fuller appears to have written in his diary much less regularly. From 1794 on, he chiefly made entries while on distant travels for the BMS.

[98]These included such journals as *The Evangelical Magazine*, *The Baptist Magazine*, *The Biblical Magazine*, and *The Baptist Register*. American religious periodicals reprinted these notices as well.

[99]The earliest editions of these journals were gathered into three volumes and reprinted later: J. W. Morris, *Periodical Accounts Relative to a Society, Formed among the Particular Baptists, for Propagating the Gospel among the Heathen*, 3 vols. (London: J. W. Morris, 1800). Any copies of the *Periodical Accounts* are extremely hard to come by today, especially in the United States. Bringing these accounts out in a reprint edition is an important need in Baptist studies.

[100]Samuel Pearce was the pastor of Cannon Street Baptist Church in Birmingham, England. He was a warm-hearted evangelical graduate of the Bristol Baptist Academy who sought to serve the BMS as a missionary. His poor health stood in the way, and he died at age 33. Fuller wrote his memoirs, with the proceeds dedicated to support Pearce's widow and children. The memoirs are included in Fuller, *Complete Works*, 3:367–446.

*Samuel Pearce A.M.*
*late. Minister of the Gospel, Birmingham, Eng.*

*A line drawing of Samuel Pearce from a frontispiece to his memoirs by Fuller.*

as much as any other pastor, he revealed the dizzying array of details that went into the oversight of this publishing venture:

> By the time No. VI comes out, many sets of the Periodical Accounts will be wanted. But there are few if any left of No. II. Should not a small edition, say 400 of that number be printed, which will come to about 12£, and about 100 or more sets be put in boards and sold at what? 6/6 the volume? Or what? It appears necessary, however, before this be done . . . to ascertain as nearly as we can what number of the others are left unsold, to bind up with it. This we propose to accomplish by writing to the principal places whither they have been sent. Could you then, since you are at Birmingham, ascertain how many they have of Nos. I,

II, III, IV, & V unsold; and give me the answer? And when you return, give me the same answer as to what you have at Olney.[101]

Work like this took time, which was always at a premium for Fuller. That he was willing to grant it reveals the importance he attached to the missionary enterprise.

Another area that required Fuller's oversight was ensuring that funds and provisions made it to the missionaries in the field. The difficulties in this undertaking came from different quarters. First, Fuller was trying to supply the Mission in India at the height of the Napoleonic Wars. Because of perils to English shipping, many parcels that were sent never reached their destination. Those same problems also plagued letters to and from the missionaries. Keeping up with what had been requested and shipped versus what had actually been received became a logistical nightmare. Second, the East India Company had sufficient regulatory control over shipping to greatly harass efforts to supply the missionaries. Some of the staples that were needed in India could be seen as a threat to the East India Company's business monopoly. Aggravating the situation was the fact that many officials in the company were hostile to the idea of mission work in general. Such packages as did get through to India were always subject to being waylaid by Indian custom officials, who were corrupt as often as not. Third, as the number of people working in the India Mission mushroomed and the scope of the work exploded, the sheer volume of items requested could be overwhelming. Fuller's supply lists he took to London to be filled had to be maddening to complete. He purchased enough books to fill a library (on all topics and in many languages), all the mechanical equipment and supplies needed to run the huge printing venture connected with the translation efforts of the missionaries, an enormous array of pharmaceutical supplies, as well as clothing and everyday goods of all sorts.[102]

A third administrative responsibility that consumed much of Fuller's mental energies during his years as secretary was corresponding with the missionaries

---

[101] A. Fuller to J. Sutcliff, January 11, 1800. This citation has been edited extensively for clarity. Fuller used shorthand frequently. In this case, the letter is in longhand with numerous abbreviations and shows signs of being composed in great haste. This is typical of Fuller's letters, especially to familiar friends.

[102] Fuller's lists of these items are often contained in his correspondence with John Sutcliff. Three of the most fascinating are A. Fuller to J. Sutcliff, February 18, 1801; November 29, 1802; and May 10, 1804.

themselves. It was through this means that he mediated the wants and desires of the missionaries on the field with those of the leadership of the society back home. No matter how much Fuller wrote, he never seemed to satisfy the need. When Carey complained that Fuller had not been sufficiently forthcoming with letters, he replied,

> You complain of my not writing. I think I must have written more than a dozen letters to you, and several of them very long ones. I am glad Brother Morris is "copious." I will encourage him to be so still, and will do the best I can myself, tho' I have ten times the writing I suppose upon my hands that he has, and not half the capacity to perform it.[103]

Fuller's correspondence with the missionaries covered a wide gamut of topics, some frivolous and some serious. For example, when one of the missionaries insisted on denouncing English monarchy in favor of democratic ideals, Fuller spent an enormous amount of time trying to warn him that this activity threatened to undermine the entire mission enterprise.[104] Perhaps the thorniest problem he had to adjudicate through the post was the temporary embrace of open communion by the mission station in India.[105]

---

[103] A. Fuller to W. Carey, August 9, 1796. Slight editing has been done for clarity. "Bro. Morris" is Fuller's friend and fellow Northamptonshire Baptist Association pastor, J. W. Morris of Clipstone.

[104] The missionary in question was John Fountain (1767–1800), who was sent out to become Carey's assistant. He rejected Fuller's advice and would likely have been recalled had he not died. The early failure of the BMS's second mission outpost (Sierra Leone, West Africa) was attributable to the political and social activism of the missionaries there.

[105] Unrest on the question of open versus closed communion was beginning to be felt with force in the latter years of Fuller's ministry. Fuller, like most of the older Particular Baptists, staunchly supported closed communion. Several of the younger missionaries, especially William Ward (1769–1823), were vigorous advocates of open communion. Ward arrived in India in 1793 and immediately began agitating for the mission station to practice open communion, especially since English travelers of many denominational persuasions often lodged and worshiped in their quarters. Though Ward's arguments initially carried the day among the missionaries, at Carey's insistence the mission deferred to Fuller's judgment. Fuller sought to persuade Ward of the rightness of the closed communion position and insisted that the mission adhere to it, for fear of alienating supporters back home. Once Fuller and Carey died, the missionaries quickly moved to the practice of open communion, as did the main body of English Particular Baptists. See especially W. Fuller to W. Ward, September 21, 1800.

All of this administrative work took a tremendous toll on Fuller's physical and emotional energy. Fuller's widow, Anne, captured the burden he carried in a letter to John Ryland:

> But to so great a degree was he absorbed in his work, as scarcely to allow himself any leisure, or relaxation from the severest application . . . I was sometimes used to remark, how much we were occupied; (for, indeed, I had no small share of care devolved upon me, in consequence;) his reply usually was, "Ah, my dear, the way for us to have any joy, is to rejoice in all our labour, and then we shall have plenty of joy." If I complained, that he allowed himself no time for recreation, he would answer, "O no: all my recreation is a change of work." If I expressed an apprehension that he would soon wear himself out, he would reply, "I cannot be worn out in a better cause. We must work while it is day;" or, "Whatever thy hand findeth to do, do it with all thy might."[106]

With justifiable grounds, Mrs. Fuller went on to be the first to offer the often-repeated assertion that her husband should be considered a martyr to the cause of missions: "I am fully persuaded, that my dear husband fell a sacrifice to the concerns of the Mission."[107] The most satisfying answer as to why he drove himself so relentlessly is that Fuller was living out the implications of his soteriological beliefs.

### Fuller's Defense of Missions

Though there is much more to the story that could be added, a final episode in Fuller's career as a missions rope holder further illustrates the transforming

---

[106] A. Fuller to J. Ryland, n.d. [other sources indicate it appeared in 1815], in Ryland, *Work of Faith*, 282. Fuller married Anne several years after the death of his first wife. She proved to be a tremendous asset to his ministry. Among the many ways she aided him was extensive service as a secretary and amanuensis. She was also actively involved in collecting the necessary materials for the publication of his collected works. For example, see a letter she wrote requesting the return of a letter Fuller had sent to a friend, which contained little-known details about his early life and conversion: A. Fuller to M. Hope, May 23, 1815 (original in the Angus Library, Regent's Park College, Oxford University, in the "Archives of the Baptist Missionary Society, 1792–1914"). These documents have been preserved on 90 rolls of microfilm. This particular letter is found on roll 21.

[107] Ryland, *Work of Faith*, 283.

impact that his doctrinal conclusions had on his life. As has already been hinted at in the mention of the case of John Fountain, Fuller had a strong aversion to political involvement by ministers.[108] He repeatedly expressed his concerns about Fountain's outspoken political views. When rumors began to surface of the young man's fiery comments, Fuller wrote to him, "All that we felt any hesitation about [in your appointment as a missionary] was your too great edge for politicks. The mission has awfully suffered in Africa thro' that folly. . . . You should have avoided every thing that would impede your main object."[109] Fountain did not heed Fuller's gentle advice and continued to make acerbic comments about English royalty. He even had the indiscretion to put such things in letters bound back for England, which were subject to being read by customs officials. Fuller feared that the authorities would begin to think that the real goal of the missionaries was to spread revolutionary political ideas, not the gospel. Within a year of his arrival, Fuller felt that Fountain's appointment had been a mistake. He wrote a letter ostensibly addressed to Carey but indicated that it should be read by all at the mission station:

> If Mr. Fountain be so infatuated with political folly, as not to be able to write a letter to England without sneering sarcasms upon Governments, "cursing" their monopolies, expressing his hope of revolution work going on &c &c, I must say once for all, It is my judgement that the Society, much as they esteem him in other respects, *will be under the necessity of publickly disowning him*, as they were obliged to disown Grigg.[110]

Probably the only thing that prevented this unpleasant step was Fountain's untimely death soon after this letter was written.

Yet when political machinations were set afoot that might jeopardize the efforts of the BMS, Fuller jumped into the political arena with full force. To be sure, he always conducted himself with due respect for the officials—the lack

---

[108] See n. 104.

[109] A. Fuller to J. Fountain, September 7, 1797. The last sentence of this citation is itself a quotation from a similar complaint that Fuller had lodged in a letter addressed to the African missionary Jacob Grigg (1769–1835). At the collapse of the effort in Sierra Leone, Grigg came to America in pursuit of political liberty. See Haykin, *One Heart and One Soul*, 243–45.

[110] A. Fuller to W. Carey, April 18, 1799; Fuller's abbreviations have been rendered in longhand.

of which was his primary complaint against Fountain. Still, that Fuller would involve himself in the political arena at all spoke volumes about how he had come to view the cause of missions. It was now seen as an obligatory component of Christian faith and practice.

Fuller tried to walk a fine line between seeking diligently to preserve Christian liberties, especially to preach and evangelize freely at any place in the British Empire, and an unhealthy entanglement with political affairs. His attitude comes across in a letter he wrote to Carey:

> We have now a dark cloud hanging over the dissenters. A bill is now preparing to be introduced in parliament, which if it pass into a law will in effect repeal the Toleration Act. I am using all the interest I can with H. Thornton and Wilberforce against it: but God knows what is coming upon us. The bill is aimed particularly against village preaching and is drawn up by a member of the Minority! For aught I know your friends here may soon be in prison. My heart however is at rest in God, All my fear is that many of us should have to suffer not *as Christians* but as *busy bodies*. O that I could say of dissenters what Tertullian said of the Christian! Then would I write an *Apology* too: but men of Mr. Fountain's spirit render me incapable.[111]

Ryland believed that Fuller was successful in maintaining proper deportment in these debates: "Mr. Fuller went to London, and obtained an interview with several persons of rank and influence, by whose advice he pursued the wisest measurers for their [the missionaries] security. It would be improper to detail particulars; but few men could have acted with equal prudence and firmness in these affairs."[112] In his latter years, Fuller repeatedly engaged in political

---

[111] A. Fuller to W. Carey, April 12, 1800; Fuller's abbreviations have been rendered in longhand. Henry Thornton (1760–1815) and William Wilberforce (1759–1833) were members of Parliament. Tertullian (c. 155–220) was one of the most influential early Latin fathers. He was especially noted for his *Apology*, in which he sought to demonstrate to magistrates that Christianity was not a threat to the Roman political order.

[112] Ryland, *Work of Faith*, 197. Fuller made repeated trips to London in 1807 and 1808 on this endeavor. The bills seeking to shackle and even recall the missionaries were all defeated. Another round of intense opposition occurred when the charter of the East India Company went up for review in 1813. Once again, Fuller spearheaded an effective lobbying campaign to ensure that measures injurious to the cause of missions were not inserted in the new charter. In addition to these behind-the-scenes lobbying efforts, which included personal interviews and many letters to persons in power, Fuller also engaged in public debate. He wrote three pamphlets responding to a

activity as he successfully defended the rights of the BMS to engage in mission work. Morden correctly notes that these out-of-character political efforts to defend the right to evangelize freely are a powerful "testimony to his commitment to the missionary cause."[113]

## FULLER AS AN APOLOGIST

In addition to his apologetic work on behalf of missions, Fuller engaged in a series of other theological debates, and each one had a direct bearing on his soteriological convictions. Of course, attention has already been given to Fuller's basic defense of what the gospel was and how it ought to be preached: *The Gospel Worthy of All Acceptation*.[114] As he feared, the publication of that work necessitated that he continue to write on the theme to defend his thesis from attack. In fact, one of Fuller's unanswered prayers was, "The Lord grant I may never enter the polemical lists!"[115]

Throughout his ministry, Fuller especially paid close attention to the progress of theological errors that threatened the integrity of the gospel. Whenever he thought he detected such a danger, he was scarcely able to suppress a reply, no matter how full his hands were of pastoral and mission administration work. As to his success in defense of what he believed, W. Williams wrote,

---

series of antimissionary publications. They were bound together and published as *An Apology for the Late Christian Mission to India: In Three Parts, with an Appendix* (1808); see Fuller, *Complete Works*, 2:763–836.

[113] Peter Morden, "Andrew Fuller as an Apologist for Missions," in Haykin, *At the Pure Fountain of Thy Word*, 255. This chapter is an excellent summary of the topic at hand. The older account by Morris (*Memoirs of the Life and Writings of the Rev. Andrew Fuller*, 141–46, 277–91) is a nice supplement to Morden's work.

[114] See chapter 3. Fuller also wrote three additional full-length books in which he sought to respond to the critiques of his signature publication. His evangelical Calvinism was attacked from High Calvinists on the right and Arminians on the left. These titles are *A Defence of a Treatise Entitled "The Gospel of Christ Worthy of All Acceptation," Containing a Reply to Mr. Button's Remarks and the Observations of Philanthropos* [Dan Taylor] (1787); *The Reality and Efficacy of Divine Grace, with the Certain Success of Christ's Kingdom, Considered in a Series of Letters: Containing Remarks upon the Observations of the Rev. Dan Taylor on Mr. Fuller's Reply to Philanthropos* (published under the pseudonym, Agnostos; 1788?); *Remarks on Mr. Martin's Publication Entitled "Thoughts on the Duty of Man Relative to Faith in Jesus Christ," in Five Letters to a Friend* (1789). Each is found in Fuller, *Complete Works*.

[115] Fuller, *Diary*, July 20, 1780.

A mere Shamgar, as it might seem, he entered the battlefield with but an ox goad against the mailed erroists [*sic;* i.e., those in error] of his time . . . He developed almost unrivalled power in theological controversies especially in detecting sophistry. His theology was clear and massive. The man who encountered him in argument generally bore from the encounter the marks of a bludgeon.[116]

This chapter concludes with an overview of Fuller's apologetic efforts against five separate theological challenges that he believed threatened the integrity of the gospel.

### *Fuller and Deism*

Fuller lived and ministered in what historians now call the Age of Enlightenment. He would never have accepted that epithet as properly descriptive of his era. "Every generation has its peculiar work," he wrote. "The present age is distinguished, you know, by the progress of infidelity."[117] Fuller charged that the gospel emerging from the clash of the church with rationalism had been stripped of "all that is interesting and affecting to the souls of men,"[118] and all that remained was "Christianity in the frigid zone."[119]

None advocated this cool, calculating approach to religion with greater force than Thomas Paine. His *Age of Reason* appeared in two parts, in 1794 and 1795. Paine wrote his diatribe against Christianity as a theological exercise. His subtitle reveals the theological thrust he intended for the treatise: "Being an Investigation of True and Fabulous Theology." Attacking the notion of supernatural revelation, Paine undercut the ground on which the gospel rests. In its place, he reared an edifice of religion in which no salvation was offered or required. Given Paine's theological claims for his book and the contempt he

---

[116]W. R. Williams, no source given, cited in W. W. Everts, "Andrew Fuller," *The Review and Expositor* 17 (1920): 414. Williams's *Lectures on Baptist History* (Philadelphia: American Baptist Publication Society, 1877) contains a portion of this citation (p. 304). Possibly Everts was citing Williams from another source, likely a periodical.

[117]Fuller, *Complete Works*, 2:105.

[118]Ibid., 2:127.

[119]Ibid., 2:127. Fuller acknowledged that he borrowed this phrase from "the ingenious Mrs. Barbauld."

had for the notion of salvation by God, it is not surprising that one of the many replies entered against *The Age of Reason* came from Fuller.

An earlier chapter focused on Fuller's reply to Paine in *The Gospel Its Own Witness*,[120] and I drew attention to Fuller's defense of the possibility of divine revelation in Scripture. It needs noting here that Fuller's soteriological convictions played a significant role in why he felt that Christians must not jettison supernatural revelation in the Scriptures.

In *The Gospel Its Own Witness*, Fuller took note of Paine's exclusive preference for natural revelation: "But that on which our opponents insist the most, and with greatest show of argument, is *the law and light of nature*. This is their professed rule on almost all occasions, and its praises they are continually sounding."[121] Fuller clarified that he had no desire to deny the value of natural revelation. The Scriptures, he acknowledged, admit that it serves an important function. And here was the rub. Where deists thought a person could live well by nature's light, Fuller believed it only provided enough information to justify God's condemnation of rebellious creatures. Its purpose was never to provide a saving revelation.

The deistic confidence in the usefulness of natural light also failed to take into account the sinfulness of humanity. Fuller made a distinction between what might be known through natural revelation and what was actually understood from that revelation: "By the *light of nature*, however, I do not mean those ideas which heathens have actually entertained, many of which have been darkness, but those which were presented to them by the works of creation, and which they might have possessed, had they been desirous of retaining God in their knowledge."[122]

In short, Fuller believed deists like Paine had misunderstood the purpose of God's revelation in creation. It was given to render men without excuse, not to give them the resources to become righteous or to order their lives as God intended. Further, because of the sinfulness of the human condition, natural revelation must always remain a resource whose potential is never fully tapped. For this reason, Fuller elevated special revelation in the Scriptures to

---

[120] See chapter 2.
[121] Fuller, *Complete Works*, 2:18.
[122] Ibid.

a place of supreme importance. Since it took away the only sure basis for the knowledge of salvation, deism was a serious soteriological threat.[123]

### *Fuller and Socinianism*

Fuller's most prized book in our day is *The Gospel Worthy of All Acceptation*.[124] Older writers were just as likely to agree with Everts's opinion that "the most celebrated of Fuller's writings" pertained to the bitter struggle of orthodoxy with Socinianism.[125] Fuller's primary responses to Socinianism were sharply polemical works. His first such effort received wide readership and praise from the orthodox of all denominations. It was titled *The Calvinistic and Socinian Systems Examined and Compared, as to Their Moral Tendency, in a Series of Letters to the Friends of Vital and Practical Religion* (1793).[126] This book was primarily intended as a rejoinder to the writings of the well-known English Unitarian, Joseph Priestly (1733–1804).[127]

A. P. F. Sell objected that in focusing on the moral tendencies of religious belief systems, Fuller's "chosen ground of argument is shaky indeed."[128] Two replies are in order. First, Fuller did not choose the ground of this particular debate. Priestly was the first to allege that orthodox Christianity, especially of the Calvinistic variety, gave "wrong impressions concerning the character and moral government of God, and as relaxing the obligations of virtue."[129]

---

[123]For a more complete treatment of this topic, see M. A. G. Haykin, "'The Oracles of God': Andrew Fuller's Response to Deism," in Haykin, *At the Pure Fountain of Thy Word*, 122–38.

[124]For excellent treatments of this subject in greater depth, see T. J. Nettles, "Christianity Pure and Simple: Andrew Fuller's Contest with Socinianism," in Haykin, *At the Pure Fountain of Thy Word*, 139–73; and A. P. F. Sell, "Andrew Fuller and the Socinians," *Enlightenment and Dissent* 19 (2000 [Festschrift issue for D. O. Thomas]): 91–115.

[125]Everts, "Andrew Fuller," 416. Faustus Socinus (1539–1604) was an early rationalistic Protestant theologian. He is especially remembered for his antitrinitarian views. In the eighteenth century, his name was generally used to describe the substantial Unitarian movement in England.

[126]Several revised editions of this book were published, with various appendices attached. The last edition is found in Fuller, *Complete Works*, 2:108–242.

[127]A man of science, letters, and the church, Priestly served as a pastor and teacher. His theology consistently declined from orthodox Presbyterianism into the most skeptical and rationalistic species of Unitarianism. His attacks on orthodoxy—both theological and political—were sufficient to provoke riots in which he nearly lost his life. In consequence, he migrated to America in 1794.

[128]Sell, "Andrew Fuller and the Socinians," 111, cited in Nettles, "Christianity Pure and Simple," 169.

[129]Fuller, *Complete Works*, 2:137. Fuller was citing Priestly at this point, but it is unclear from which of Priestly's many books this quotation is taken.

Fuller was merely replying to the charge that orthodoxy led to moral degeneration in kind. Second, Nettles has appropriately noted that Fuller confined himself to tracing the outflow of theological principles and did not descend to branding Socinianism wrong because of the behavior of individuals.[130] Still, the polemical and somewhat restricted focus of *The Calvinistic and Socinian Systems Compared* do not make it best suited for grasping Fuller's theological objections to Socinian doctrine.

Fuller's second major work in the debate was only an extension of the first. Its title formed an abstract to the whole: *Socinianism Indefensible on the Ground of Its Moral Tendency: Containing a Reply to Two Late Publications; the One by Dr. Toulmin, Entitled* The Practical Efficacy of the Unitarian Doctrine Considered*; the Other by Mr. Kentish, Entitled* The Moral Tendency of the Genuine Christian Doctrine.[131] Soon after Fuller's broadside against Priestly, the latter had to flee the country and was in no position to reply to Fuller's critique. Morris reported that the two critics Fuller refuted in this book were unworthy opponents. Of Toulmin, Morris quipped, "He was scarcely a breakfast for his antagonist."[132] As with his former treatise, this one is largely consumed with answering specific charges of the Unitarian party.

Fuller's clearest theological exposition of why he felt Socinianism was a danger was contained in an essay he wrote a few years later: "The Deity of Christ Essential to the Atonement."[133] In a passage that reveals an accurate grasp of Christian history, Fuller gets to the heart of why Unitarianism must be rejected:

> In short, the Deity and atonement of Christ have always, among thinking people, stood or fallen together, and with them almost every other important doctrine of the gospel. The person of Christ is the foundation-stone on which the church is built. An error, therefore, on this subject affects the whole of our preaching, and the whole of our religion. In the esteem of the apostle Paul, that which nullified *the death of Christ* was accounted to be *another gospel*; and he expressed his wish that those who propagated it, and so troubled the churches, were *cut off*.

---

[130] Nettles, "Christianity Pure and Simple," 169–70.
[131] Fuller, *Complete Works*, 2:243–87.
[132] Morris, *Memoirs of the Life and Writings of the Rev. Andrew Fuller*, 262.
[133] Fuller, *Complete Works*, 3:693–97.

The principle maintained by the Galatians, it is true, did not consist in a denial of the Deity of Christ; but the consequence is the same. They taught that justification was by the works of the law, from whence the apostle inferred that "Christ is dead in vain." And he who teaches that Christ is a mere creature holds a doctrine which renders his sufferings of none effect. If the Deity of Christ be a Divine truth, it cannot reasonably be denied that it is of equal importance with the doctrine of justification by his righteousness. If therefore a rejection of the latter was deemed *a perversion of the gospel*, nothing less can be ascribed to the rejection of the former.[134]

Whenever and wherever heresy has undermined the deity of Christ, the gospel has been lost and with it the souls of men. Because of this, Fuller's soteriological and missiological commitments compelled him to oppose Socinianism tooth and nail.

### Fuller and Universalism

Universalism[135] was another heresy with profound soteriological ramifications that Fuller attacked.[136] The occasion of his involvement in this particular controversy was the defection of an erstwhile Baptist minister, whom Fuller knew personally, to the ranks of the universalists. This pastor, William Vidler (1758–1816), was converted to universalistic sentiments through the preaching of the American apostle of universalism, Elhanan Winchester (1751–97). Vidler split the Baptist Church in Battle, Sussex, over his embrace of the doctrine of universal salvation. He took Winchester's place as an avant-garde London pastor at his mentor's death.

Upon hearing of Vidler's public avowal of universalism, Fuller wrote him a private letter in 1793 attempting to recall him to orthodox sentiments. When no reply was forthcoming, Fuller expunged any personal references and ran it as a general interest piece in the *Evangelical Magazine* (1795), under the pen name "Gaius." Once in London, Vidler became the founding editor of a

---

[134]Ibid., 3:695.

[135]For a more complete treatment of this theme, see B. Howson, "Andrew Fuller and Universalism," in Haykin, *At the Pure Fountain of Thy Word*, 174–202. His overview of the history of universalistic thought within the Christian tradition is particularly helpful.

[136]Fuller, *Complete Works*, 2:292–327.

pro-universalist publication, *The Universalist's Miscellany*. Some of his initial issues (1799–1800) were taken up in responding to Fuller's letter. Fuller replied to Vidler's editorials in a series of seven letters that Vidler included in *The Universalist's Miscellany*. Eventually, all eight of Fuller's letters were collected and published as a freestanding volume, *Letters to Mr. Vidler, on The Doctrine of Universal Salvation* (1802).[137]

Three of Fuller's arguments against Vidler are especially cogent. First, he thought that to seek to support universalism from the Scriptures required one to engage in textual cherry-picking. The universalist could well be expected to question his soteriological conclusions from the simple consideration that "the whole tenor of Scripture saith 'to the righteous, it shall be well with him; and to the wicked, it shall be ill with him.'"[138] In letter five, Fuller presented the scriptural evidence that must be overlooked in order to embrace universalism. He gathered well over 50 texts under four heads and accompanied each listing of verses with exegetical support for the interpretation he was assigning them. The categories he suggested for these texts were (a) verses that describe "the future state of men in contrast"; (b) verses that "speak of the duration of future punishment by the terms 'everlasting, eternal, for ever, and for ever and ever'"; (c) verses "which express the duration of future punishment by implication, or by forms of speech which imply the doctrine in question"; and (d) those texts "which intimate that a change of heart, and a preparedness for heaven, are confined to the present life."[139]

Second, Fuller dealt at length with one of the universalist's favored lines of evidence; namely, that mistranslation of key biblical terms had led the church erroneously to embrace the idea of eternal punishment. In letters two and six, Fuller proved that Ryland's tutoring in Greek and Hebrew had not been in vain.

Third, Fuller responded to the argument of the universalists that has perhaps had the greatest currency across the years. Vidler wrote, "The character of God is LOVE; which is expressly against the horrible idea of the endless misery

---

[137] Ibid.

[138] Ibid., 2:293.

[139] Ibid., 2:306–12. Morris's remark (*Memoirs of the Life and Writings of the Rev. Andrew Fuller*, 267) about this letter may still be valid: "It may be doubted whether such a mass of striking and satisfactory evidence on this subject has ever been exhibited, within the same compass, in the English language."

of any of his rational creatures."[140] Fuller thought that such a line of argument was based on reason, not Scripture, and was therefore of little relative weight. Nevertheless, he also challenged its cogency on purely rational grounds. He made the point that in passing judgment on evildoers, a king's goodness was not eclipsed. If anything, God's righteousness and holiness demanded the doctrine of hell be preserved in its orthodox explanation.

Once again, it can easily be demonstrated that Fuller's soteriological and missiological beliefs led him to active involvement in this debate. In his initial private letter to Vidler, Fuller begged his friend to recall what was at stake: "It is certainly a very serious matter that we *do not err* in our ministrations. Error in a minister may affect the eternal welfare of many."[141] Fuller warned that universalism was simply a repackaging of the primordial heresy from the garden of Eden:

> Consider whether your ministration, on this principle, will not savour of his who taught our first parents, "Ye shall not surely die." If you should raise the hopes of the ungodly part of your audience [that an eternal hell is delusory] and if all at last should prove a deception, think how you will be able to look *them* in the face another day; and, what is still more, how you will be able to look *Him* in the face who hath charged you to be "free from the blood of all men."[142]

### Fuller and Sandemanianism

Sandemanianism was an eighteenth-century Christian movement that had its roots in Scotland.[143] It eventually resulted in a sort of loose network of like-minded churches that embraced the viewpoints of the principle spokesman for

---

[140]Cited without data by Fuller in his final letter (*Complete Works*, 2:325).

[141]Ibid., 2:293.

[142]Ibid., 2:294.

[143]For more information on this important controversy, see M. A. G. Haykin, "Andrew Fuller and the Sandemanian Controversy," in Haykin, *At the Pure Fountain of Thy Word*, 223–36; D. M. Lloyd-Jones, "Sandemanianism," in *The Puritans: Their Origins and Successors, Addresses Delivered at the Puritan and Westminster Conferences 1959–1978* (Edinburgh; Carlisle, PA: Banner of Truth, 1987), 170–90; T. J. South, "The Response of Andrew Fuller to the Sandemanian View of Saving Faith" (Th.D. dissertation, Mid-America Baptist Theological Seminary, 1993).

the movement, Robert Sandeman (1718–71).[144] Though as a sect it remained numerically insignificant, one aspect of the Sandemanian position gained currency in quite a number of churches: its view of what constituted saving faith.[145] Sandeman's position was that saving faith was merely a notional event. All that was required for justification was the simplest assent that the facts of the gospel were so. In his own words, Sandeman defined saving faith: "The whole benefit of this event [the atonement] is conveyed to men only by the Apostolic report concerning it, that everyone who understands this report to be true, or is persuaded that the event actually happened as testified by the Apostles, is justified and finds relief to his guilty conscience."[146]

This Sandemanian view of saving faith was embraced by Archibald McLean (1733–1812), the leading figure among Scottish Baptists in the eighteenth century. Fuller's five trips to Scotland on behalf of the BMS meant that he frequently encountered churches that had adopted the Sandemanian position on faith. McLean himself became a warm supporter of the missionary work and a sometime traveling companion of Fuller. Though he respected and liked his Scottish friend, Fuller believed that Sandemanianism was a significant threat to the purity of the gospel and that it led inevitably to lifeless churches. Given what was at stake, Fuller refused to allow his personal feelings for McLean to silence his criticisms of this spreading aberrant view of saving faith.

---

[144] Sandeman popularized and developed ideas he first learned from his father-in-law, John Glas (1695–1773). The Sandemanians are sometimes called "Glasites."

[145] South devoted about 25 percent of his dissertation to exploring the connection between Sandemanianism and the modern debate concerning "lordship salvation." He concluded that though "there are no direct connections between Sandemanianism and the current debate," the root error of the two movements is identical—an inadequate definition of saving faith. I agree with the last point but remain unconvinced that a more direct historical link between the two could not be established. It is a matter that needs further investigation. See South, "The Response of Andrew Fuller to the Sandemanian View of Saving Faith," 149–96. The citation is on p. 152. Lloyd-Jones, speaking about Sandemanianism prior to the outbreak of the lordship-salvation controversy, believed that the Sandemanian position on saving faith had largely supplanted a more robust and biblical definition. In 1967, he said, "If I understand the condition of the church today—and, indeed, during the last fifty years or so—I would say that its great trouble has been that it has fallen into this particular error" ("Sandemanianism," 170).

[146] R. Sandeman, *Letters on Theron and Aspasio. Addressed to the Author* [James Hervey], 2 vols. (Edinburgh: Sands, Donaldson, Murray, and Cochran, 1757). This is not to be confused with J. Hervey's prior publication, *Dialogues between Theron and Aspasio*, which had argued for the traditional view of saving faith as encompassing more than intellectual assent.

Fuller responded to the Sandemanian error in three primary venues. First, he broached the topic in an appendix added to the second edition of *The Gospel Worthy of All Acceptation*: "On the Question Whether the Existence of a Holy Disposition of Heart be Necessary to Believing."[147] Second, he wrote a gospel tract expressly designed to counteract the Sandemanian view. This piece was called "The Great Question Answered."[148] His most thorough response was a series of letters bound together and published as *Strictures on Sandemanianism: in Twelve Letters to a Friend* (1810). Of this last work, Lloyd-Jones remarked, "It is generally agreed that Fuller more or less demolished Sandemanianism in those twelve letters."[149]

Fuller justly defined the Sandemanian position on saving faith as "the bare belief of the bare truth."[150] In arguing instead for a "holy disposition of heart," Fuller was careful not to give back the ground he had taken from the High Calvinists. He wrote,

> For a minister to withhold the invitations of the gospel till he perceives the sinner sufficiently, as he thinks, convinced of sin, and then to bring them forward as something to which he is entitled, holding up his convictions and distress of mind as signs of grace, and persuading him, on this ground, to think himself one of God's elect, and warranted to believe in Christ, is doing worse than nothing.[151]

Still less did Fuller intend to deny the Reformation dictum *sola fides*: "If anything I have advanced [is] inconsistent with justification by faith alone . . . I am

---

[147] Fuller, *Complete Works*, 2:393–416.

[148] Ibid., 3:540–49. It is worth mentioning that the very length of this tract—nine full pages of very small print with narrow margins—makes an interesting contrast to the typical gospel tract of the present day. The brevity with which present-day evangelicals consistently express the gospel lends credence to Lloyd-Jones's assertion that Sandemanianism has largely won the day. Fuller's tract enjoyed a very wide circulation and was kept in print long after his death by the American Baptist Publication Society. It was also translated into numerous languages. For Fuller's anti-Sandemanian statement of purpose in writing the tract, see Fuller, *Complete Works*, 2:561.

[149] Lloyd-Jones, "Sandemanianism," 173. South ("The Response of Andrew Fuller to the Sandemanian View of Saving Faith," 201) agreed with this reading: "Fuller's arguments have never been satisfactorily answered and are still valid."

[150] Fuller, *Complete Works*, 2:566 (emphasis in original).

[151] Ibid., 2:563.

not aware of it."[152] Nonetheless, Sandemanianism was certainly to be censured because it had "reduced faith to a nullity."[153]

Reducing saving faith to mental assent to the facts of the gospel message was Sandeman's "easy view."[154] To name but one line of argument he took in refuting this position, Fuller denied that it did adequate justice to the full biblical revelation on the topic of saving faith:

> The holy nature of living faith may be difficult, and even impossible, to be ascertained but by its effects . . . [but] how was it that the Corinthians, who, by their unworthy spirit and conduct, had rendered their being Christ's disciples *indeed* a matter of doubt, should be told to *examine themselves* whether they were in the faith . . . on the principle here opposed, they should have examined, not themselves, but merely their creed, or *what* they believed, in order to know whether they were in the faith.[155]

In Sandeman's view, decisions for Christ might be easier to come by, but the long-term effects could not help but be disastrous. Sandemanianism had hollowed out the nature of saving faith in the Scottish churches, and Fuller believed he could see where the trajectory of the doctrine must go: "If we may judge from its effects during the last fifty years, it would lead the Christian world, if not to downright infidelity, yet to something that comes but very little short of it."[156] In consequence, Fuller warned Baptists of the dangers of this hidden reef.

---

[152] Ibid., 2:614.

[153] Ibid., 2:572.

[154] Ibid.

[155] Ibid., 2:587–88.

[156] Ibid., 2:646. Sandemanianism was also influential in Wales. The great Welsh Baptist preacher Christmas Evans (1766–1838) accepted it for a time. His testimony of its effects agrees with Fuller's fears: "The Sandemanian heresy affected me so far as to quench the spirit of prayer for the conversion of sinners . . . I lost the strength which clothed my mind with zeal, confidence and earnestness in the pulpit for the conversion of souls." Cited without source in Lloyd-Jones, "Sandemanianism," 186.

## Fuller and Antinomianism

The final major theological controversy in which Fuller played a significant role was the antinomian debate.[157] In many ways, it is difficult to separate this from Fuller's broader work against High Calvinism. That is because certain doctrines commonly found among the High Calvinists had a built-in tendency toward forms of antinomianism.[158] For example, John Gill had advocated the doctrine of eternal justification. That placed the act of justification in the past decrees of God, not in the lifetime of the believer. Though few would accuse Gill of antinomian teaching or practice, it is obvious that only a small step was required from his position on justification to antinomian sentiments. Similarly, many of Fuller's arguments against the Sandemanians could be made to serve double duty against antinomians.

Still, there was a particular form of antinomianism that was making inroads into English Particular Baptist life during Fuller's ministry. He addressed it in quite a number of shorter works. What was intended to be a full-length treatment of the issue remained unfinished at his death.[159] In the eighteenth-century English context, antinomianism was used to speak "of those who insisted that the Moral Law is not the Christian's rule of life."[160] This was contrary to the view of most Reformed theologians, especially those who stood in the Puritan tradition like the Particular Baptists.[161] The *Second London Confession* (1677, 1689) was in complete conformity with the Puritan legacy on this point: "The moral Law doth forever bind all, as well justified persons and others, to the

---

[157] This controversy is treated by C. Daniel, "Andrew Fuller and Antinomianism," in Haykin, *At the Pure Fountain of Thy Word*, 74–82. For a helpful introduction to the relationship of Particular Baptists and Antinomianism, see Oliver, "The Emergence of a Strict and Particular Baptist Community," 120–46.

[158] Daniel ("Andrew Fuller and Antinomianism," 78) agreed with this assessment of High Calvinism's tendency.

[159] This fragment was published posthumously as *Antinomianism Contrasted with the Religion Taught and Exemplified in the Holy Scriptures* (1817); it is found in Fuller, *Complete Works*, 2:737–62. In the introduction to this book, Fuller explained one reason he had been reluctant to give attention to this conflict: "There is something so low, foul, and scurrilous in the generality of the advocates of this system, that few have cared to encounter them, lest they should bring upon themselves a torrent of abuse" (p. 737). As expected, that was exactly what Fuller received. See Morris, *Memoirs of the Life and Writings of the Rev. Andrew Fuller*, 238–45.

[160] Oliver, "The Emergence of a Strict and Particular Baptist Community," 121.

[161] See the classic study by E. F. Kevan, *The Grace of the Law: A Study of Puritan Theology* (London: Carey Kingsgate Press, 1976; repr., Morgan, PA: Soli Deo Gloria Publications, 1993).

obedience thereof . . . Neither doth *Christ* in the Gospel any way dissolve, but much strengthen this obligation."[162]

As Fuller saw it, the antinomian error had two roots. For some it was High Calvinism, especially an abuse of the doctrine of election. Convinced they were the chosen of God from all eternity past, some had drawn the further implication that a holy life on earth was not incumbent on them. Others arrived at nearly the same position from a Sandemanian starting point. Since saving faith had been distilled away from all other biblical teaching until it was only mental assent to a bare list of facts, the law was not binding. Whereas Fuller could fellowship with High Calvinists and Sandemanians, he drew the line with antinomians.[163]

Fuller traced the practice of antinomians to a faith void of true love for God—dead faith. He wrote, "The love of God *as God*, or an affection to the Divine character as holy, is not in it."[164] The lack of love extended to every aspect of their lives, including the hateful way antinomians responded to critics. The bottom line was that Fuller thought antinomians were only pretenders, not true Christians: "True Scriptural conversion consists in 'repentance toward God, and faith toward our Lord Jesus Christ.' But in many of these conversions there is no appearance of one or the other."[165]

Fuller believed that Antinomianism had become a Trojan horse that must be identified and exposed. He warned, "It is one of the arts of the wily serpent, when he cannot prevent the introduction of the gospel into a place, to get it corrupted, by which means it is not only deprived of its wonted efficacy, but converted into an engine of destruction."[166] Thus, opposing antinomianism was a logical extension of Fuller's overall ministry designed to preserve the effectiveness of the church in bringing salvation to the lost.

---

[162] "Second London Confession (1677)," in Lumpkin, *Baptist Confessions of Faith*, 276–77.
[163] Oliver, "The Emergence of a Strict and Particular Baptist Community," 125.
[164] Fuller, *Complete Works*, 2:738.
[165] Ibid., 2:739.
[166] Ibid., 2:737.

## CONCLUSION

Fuller was a powerful apologist for the integrity of the gospel in the eighteenth and nineteenth centuries. Though he was enormously busy with his duties as a pastor and as secretary to the BMS, he made time to respond to a wide variety of theological heresies and aberrations. His motivation for this unpleasant work frequently traces back to his conviction that souls hung in the balance of the diligence with which pastor-theologians worked to preserve the purity of the gospel.

# Chapter 5

# Conclusion

## Andrew Fuller as a
## Pastor-Theologian

### INTRODUCTION

This study has examined Andrew Fuller's ministry with the goal of presenting him as a model Baptist pastor-theologian. This final chapter concludes with three sections that qualify, clarify, and highlight Fuller in this role.

### THE LIMITATIONS OF THIS STUDY

The soteriological debates that filled eighteenth-century English Particular Baptist life had a profound impact on the future theological direction of Baptists in general. Because of Fuller's prominence in these debates, he is chiefly remembered for his contributions to soteriology and missiology. But it is a mistake to paint Fuller as a one-dimensional theologian. Although it is true that soteriology was Fuller's favorite theme, he made contributions in other fields as well. Additional work needs to be done to provide contemporary students of Fuller with a better-rounded look at his life and ministry. A number of areas beckon for further work.

The first of these is Fuller's doctrine of God. Though the present study has touched on Fuller's defense of the deity of Christ in connection with his conflict with Socinianism, there is much more that could be said. Fuller was a major figure in preserving orthodox Christology among Baptists at a time when traditional views were under intense attack. Fuller also ably defended the trinitarian understanding of the Godhead.[1]

A second area of Fuller's thought that has been insufficiently studied is his doctrine of revelation. In this book Fuller's doctrine of revelation was briefly considered in connection with his theological method and his apology against deism. Once again, all that this study has been able to do is extract the highlights. Fuller's doctrine of revelation could be fleshed out in far greater detail. His reverence for the Scriptures joins with a chorus of Baptist voices reminding the present generation of the need for constant vigilance on this point.[2]

A third area that would repay additional study is Fuller's view of the ordinances. Baptism and the Lord's Supper were important themes in his writings and significant events in his local church ministry. Although the issue of open versus closed communion in Baptist life has been the subject of much research, Fuller's views have been largely neglected. Fuller's defense of closed communion was a noteworthy factor in the delay of the acceptance of open communion in English Baptist life. He also had a tremendous impact on Joseph Kinghorn, who became the primary challenger to Robert Hall's influential defense of open communion in the years immediately following Fuller's death.[3]

Fourth, Fuller's eschatology is an excellent representation of the hopeful postmillennialism that was characteristic of his time. There is a strong and vital link between this eschatological position and the formation of the Baptist Missionary Society (BMS). Since Fuller published a full-length exposition of the book of Revelation, his postmillennial eschatology could be explicated in some depth.[4]

---

[1] Fuller wrote several short pieces pertaining to Christology. Some of these were essays and others were originally letters, later published as essays (see Fuller, *Complete Works*, 3:693–704). Fuller's mature thoughts on the Trinity were some of the last words he ever put to paper. In fact, the last of his "Letters on Systematic Divinity" that he was able to complete before his final illness was on the Trinity (see ibid., 1:707–11).

[2] One area of Fuller's doctrine of Scripture that has been largely neglected by previous research is his effort to vindicate the complete trustworthiness of the Bible. He wrote a series of essays designed to resolve apparent contradictions between certain texts of Scripture (see ibid., 1:667–84). Also, three of Fuller's "Letters on Systematic Divinity" pertain to the doctrine of revelation (see ibid., 1:695–704).

[3] I have prepared a paper on Fuller's defense of closed communion that I hope to see published in the future.

[4] In 2004, I prepared an unpublished paper titled, "Postmillennialism and the Formation of the Baptist Missionary Society." Since that time, B. Howson published a paper in which he reached

Finally, the whole subject of Fuller's impact on American Baptists has never been sufficiently investigated. Two recently published biographies of early Southern Baptist leaders have underscored the need for further research in this direction.[5] Both of these books make the claim that Fuller's evangelical Calvinism was widely adopted by early Baptist leaders in the South. Fuller's impact on numerous other American Baptists needs to be better documented.[6]

## FULLER'S STRENGTHS AND WEAKNESSES
## AS A PASTOR-THEOLOGIAN

In contemplating Fuller as a model pastor-theologian, it is important to keep in mind both his strengths and his weaknesses. This section draws attention to several aspects of his ministry in each category.

### Fuller's Weaknesses as a Pastor-Theologian

Although I am sympathetic to many of Fuller's theological conclusions, I also recognize that no human model is perfect. Fuller is no exception. Those who look toward Fuller as a model should be careful to avoid several pitfalls that his ministry illustrates.

### Achieving Balance

Even Fuller's most sympathetic biographer admits that he became so consumed in his work as secretary to the BMS that his local church ministry suffered to some extent. For example, Ryland wrote, "But after he became involved in the Mission, its concerns gradually grew to such a magnitude, as, in great measure,

---

a similar conclusion: a significant change in eschatological outlook occurred between the time of John Gill and Andrew Fuller. This changed perspective was essential to the development of a missionary theology. See Howson, "The Eschatology of the Calvinistic Baptist John Gill (1697–1771) Examined and Compared," *Eusebeia: The Bulletin of the Jonathan Edwards Centre for Reformed Spirituality* 5 (2005): 33–66. The Jonathan Edwards Centre has recently been renamed in honor of Fuller, as more befitting the Baptist heritage of the sponsoring institution, the Southern Baptist Theological Seminary. (Originally, the Centre was sponsored by Toronto Baptist Seminary.)

[5]A. L. Chute, *A Piety Above the Common Standard*, and J. Burch, *Adiel Sherwood*.

[6]Not all American Baptists embraced Fuller's soteriological views warmly. The Primitive Baptist reaction against the spread of Fullerism is a significant part of his impact in America.

to incapacitate him from the due discharge of his other duties."[7] Morris added that overwork made him somewhat unapproachable to his people: "Those who wished for more of his pastoral advice, were fearful of breaking in upon his retirements, or of interrupting the career of his labours."[8] It seems that Fuller did not always model the best balance between the various aspects of his ministry.

In a related matter, Mrs. Fuller's lament over her husband's workaholic habits should be kept in mind.[9] Ministerial obligations ought not to become so consuming that the pastor neglects the legitimate needs of his family. When such is the case, it is probably a sign that the pastor has taken more upon himself than God intended.

Perhaps the root of both of these shortcomings is to be found in another weakness. Fuller was reluctant to delegate responsibilities to others. In the case of Kettering Baptist Church, he postponed bringing in an associate pastor until the congregation almost forced it upon him. In a similar fashion, he resisted the repeated advice of friends that the BMS hire an assistant to work alongside him in the mission. Ryland explained Fuller's thoughts on this issue: "While on a journey with a confidential friend, he once remarked, 'Friends talk to me about coadjutors and assistants, but I know not how it is, I find a difficulty.'"[10] Fuller went on in this quote to clarify exactly why he was reluctant to hire an assistant. He felt like his promise to Carey to "hold the rope" would somehow be abrogated if he entrusted things to others. But surely Fuller was mistaken in his opinion at this point.

Although Fuller may legitimately be criticized for allowing his local church ministry and family responsibilities to be crowded out by other concerns, his sacrificial service to the kingdom of God still calls forth great admiration. It is easy to excuse his failings in this area as Ryland did: "But what could he do? The demands of the Mission were imperious; the powers of man, both mental and corporeal, are limited; and though it may truly be said of him, that he 'rejoiced in all his labours,' yet his exertions proved greater than nature was able to sustain, and he sank under them into a premature grave."[11]

---

[7] Ryland, *Work of Faith*, 358.

[8] Morris, *Memoirs of the Life and Writings of the Rev. Andrew Fuller*, 86.

[9] See chapter 4.

[10] Ryland, *Work of Faith*, 144.

[11] Ibid., 358.

*The Trajectory of a Governmental View of the Atonement*

The chapter on Fuller's soteriology called attention to Fuller's fondness for governmental language in describing the atonement.[12] This practice has probably drawn more fire on Fuller's theology than anything else he ever said or wrote. In consequence, he was accused of denying the doctrine of a substitutionary atonement, together with the related concept of imputation. Ella spoke for many of Fuller's critics:

> There is thus in Fullerism no imputation of sin, no transfer of guilt and punishment, no substitution, no satisfaction, no indwelling righteousness of Christ. Indeed, the whole work of Christ in His redemptive sufferings and death, for Fuller, was an arbitrary sham merely to shake man into an awareness of his natural duties to shun evil and seek God and thus grasp out and take the forgiveness that is his for the asking.[13]

Three replies are in order. First, Ella and the many critics he represents have grossly misunderstood Fuller. Haykin is correct to argue that, in using governmental imagery to discuss the atonement, "Fuller did not surrender his commitment to particular redemption. Nor did he abandon his conviction that Christ died in the stead of sinners."[14] Nettles reads the evidence the same way:

> Some evidence exists in Fuller's unpublished correspondence that to a degree he came under the influence of the resurrected government theory of the atonement, propounded by several New England theologians. His appreciation for the insights of this view diminished in no instance Fuller's commitment to particular atonement. Instead, his commitment to the concept seemed strengthened and set within a more comprehensive framework. Fuller's use of governmental language did not involve him in the mistakes

---

[12]See chapter 3.

[13]George M. Ella, "Why I Am Not a Follower of Andrew Fuller." Accessed September 17, 2006. Online: http://www.evangelica.de/Why%20I%20Am%20Not%20a%20Follower%20of%20 Andrew%20Fuller.htm. In keeping with his views, Ella went on to warn that "Fullerism is the work of the serpent . . . and is the greatest heresy that ever strove to corrupt the Bride of Christ from within her retinue." G. M. Ella, "The Evangelical Liberalism of Andrew Fuller." Accessed September 9, 2006. Online: http://www.evangelica.de/The_Evangelical_Liberalism_of_Andrew _Fuller.htm.

[14]Haykin, "Particular Redemption in the Writings of Andrew Fuller," 128.

of the governmentalists; the atonement never became merely symbolic of justice, but maintained its character as an actual act of justice.[15]

In other words, it is possible to retain full belief in the substitutionary nature of Christ's work on the cross for sinners and at the same time allow that God has vindicated his justice in that act. These different models for understanding the atonement can be made complementary and do not have to be seen as standing at cross-purposes.

Second, it must be admitted that several illustrations Fuller used to discuss the atonement could be misleading if allowed to stand alone as expressive of his views on the subject. The same could be said of his frequent use of phrases that speak of the atonement in terms of its moral justice. Both of these traits show up in *The Gospel Its Own Witness*. Fuller developed an elaborate illustration there of why the atonement was not contrary to sound principles of morality, as Thomas Paine had alleged. In that illustration, the son of a king agrees to be punished in the stead of wrongdoers in order to make manifest the king's "displeasure against their wicked conduct."[16] Language like this, and indeed the general thrust of the illustration, is clearly compatible with a governmental view of the cross as a display of God's determination to punish sin. Yet even here, one must go rather far out of the way to miss important qualifiers whereby Fuller clarified that he was not denying the substitutionary nature of the atonement.[17] Haykin argued fairly that Fuller did not "abandon his conviction that Christ died in the stead of sinners, though, it must be admitted that his fondness for governmental language about the atonement hampered, rather than helped, a clear expression of this conviction."[18]

---

[15]Nettles, *By His Grace*, 128. As has already been demonstrated, Fuller's embrace of governmental imagery and language was not confined to his private correspondence. His first use of the governmental view was in *The Gospel Its Own Witness* (1799). Such arguments were also featured prominently in the second edition of Fuller's signature book, *The Gospel Worthy of All Acceptation* (1801). See chapter 3.

[16]Fuller, *Complete Works*, 2:77.

[17]For example, Fuller himself acknowledged the imperfection of his illustration. He suggested that his illustration compared to the reality of the atonement like a few man-made electrical sparks compared to lightning and thunder (ibid., 2:80). Beyond this, though he expressed the sacrifice of the king's son in governmental language, the basic structure of the illustration was substitutionary. The son takes the place of the wicked men.

[18]M. A. G. Haykin, "Particular Redemption in the Writings of Andrew Fuller," in *The Gospel in the World: International Baptist Studies*, ed. D. W. Bebbington, SBHT (Carlisle, UK; Waynesboro, GA: Paternoster, 2002), 1:128.

Third, Fuller may be legitimately criticized for not realizing the trajectory to which an embrace of the governmental view must tend. For example, Fuller had imbibed his governmental views especially from the influence of the New Divinity theologians working in New England.[19] The modifications these writers made to Edwardsean Calvinism would lead to serious declensions away from orthodoxy within a short number of years. Morden correctly argued that Fuller was careful to sift the work of the New Divinity men thoroughly and therefore avoided being led away into error.[20] Many who followed Fuller were not as careful to take doctrines back to the Scriptures, and in time radical changes were introduced to Baptist theology through this open door.

## Fuller's Strengths as a Pastor-Theologian

Accolades for Fuller's work continue to come in even though it is approaching 200 years since he died. Perhaps the latest expression of this contemporary interest is the launch of a new Web site dedicated to Fuller studies: "The Elephant of Kettering: Andrew Fuller."[21] Fuller's strengths as a pastor-theologian make him an attractive figure for study and emulation. Five of those strengths are spotlighted below.

### Never Keep Back the Truth

The book of Jude admonishes pastors to "contend earnestly for the faith which was once handed down to the saints" (Jude 3, NASB). Fuller modeled adherence to this principle. The first entry in his diary is titled "A Solemn Vow or Renewal of Covenant with God."[22] Taking note of the diversity of interpretation to be found in the church, Fuller pled for God to guide him into the truth through the Scriptures. He concluded the covenant with a prayer:

---

[19]For a helpful discussion of the influence of the New Divinity School on Fuller, see Morden, *Offering Christ to the World*, 89–97. For a recent study of the New Divinity School, see D. A. Sweeney and A. C. Guelzo, eds., *The New England Theology: From Jonathan Edwards to Edwards Amasa Park* (Grand Rapids: Baker, 2006).

[20]Morden, *Offering Christ to the World*, 93–97.

[21]The address is http://andrewfuller.blogspot.com/. The site was begun in November 2006.

[22]Fuller, *Diary*, January 10, 1780. Ryland (*Work of Faith*, 116–17) cited from this document and concurred as to the date of its composition, but he apparently viewed it as a free-standing piece.

One thing in particular I would pray for; namely, that I may not only be kept from erroneous principles, but may so *love* the truth as never to keep it back. O Lord, never let me, under the specious pretence of preaching *holiness*, neglect to promulgate the truths of thy word; for this day I see, and have all along found, that holy practice has a necessary dependence on sacred *principle*. O Lord, if thou wilt open my eyes to behold the wonders of thy word, and give me to feel their transforming tendency, then shall the Lord be my God; then let my tongue cleave to the roof of my mouth, if I shun to declare, to the best of my knowledge, the whole counsel of God.[23]

When Fuller's search for theological truth led him to views that he knew would meet with strong opposition, this vow stiffened his resolve to engage in debate. For example, on the eve of the release of *The Gospel Worthy of All Acceptation*, his diary records this struggle: "Feel some pain in the thought of being about to publish something on the *Obligations of Men to Believe in Christ*, as supposing I shall thereby expose myself to plenty of abuse, which is disagreeable to the flesh. Had I not a satisfaction that 'tis *the cause of God and truth*, I would drop all thoughts of printing."[24] In the course of his ministry, Fuller came to that same conviction time and again. His passion to protect the integrity of the gospel repeatedly drove him to engage in theological debate.

At the same time, it should be noted that Fuller was careful to choose what topics were worthy of conflict. To use Mohler's phrase, he practiced "theological triage."[25] The topics to which he devoted most attention invariably had to do with the central matters of Christian faith and practice. Roberts explained why: "For Fuller correct doctrine and theology were not the niceties of the faith but indispensable building blocks of the kingdom of God."[26] As has already been seen, this exactly captures Fuller's sentiment "that holy practice has a necessary dependence on sacred *principle*."[27]

Put another way, Fuller believed that doctrine mattered. He recognized that not every Christian had the same capacity to distinguish theological truth from

---

[23]Fuller, *Diary*, January 10, 1780.

[24]Ibid., October 31, 1784.

[25]Mohler, "The Call for Theological Triage and Christian Maturity," 2.

[26]Roberts, "Andrew Fuller," 47.

[27]Fuller, *Diary*, January 10, 1780 (see Fuller's prayer just quoted).

error. But he thought that this responsibility lay at the heart of the pastoral calling. In one of his ordination sermons, Fuller counseled,

> By your public ministry root out errors in doctrine. Overturn them—not by empty declamation, but by solid Scriptural evidence—not by the wild fury of a bigot, but with the pure love of the Christian pastor, whose care it should be to preserve his charge from things that tend to the ruin of their souls. . . . If you love *Christ*, you will root up those principles which degrade his dignity and set aside his atonement. If you love *your people*, you will root up those principles which endanger the salvation of their souls.[28]

Defending and clarifying the Christian faith came with its own reward because "the salvation of his hearers is the reward of a faithful minister."[29]

### Biblical Theology

Calvin's biblical commentaries remain remarkably usable today, even though they were written over 450 years ago. One reason for this is that they tend to be rigorously focused on expounding the actual text of Scripture. In a similar way, Fuller's theological writings have had lasting appeal because he sought to ground his positions firmly on a biblical footing.[30]

That service to the church was all the more valuable as the tenor of Fuller's era tended to discount the value of the Bible. Though he felt obliged to meet Paine's attacks directed against the integrity of the Bible, Fuller claimed he had no concerns for the ultimate outcome of the debate. God would not allow His word or his cause to fail.[31] Years later, Fuller recalled the famous boast Paine had made in *The Age of Reason*: "A few years ago, a certain infidel braggadocio pretended to have gone through the wood and cut down the trees,

---

[28] Fuller, *Complete Works*, 1:487 (some italics in the original have been omitted).

[29] Ibid., 1:542.

[30] John Piper delivered a biographical address on Andrew Fuller at the Desiring God 2007 Conference for Pastors. In that address, he identified Fuller's Scripture-centeredness as "one of the main reasons why it is profitable to read Fuller to this very day: He is so freshly biblical." See J. Piper, "Holy Faith, Worthy Gospel, World Vision: Andrew Fuller's Broadsides Against Sandemanianism, Hyper-Calvinism, and Global Unbelief," an address given at the Desiring God 2007 Conference for Pastors, Bethlehem Baptist Church, Minneapolis, MN, February 6, 2007.

[31] See the preface to Fuller, *The Gospel Its Own Witness* (Fuller, *Complete Works*, 2:4).

which the priests, he said, might stick in again, but they would not grow!"[32] Reflecting back on the tremendous upswing in Bible distribution efforts in the first decade of the nineteenth century, Fuller felt that his earlier optimism had been vindicated: "And have the sacred Scriptures been less in request since that time [of Paine's challenges] than they were before? Rather have they not been much more so? Infidelity, by overacting its part, has given itself a wound; and its abettors, like Herod, have been eaten of worms, and have died. But the word of the Lord has grown and been multiplied."[33]

## *The Heart of Pastoral Theology: The Gospel*

A third strength of Fuller's work as a pastor-theologian is that he modeled the need for this group of leaders to be absolutely clear on all facets of the gospel. Pastors need to be able to articulate the gospel in speech and in print. They also need to be able to superintend the work of the gospel in the souls of those who hear it proclaimed. Roberts also pointed out this strength:

> Fuller manifested a willingness to deal with the intricate issues of conversion and salvation that today are often treated glibly and superficially. The two enemies in the camp, so to speak, of evangelical Calvinism were in his view an antimissionary, unbalanced hyper-Calvinism and a mechanical, rationalistic Sandemanianism. In taking the stand that he did, he demonstrated the value of a thoughtful, biblical theology of conversion as an incentive to evangelism and as a check to mental assent alone as being synonymous with genuine repentance and faith.[34]

Wells noted that the number of tasks pastors are expected to perform competently has steadily increased across the years.[35] One unintended consequence of that expanded breadth is that pastors today are much less theological in their basic orientation to ministry. Although that tendency bodes ill for the church in many regards, it is especially dangerous when that superficiality pertains to how pastors comprehend and proclaim the gospel. In contrast to much of what

---

[32] Fuller, *Complete Works*, 1:702.

[33] Ibid., 2:702. Fuller was active in support for efforts at Bible translation and distribution. He took great delight in the success of the societies engaged in this work.

[34] Roberts, "Andrew Fuller," 46.

[35] Wells, *No Place for Truth*, 232–33.

goes on under the umbrella of evangelicalism today, Fuller's ministry models the elevation of the gospel to the place of prominence that it deserves.

*Theology Wed to Ministry*

A fourth strength of Fuller's ministry is that he wed theology to everyday pastoral ministry. Wells pointed out that theology is being increasingly marginalized in evangelical churches. He argued that though the amount of theological literature being produced by evangelicals has skyrocketed in recent years, it is consistently aimed at a smaller and smaller circle of professional theologians.[36] A dichotomy has developed between what Wells calls "professional scholars" and "theorizers of practice,"[37] that is, between theologians and pastors. The result is that theology has an ever-weakening impact on the church.

Fuller's ministry models how theological reflection can be carried on in the context of active ministry. It also illustrates the need for such theologizing to be targeted more broadly than to a professional class of scholars. In Fuller's context, sound theological reflection was desperately needed in the areas of soteriology and missiology. As much as any other person, Fuller was used of God to bring about revitalization in British Particular Baptist life through his challenge to the theological assumptions then current.

*Integrity in Ministry*

A final strength of Fuller's ministry is that he carried it out with complete moral integrity. In a day when ethical and moral failures among evangelical leaders have become so common that they fail to be shocking, Fuller's contrary example deserves to be highlighted. After drawing attention to Fuller's tendency to sometimes be too rough and severe in dealing with fellow ministers, Morris concluded his sketch of Fuller with this tribute to his character:

His entire character was formed of STERLING INTEGRITY, ramified into all his actions. In principle, as well as in doctrine, he "shewed incorruptness," and great "sincerity." The severest suspicion could never reach him; his elevation on this part of the moral scale placed him far beyond the eye of jealousy, and nearer to the throne of eternal justice

---

[36] Ibid., 109.
[37] Ibid.

than is common to the most distinguished mortals. His sense of honour
and fidelity, allowed of no resort to the schemes of interest, or the too
common arts of dishonest temporising. No hopes, no fears, no consider-
ations whatever, could cause him to deviate from what he judged to be
the path of uprightness. Never was human integrity found more inflex-
ible, or honesty more true to her intention.[38]

Coming as they do from one who bore heavy criticisms from Fuller, these
words speak volumes about Fuller's character. Of all the areas in which pastor-
theologians might opt to follow Fuller's lead, none is more important than
embracing his concern for ministerial integrity.

## CONCLUDING REFLECTIONS

This book has argued that Fuller provides an example of the Baptist pastor-
theologian that is worthy of emulation. Several reflections related to that theme
are now offered to conclude the study.

### *Retrieving the Value of Theology*

Fuller's ministerial context is far removed from the present day. Of the numerous barriers that one would expect to find in seeking to model pastoral ministry
on so distant an example, none is perhaps as serious as the church's devalua-
tion of theology. Wells's insights at this point are worth quoting at length:

> It should now be clear that there are two quite different models of min-
> istry at work in the evangelical Church today, and theology is located
> quite differently in each. In the model of the Church that has its roots in
> the Reformation and in the Puritanism that followed, theology is essen-
> tial and central; in its modern-day evangelical descendants, however,
> theology is often only instrumental and peripheral. In the one, theology
> provides the culture in which ministry is understood and practiced; in
> the other, this culture is provided by professionalization.

---

[38] Morris, *Memoirs of the Life and Writings of the Rev. Andrew Fuller*, 374.

The difference between the two models is not that theology is present in the one but not in the other. Theology is professed and believed in both. But in the one, theology is the reason for ministry, the basis for ministry; it provides the criteria by which success in ministry is measured. In the other, theology does none of these things; here the ministry provides its own rationale, its own criteria, its own techniques. The second model does not reject theology; it simply displaces it so that it no longer gives the profession of ministry its heart and fire.[39]

If Wells is correct, as I believe he is, it means an aspiring Baptist pastor-theologian today may find that his vision for the work of a pastor differs significantly from the model accepted in many churches. Almost inevitably, this leads to problems. Offering a theologically centered ministry can reasonably be expected "to collide head-on with the self-absorption and anthropocentric focus that are now normative in so many evangelical churches."[40] Thus, contemporary Baptist pastor-theologians may have to demonstrate by patient and faithful ministry that churches need to learn again to place a premium on theological matters.

Positively, it would appear that Baptist churches and leaders are, in fact, awakening to this need. For example, several key leaders in the Southern Baptist Convention (SBC) have recently begun to speak of the need for a recovery of theology in Baptist church life. Two men who are strategically placed to lead in such a recovery may be mentioned as illustrative of a broader trend.

First, President R. Albert Mohler Jr. of the Southern Baptist Theological Seminary (Louisville, Kentucky) has written an article on this theme in which he argued,

Every pastor is called to be a theologian. This may come as a surprise to some pastors, who see theology as an academic discipline taken during seminary rather than as an ongoing and central part of the pastoral calling. Nevertheless, the health of the church depends upon its pastors

---

[39] Wells, *No Place for Truth*, 255.
[40] Ibid., 256.

functioning as faithful theologians—teaching, preaching, defending, and applying the great doctrines of the faith.[41]

Mohler's comments would be completely appropriate as a summary of Fuller's life and work. Thus, if Mohler's analysis of the need is on target, then Fuller has much to teach contemporary pastors about how to fulfill the role of pastor-theologian.

Second, President Daniel Akin of Southeastern Baptist Theological Seminary (Wake Forest, North Carolina) echoed this theme in a recent address. Speaking at the annual pastor's conference for the South Carolina Baptist Convention, Akin also stressed the need for a return to theological literacy among Baptist pastors. He addressed the pastors on the topic of "The Pastor as Theologian."[42] Akin lamented the fact that theological literacy is at a low ebb among Southern Baptists. He attributed part of the conflict within the SBC to the fact that controversial theological matters like tongues and Calvinism are being handled in a manner that is "sloppy" and "ill-informed."[43] Akin traced these failures back to a loss of a theological component in pastoral ministry: "I have a tremendous burden about the fact that evangelicals, Southern Baptists, are in serious, serious trouble. Much of that fault lies in the pulpit, with men who are not fulfilling the assignment of being the pastor-teacher, the pastor-theologian."[44] Like Mohler, Akin wants to work to reverse this trend.

---

[41] R. A. Mohler Jr., "The Pastor as Theologian," *The Tie* 74 (2006): i. This article is circulating widely in the SBC. It has been featured on the Baptist Press Web site and also in several state convention publications.

[42] D. L. Akin, "The Pastor as a Theologian," an address given at the Pastors' Conference of the South Carolina Baptist State Convention, Brush Creek Baptist Church, Taylors, SC, November 13, 2006. I have served as a Southern Baptist pastor since 1990. During those years, I have attended perhaps 20 pastor's conferences sponsored by state and national conventions. The sad truth is that the vast majority of those conferences—designed to enable pastors to fulfill their calling—had very little theological focus or content. In fact, they were decidedly atheological. My experience in these settings was part of what motivated me to return to seminary in the quest for additional theological training in ministry. There appears to be a theological hunger, especially among younger Southern Baptist pastors, that these two seminary presidents have noticed.

[43] Ibid.

[44] Ibid.

## *Theology and the Pace of Local Church Ministry*

Most Baptist pastors would probably agree that their own theological commitments form an important part of their ministerial foundation. In considering Fuller as a model of the Baptist pastor-theologian, however, they might object that the present pace of local church ministry does not allow for pastors to be theologically involved at that depth. Fuller's influence through a writing ministry may seem especially out of reach. Several replies are in order.

First, it is undoubtedly true that not every pastor is gifted or situated to fulfill a role similar to Fuller's. Each minister must be encouraged to be faithful to his own unique calling. But again it must be stressed that biblical and doctrinal understanding remains at the heart of the pastoral calling. They are nonnegotiables for Christian pastoral ministry.

Second, it may readily be granted that the changing circumstances of the last several hundred years have nearly necessitated the rise of a professional class of theologians and biblical scholars whose work is primarily aimed at academic and seminary audiences. Even in Fuller's day, the rise of formal theological education was leading to increasing specialization in various ministry-related fields. Though Fuller never received formal theological training, he sometimes lamented his lack of it and encouraged those who could to pursue ministerial training in this direction.[45] He also supported some pastors redirecting their ministries to serve the needs of the classroom. For example, here is part of Fuller's encouragement to Ryland when the latter agreed to accept the post as the leader of the Bristol Baptist College:

> I am satisfied that you are in the path of duty. . . . Your views of divine truth, I consider as of great importance in the Christian ministry. Go then, my Brother, pour them into the minds of the rising generation of ministers. Perhaps, there could not have been a station in which you would have had so fair an opportunity of propagating gospel-truth. Let us do all we can in our different stations.[46]

---

[45] His nephew, Joseph Fuller, is notable in this regard. The nephew lived with Fuller for some years in a mentoring relationship. But Fuller also encouraged Joseph to attend the Bristol Baptist Academy. The young man died before completing his studies. Joseph is often mentioned in Fuller's diary and correspondence, and his loss was deeply felt. See Ryland, *Work of Faith*, 295–99.

[46] Ibid., 213.

Third, contemporary pastor-theologians should not underestimate the value of writing as a tool to use in arriving at clarity of thought in a given area. Fuller initially penned his thoughts on the "modern question" as a personal exercise in thinking carefully, biblically, and accurately about this critical topic. The passage of time has done nothing to diminish the need for clear theological understanding in pastors. In spite of all the tools and innovations that technology has introduced to the ministry, it may be doubted that a surer way to theological clarity will ever be found than through the hard discipline of committing one's views to writing. When those writings are exposed to the critique of others, as Fuller's were, the value of the exercise increases all the more.

Finally, it should be noted that many of Fuller's published writings were either short pieces designed for release in journals or longer works composed of smaller building blocks. One of his favorite techniques when dealing with topics that demanded greater length was to handle them in a series of letters on the topic. When completed, these individual letters could then be published as a whole treatise.[47] These writing techniques lend themselves to use by busy pastors.

When the theological reflection of the church on a given issue is devoid of input from those who actually serve as pastors, it is significantly incomplete. Yet a great deal of contemporary theology is written by a professional class of theologians with limited pastoral involvement. In this environment, care is needed to ensure that the pastoral voice is not neglected. More pastors need to follow the example of Fuller and find ways to contribute to ongoing theological discussions.

### The Unique Value of Fuller in the Present Theological Climate

Quite a number of voices agree that Calvinism is growing in popularity among American evangelicals generally and among Southern Baptists in particular.[48] Given this situation, Fuller's life and work become all the more relevant.

---

[47]At least six of Fuller's apologetic pieces were composed in this manner.

[48]For documentation of this trend, see C. Hansen, "Young, Restless, Reformed: Calvinism Is Making a Comeback—and Shaking Up the Church," *Christianity Today* 50 (September 2006): 32–38; cf. S. W. Lemke, "The Future of Southern Baptists as Evangelicals" (paper presented to the "Maintaining Baptist Distinctives Conference," Mid-America Baptist Theological Seminary, April 2005. Accessed May 1, 2005. Online: http://www.nobts.edu/Faculty/ItoRLemkeSW/Personal/SBCfuture), where he wrote that "among Southern Baptists, Calvinism has been on the

*Fuller's Work as a Reminder of the Dangers Inherent in Hyper-Calvinism*
In an era of resurgent Calvinism, Baptists would do well to keep in mind the theological and spiritual dangers inherent in hyper-calvinism. Chute recently made this point in his fine study of Jesse Mercer.[49] He expressed his hope that "those who appeal to the founders of the Southern Baptist Convention as examples of Calvinistic Baptists will carefully note the pitfalls into which Primitive Baptists fell and avoid them like the plague."[50]

The Primitive Baptists were a loosely organized offshoot of the American Baptist family who especially protested the advance of a missionary theology in denominational life. Doctrinally, they preferred High Calvinistic sentiments, which they characteristically classified as belonging to Gill and opposed to Fuller. They may be regarded as very similar doctrinally to the British High Calvinists whom Fuller opposed. The sad history of their precipitous decline to near extinction stands as its own powerful warning of the potentially destructive effects of High Calvinism.

No Baptist theologian can be read to greater profit on the dangers of hyper-Calvinism than Fuller. With Calvinism on the rise in Baptist life, those involved in the theological education of ministers would do well to recommend the writings of Fuller.

*Fuller's Work as a Testimony to the Spiritual*
*Vitality of Evangelical Calvinism*
Perhaps the most common reaction to the resurgence of Calvinism among Baptists in America is a fear that this doctrinal position will deaden effectiveness in evangelism and missions.[51] Among Southern Baptists, few leaders

---

rise for the past few decades" (p. 12). Yet another article noticing this trend is C. D. Weaver and N. A. Finn, "Youth for Calvin: Reformed Theology and Baptist Collegians," *BHH* 39 (2004): 19–41. See also E. Stetzer, "Calvinism, Evangelism, and SBC Leadership," in *Calvinism: A Southern Baptist Dialogue*, ed. E. R. Clendenen and B. J. Waggoner (Nashville: B&H, 2008), 13–26.

[49]Chute, *A Piety above the Common Standard*. Jesse Mercer was a hugely influential Southern Baptist pioneer.

[50]Ibid., xiii.

[51]One clear expression of this is found in F. S. Page, former president of the SBC, who wrote, "If one studies the pages of history, one will see that Calvinistic theology (five point) has encouraged a slackening of aggressive evangelistic and missionary heartbeat of the church." *Trouble With the Tulip*, p. 75. Many agree with Page, as evidenced by the recent "John 3:16 Conference." The conference was jointly sponsored by a number of entities, including three of the six Southern Baptist seminaries: Midwestern, Southwestern, and New Orleans. The conference was held at the First

have been more outspoken in this regard than Steve Lemke, provost of New Orleans Baptist Theological Seminary, one of six seminaries supported by the SBC. Addressing fellow Southern Baptists in a recent paper, Lemke offered the opinion that Calvinism "is potentially the most explosive and divisive issue facing us in the near future."[52] He went on to pinpoint why he fears resurgent Calvinism: "My concern is that Southern Baptists could suffer decline in our evangelism and missions due to overzealous and misinformed application of Calvinistic theology."[53]

In reply, it could be argued that Southern Baptists have long since suffered exactly such a decline, especially in the area of evangelistic effectiveness.[54] But given the fact that only 10 percent of Southern Baptist pastors presently identify themselves as five-point Calvinists, it is difficult and unfair to pin the blame for this decline on the rise of Calvinism.[55] Beyond that, it is inaccurate

---

Baptist Church of Woodstock, Georgia, November 6–7, 2008. See D. L. Allen and S. W. Lemke, eds., *Whosoever Will: A Biblical-Theological Critique of Five-Point Calvinism (Reflections from the John 3:16 Conference)* (Nashville: B&H Academic, 2010).

[52] Lemke, "The Future of Southern Baptists as Evangelicals," 14.

[53] Ibid., 17. Similar sentiments were expressed by M. B. Yarnell III (associate professor of systematic theology at Southwestern Baptist Theological Seminary, Ft. Worth, Texas). See "The TULIP of Calvinism: In Light of History and the Baptist Faith and Message," *SBC Life* 14 (April 2006): 9; id. "Calvinism: Cause for Rejoicing, Cause for Concern," in Clendenen and Waggoner, *Calvinism*, 73–95; id., "The Potential Impact of Calvinist Tendencies upon Local Baptist Churches," in Allen and Lemke, *Whosoever Will*, 213–32. Another key Southern Baptist leader, William Harrell, has echoed these concerns in recent days. (Harrell serves as the chairman of the SBC's executive committee.) He believes that Southern Baptists "have two important issues to solve in our Convention," one of which he identifies as Calvinism. See J. G. Harris, "Martinez Pastor [William Harrell] on National Stage Representing Georgia Baptists," *The Christian Index* 185 (October 26, 2006): 9. Accessed November 1, 2006. Online: http://www.christianindex.org/2715.article.print. Finally, respected Georgia Baptist leader Nelson Price has recently opined that "evangelical Calvinism is an oxymoron." In an open letter to *The Index*, he asserts that "Calvinism is a dagger in the heart of evangelism." See Price, "Evangelical Calvinism Is an Oxymoron," *The Christian Index* 185 (November 23, 2006): 8–9. Accessed November 27, 2006. Online: http://www.christianindex.org/2780.article.print.

[54] See especially the compelling research of E. Stetzer in "Disturbing Trends in Baptisms," unpublished article. Accessed December 1, 2006. Online: http://www.namb.net.

[55] For a summary of the survey that arrived at the 10 percent figure, see L. Lovelace, "10 Percent of SBC Pastors Call Themselves 5-Point Calvinists," Baptist Press online article. Accessed November 21, 2006. Online: http://www.bpnews.net/printerfriendly.asp?ID=23993. See also Stetzer, "Calvinism, Evangelism, and SBC Leadership," 13–26. It should be kept in mind that this figure of 10 percent represents the number of five-point Calvinists *after* what Lemke has characterized as several decades of a Calvinistic upswing.

to equate five-point Calvinism with hyper-Calvinism.[56] Although Lemke made considerable efforts to distinguish between Calvinism and hyper-Calvinism in his paper, he was not always successful. For example, it is both surprising and misleading to find him characterizing the Calvinism advocated by the Synod of Dort as "hyper-Calvinism."[57] In a similar vein, Lemke also characterized the Dortian position on irresistible grace as a "mechanical and deterministic process" that minimizes "human responsiveness to God's persistent wooing."[58] Although salvation that was "mechanical and deterministic" and that downplayed the need for a human faith-response would be expressive of hyper-Calvinism, it is wrong to imply that the Calvinism upheld at Dort advocated such views.[59] More to the point, though many Calvinistic Baptists have

---

[56]The term "hyper-Calvinism" is sometimes used to mean little more than "someone more Calvinistic than myself." Properly speaking, the term has a long history of careful definition and use. See P. Toon, "Hyper-Calvinism," in *New Dictionary of Theology*, ed. S. B. Ferguson, D. F. Wright, and J. I. Packer (Leicester, UK; Downers Grove, IL: IVP, 1988), 324–25.

[57]Lemke, "The Future of Southern Baptists as Evangelicals," 14. Lemke believes that the Calvinism signified by the familiar TULIP acrostic is "hard-Calvinism." He goes on to characterize the TULIP as expressive of what he calls "Synod of Dort hyper-Calvinism." Compare Lemke's opinion to a more widely accepted view, as expressed by G. P. Fisher, who characterized the position of Dort as "the more moderate type of Calvinism," "unadulterated," yet not "extreme." See Fisher, *History of Christian Doctrine*, ed. Charles A. Briggs and Stewart D. F. Salmond, The International Theological Library (New York: Charles Scribner's Sons, 1906), 4:339. J. T. Young, emeritus professor of theology at New Orleans Baptist Theological Seminary, also stated that "the Calvinism most often encountered among Southern Baptists today is hyper-Calvinism, the more rigid form that is based upon the Canons of the Synod of Dort." This opinion was expressed in Young's review of the book *God So Loved the World: Traditional Baptists and Calvinism*, by F. Humphreys and P. Robertson (New Orleans: Insight Press, 2001). Like Young, Humphreys and Robertson once taught theology at New Orleans Baptist Theological Seminary. See Young, "Review of *God So Loved the World: Traditional Baptists and Calvinism*," *Christian Ethics Today: Journal of Christian Ethics* 35 (August 2001). Accessed April 1, 2006. Online: http://www.christianethicstoday.com.

[58]Lemke, "The Future of Southern Baptists as Evangelicals," 14.

[59]The Canons of Dort are very clear that human means are required in salvation—both in terms of the responsibility of Christians to preach the gospel and of those who hear to respond in faith. See especially "The Canons of Dort, Third and Fourth Heads of Doctrine: Of the Corruption of Man, His Conversion to God, and the Manner Thereof," especially article 17. It reads in part, "For grace is conferred by means of admonitions [gospel preaching]; and the more readily we perform our duty [especially to believe], the more eminent usually is this blessing of God working in us, and the more directly is his work advanced." P. Schaff, *The Creeds of Christendom with a History and Critical Notes*, 4th rev. ed. (New York: Harper & Bros., 1877; repr., Grand Rapids: Baker, 1950), 3:592. P. E. Johnson has also noticed that misreading Dortian Calvinism has become common in certain circles of Southern Baptist scholarship. In discussing the views of Young,

affirmed their agreement with the basic soteriological conclusions expressed in the Canons of Dort, they have generally been careful to avoid embracing the extremes of hyper-Calvinism.[60]

Fuller's life and ministry stand as a significant testimony to the spiritual vitality of evangelical Calvinism in Baptist life. The tenor of his soteriology was clearly Calvinistic. The depth of his theological influence on Baptists was profound. That spiritual health and vitality attended the embrace of his views is beyond serious dispute. Those who would argue that the presence of Calvinism in Baptist life is a problem that must be overcome or that Calvinism kills evangelism will find Fuller's life and work a huge impediment to the successful advancement of their thesis. That this idea has already found a wide embrace in Southern Baptist life is an indictment on the poor historical and theological training of far too many Southern Baptist pastors and leaders.[61]

## The Centrality of the Gospel

Regardless of differences of opinion among Baptists concerning Calvinism, there is widespread agreement that the gospel must remain the center point in Baptist theology. Above all else, Fuller's ministry models a commitment to the centrality of the gospel. Because he believed it stood at the center of the Christian religion, Fuller handled the gospel with care both in regard to its doctrinal expression and its pastoral application.

---

Humphreys, and Robertson, Johnson argued ("Baptists and 'Calvinism': Discerning the Shape of the Question," *BHH* 39 [Spring 2004]: 63) that "while the 'Canons of Dort' do indeed manifest what we might call a 'scholastic' or 'orthodox Calvinism,' they bear but the faintest resemblance to hyper-Calvinism, a phenomenon that arose roughly a century later in England."

[60] It should be noted that Lemke acknowledged Calvinism as a viable doctrinal position with a long and respectable history in the SBC. Apparently, he was arguing more against future Calvinistic extremism than against any current example of hyper-Calvinism. Still, his blurred lines between Calvinism and hyper-Calvinism are not particularly helpful in the present climate.

[61] The aforementioned "John 3:16 Conference" was held after this book was completed. Nevertheless, several of the presentations given at that conference go a long way toward validating the concern that many Southern Baptist leaders are ill-informed about the compatibility of Calvinism and a robust embrace of evangelism and missions. A greater awareness of Fuller—and indeed the entire chapter of Baptist history and theology that he represents—would go a long way toward allaying the fears of a resurgence of Calvinism in Baptist life.

Fuller should remain an important figure in Baptist studies. Clipsham's point, made a generation ago, still holds true: "Many of the soteriological errors confronting Fuller are in one form or another a perennial danger to the Church's faith. Fuller's answers are therefore of lasting significance."[62] For this reason, those who aspire to faithfulness as a Baptist pastor-theologian would do well to consider Fuller a helpful model.

---

[62]Clipsham, "Andrew Fuller," 275.

# Andrew Fuller's
# Confession of Faith

O rdination services for Particular Baptist ministers in the eighteenth century were carefully planned and conducted affairs.[1] Most of them included a time at which the candidate for ordination would deliver a rather full confession of his faith before the assembled ordaining body. Often this confession was written in advance. These personal confessions of faith were also sometimes used as a means of introduction and advisement when a pastor was invited to speak or was under consideration for the pastoral office at other churches. The confession of faith reproduced below is in that pattern.[2] Andrew Fuller drew up this confession for the benefit of the Particular Baptist Church at Kettering when that church was in the process of considering him to be their pastor. It was composed in 1783 and represents Fuller's mature theological position in which he is equally committed to a theology that is both solidly Calvinistic and warmly evangelical.

I. When I consider the heavens and the earth with their vast variety, it gives me reason to believe the existence of a God of infinite wisdom, power, and goodness that made and upholds them all. Had there been no written revelation of God given to us, I should have been without excuse, if I had denied a God or refused to glorify him as God.

II. Yet, considering the present state of mankind, I believe we needed a revelation of the mind of God to inform us more fully of his and our

---

[1] See K. S. Grant, "'Very Affecting and Evangelical': Andrew Fuller (1754–1815) and the Evangelical Renewal of Pastoral Theology" (Th.M. thesis, Regent College, Vancouver, BC, 2007), 69–70. Grant identifies nine elements consistently used in such ordination services; Fuller's own ordination service included all nine elements.

[2] See Belcher, *The Last Remains of the Rev. Andrew Fuller*, 209–17. This confession was delivered by Fuller on the occasion of his installation as pastor of the Baptist Church in Kettering on October 7, 1783.

own character, of his designs towards us, and will concerning us. And such a revelation I believe the Scriptures of the Old and New Testament to be, without excepting any one of its books, and a perfect rule of faith and practice. When I acknowledge it as a perfect rule of faith and practice, I mean to disclaim all other rules as binding on my conscience, and as well to acknowledge that if I err, either in faith or practice, from the rule, it will be my crime. For I have ever considered all deviations from divine rules to be criminal.

III. From this divine volume, I learn many things concerning God, which I could not have learned from the works of nature, and the same things in a more convincing light. Here I learn especially the infinitely amiable moral character of God. His holiness, justice, faithfulness, and goodness are here exhibited in such a light by his holy law and glorious gospel as is nowhere else to be seen.

Here, also, I learn that though God is one, yet he also is three—the Father, the Son, and the Holy Spirit. The idea which I think the Scriptures give us of each of the sacred three is that of person.

I believe the Son of God to be truly and properly God, equal with the Father and the Holy Spirit. Everything I see in this sacred mystery appears to me above reason, but nothing contrary to it.

IV. I believe, from the same authority, that God created man in the image of his own glorious moral character, a proper subject of his moral government, with dispositions exactly suited to the law he was under and capacity equal to obey it to the uttermost against all temptations to the contrary. I believe if Adam, or any holy being, had had the making of a law for himself, he would have made just such an one as God's law is, for it would be the greatest of hardships to a holy being not to be allowed to love God with all his heart, and with all his soul, and all his mind.

V. I believe the conduct of man, in breaking the law of God, was most unreasonable and wicked in itself, as well as fatal in its consequences to the transgressor, and that sin is of such a nature that it deserves all the wrath and misery with which it is threatened, in this world, and in that which is to come.

VI. I believe the first sin of Adam was not merely personal, but that he stood as our representative. So that when he fell, we fell in him, and became liable to condemnation and death. And what is more, [we] are all born into the world with a vile propensity to sin against God. I own there are some things in these subjects, which appear to me profound and awful. But seeing God hath so plainly revealed them in his Word, especially in the fifth chapter of the epistle to the Romans, I dare not but bow my shallow conceptions to the unerring testimony of God, not doubting but that he will clear his own character sufficiently at the last day. At the same time, I know of no other system that represents these subjects in a more rational light.

VII. I believe, as I before stated, that men are now born and grow up with a vile propensity to moral evil, and that herein lies their inability to keep God's law, and as such, it is a moral and a criminal inability. Were they but of a right disposition of mind, there is nothing now in the law of God but what they could perform; but, being wholly under the dominion of sin, they have no heart remaining for God, but are full of wicked aversion to him. Their very "mind and conscience are defiled."[3] Their ideas of the excellence of good and of the evil of sin are as it were obliterated.

These are subjects which seem to me of very great importance. I conceive that the whole Arminian, Socinian, and Antinomian systems, so far as I understand them, rest upon the supposition of these principles being false. So that, if it should be found, at last, that God is an infinitely excellent being, worthy of being loved with all the love which his law requires; that, as such, his law is entirely fair and equitable and that for God to have required less, would have been denying himself to be what he is; and if it should appear, at last, that man is utterly lost, and lies absolutely at the discretion of God; then, I think it is easy to prove, the whole of these systems must fall to the ground. If men, on account of sin, lie at the discretion of God, the equity, and even necessity, of predestination cannot be denied, and so the Arminian system falls. If the law of God is right and good, and arises from the very nature of God, Antinomianism cannot stand. And if we are such great sinners, we need a great Saviour, infinitely greater than the Socinian Saviour.

VIII. From what I have said, it must be supposed that I believe the doctrine of eternal personal election and predestination. However, I

---

[3] Titus 1:15.

believe that though in the choice of the elect, God had no motive out of himself, yet it was not so in respect to punishing the rest. What has been usually, but perhaps, improperly, called the decree of reprobation, I consider as nothing more than the divine determination to punish sin, in certain cases, in the person of the sinner.

IX. I believe that the fall of man did not at all disconcert the great Eternal, but that he had from eternity formed a plan upon the supposition of that event (as well knowing that so it would be) and that, in this everlasting covenant, as it is called, the Sacred Three (speaking after the manner of men) stipulated with each other for the bringing about their vast and glorious design.

X. The unfolding of this glorious plan to view, I believe, has been a gradual work from the beginning. First, it was hinted to our first parents, in the promise of the woman's seed. Then, by the institution of sacrifices, by types, prophecies, and promises, it was carried on throughout the Mosaic dispensation. At length the Son of God appeared, took our nature, obeyed the law, and endured the curse, and hereby made full and proper atonement for the sins of his own elect, rose again from the dead, commissioned his apostles to go into all the world and preach his gospel, and then triumphantly ascended above all heavens, where he sitteth at the right hand of God, interceding for his people, and governing the world in subserviency to their welfare, till he shall come a second time to judge the world.

I cannot reflect upon this glorious procedure, with its all-glorious Author, without emotions of wonder and gratitude. As a workman, he might be truly said to have "his work before him!" At once he glorified the injured character of God, and confounded the devil—destroyed sin and saved the sinner.

XI. I believe that such is the excellence of this way of salvation that every one who hears, or has opportunity to hear it proclaimed in the gospel, is bound to repent of his sin, believe, approve, and embrace it with all his heart; to consider himself, as he really is, a vile, lost sinner; to reject all pretensions to life in any other way; and to cast himself upon Christ that he may be saved in this way of God's devising. This I think to be true faith, which whoever have, I believe, will certainly be saved.

XII. But, though the way of salvation is in itself so glorious, that a man must be an enemy to God, to mankind, and to himself, not to approve it, yet I believe the pride, ignorance, enmity, and love to sin in men, is such that they will not come to Christ for life; but, in spite of all the calls and threatenings of God, will go on, till they sink into eternal perdition. Hence, I believe, arises the necessity of an almighty work of God the Spirit, to new-model the whole soul, to form in us new principles or dispositions, or, as the Scriptures call it, to give us "a new heart and a right spirit."[4] I think, had we not first degenerated, we had stood in no need of being regenerated. But as we are by nature depraved, we must be born again. The influence of the Spirit of God, in this work, I believe to be always effectual.

XIII. I believe the change that takes place in a person at the time of his believing in the Lord Jesus Christ, is not only real, but relative. Before our believing in Christ, we are considered and treated by God, as a lawgiver, as under condemnation; but having fled to him for refuge, the law, as to its condemning power, hath no more dominion over us, but we are treated, even by God the judge, as in a state of justification. The subject-matter of justification, I believe to be nothing of our own moral excellence, but the righteousness of Christ alone, imputed to us and received by faith.

Also, I believe that before we believe in Christ, notwithstanding the secret purpose of God in our favour, we are considered by the moral governor of the world as aliens, as children of wrath, even as others; but that, on our believing on his Son, we are considered as no more strangers and foreigners, but are admitted into his family and have power, or privilege, to become the sons of God.

XIV. I believe that those who are effectually called of God never fall away so as to perish everlastingly, but persevere in holiness till they arrive at endless happiness.

XV. I believe it is the duty of every minister of Christ plainly and faithfully to preach the gospel to all who will hear it. And, as I believe the inability of men to spiritual things to be wholly of the moral, and therefore of the criminal kind—and that it is their duty to love the Lord

---

[4]Ezek 18:31; see 36:26.

Jesus Christ and trust in him for salvation, though they do not—I, therefore, believe free and solemn addresses, invitations, calls, and warnings to them, to be not only consistent, but directly adapted, as means in the hands of the Spirit of God to bring them to Christ. I consider it as a part of my duty, which I could not omit without being guilty of the blood of souls.

XVI. I believe the ordinances which Christ, as king of Zion, has instituted for his church to be found in, throughout the gospel day, are especially two, namely, Baptism and the Lord's Supper. I believe the subjects of both to be those who profess repentance towards God and faith towards our Lord Jesus Christ, and on such I consider them as incumbent duties. I believe that it is essential to Christian baptism that it be by immersion, or burying the person in water, in the name of the Father, the Son, and the Holy Ghost. I likewise believe baptism as administered by the primitive church to be prerequisite to church communion. Hence I judge what is called strict communion to be consistent with the word of God.

XVII. Although I disclaim personal holiness as having any share in our justification, I consider it absolutely necessary to salvation, for without it "no man shall see the Lord."[5]

XVIII. I believe the soul of man is created immortal, and that, when the body dies, the soul returns to God who gave it and there receives an immediate sentence, either to a state of happiness or misery, there to remain till the resurrection of the dead.

XIX. As I said that the development of God's plan has been gradual from the beginning, so I believe this graduation will be beautifully and gloriously carried on. I firmly and joyfully believe that the kingdom of Christ will yet be gloriously extended by the pouring out of God's Spirit upon the ministry of the Word. And I consider this as an event, for the arrival of which it becomes all God's servants and churches most ardently to pray! It is one of the chief springs of my joy in this "day of small things" that it will not be so always.

XX. Finally, I believe that Christ will come a second time, not as before, to save the world, but to judge the world. There, in the presence

---

[5] See Heb 12:14.

of an assembled universe, every son and daughter of Adam shall appear at God's tremendous bar and give an account of the things done in the body. There sinners, especially those who have rejected Christ, God's way of salvation, will be convicted, confounded, and righteously condemned! These shall go away into everlasting punishment. But the righteous, who through grace have embraced Christ and followed him whithersoever he went, shall follow him there likewise and enter with him into the eternal joy of their Lord. This solemn event, I own, on some accounts strikes me with trembling. Yet, on others, I cannot but look on it with a mixture of joy. When I consider it as the period when God will be vindicated from all the hard thoughts which ungodly sinners have indulged and the hard speeches which they have spoken against him; when all wrongs shall be made right, truth brought to light, and justice done where none here could be obtained; when the whole empire of sin, misery, and death shall sink like a mill-stone into the sea of eternal oblivion and never rise more. When, I say, I consider it in this view, I cannot but look upon it as an object of joy and wish my time may be spent in this world in "looking for and hasting unto the coming of the day of God."[6]

---

[6] 2 Pet 3:12.

# Fuller's Theological Dictionary
# Entry on Calvinism

H annah Adams (1755–1831) was a pioneering woman-researcher and author.[1] In 1784, she published a one-volume religious and theological dictionary, which ran through numerous editions in both the United States and England.[2] A Unitarian, Adams sought to provide an unbiased view of each religious group or doctrine she described. Andrew Fuller helped edit the first British edition of Adams's book, for which he also wrote the preface.

Fuller wrote several of the entries in this edition, including the one for "Calvinism." This article is reproduced below.[3] Though Fuller used Adams's 1784 entry as the loose basis for this entry, he substantially reworked it in keeping with the modifications to Calvinism that he had helped popularize. Some of these changes are highlighted by notes in brackets.

It should also be noted that Charles Buck (1771–1815) reproduced Fuller's entry in his own theological dictionary.[4] The net result was that in two of the

---

[1] For a recent study on Adams, see G. D. Schmidt, *A Passionate Usefulness: The Life and Literary Labors of Hannah Adams* (n.p.: University of Virginia Press, 2004).

[2] The first edition bore the title *An Alphabetical Compendium of All the Various Sects Which Have Appeared from the Beginning of the Christian Era to the Present Day* (Boston: B. Edes & Sons, 1784). The second and third editions were considerably revised and retitled *A View of Religions in Two Parts* (Boston: John Folsom, 1791; Boston: Manning and Loring, 1801). The fourth edition was retitled yet again as *A Dictionary of All Religions and Religious Denominations, Jewish, Heathen, Mahotmetan, and Christian, Ancient and Modern* (Boston: Cummings and Hilliard, 1817). The core of the contents remained the same in all editions.

[3] The version reproduced is taken from Belcher's *The Last Remains*, with slight modernization to the punctuation. Belcher made only slight stylistic changes to the original found in Adams.

[4] C. Buck, *A Theological Dictionary: Containing Definitions of all Religious Terms, A Comprehensive View of Every Article in the System of Divinity and Impartial Account of All Principle Denominations which have Subsisted in the Religious World* (London: n.p., 1803).

most common religious reference books of the day, Fuller's type of Calvinism was held up as the norm.


## "CALVINISM"

The leading principles taught by Calvin were the same as those of Augustine. Those by which Calvinists are distinguished from Arminians are reduced to five articles; and which, from their being the principle points discussed at the Synod of Dort, have since been denominated *the five points*. These are predestination, particular redemption, total depravity, effectual calling, and the certain perseverance of the saints.

The following statement is taken principally from the writings of Calvin, and the decisions at Dort, compressed in as few words as possible—

1. Calvinists maintain that God hath chosen a certain number of the fallen race of Adam in Christ, before the foundation of the world, unto eternal glory, according to his immutable purpose, and of his free grace and love, without the foresight of faith, good works, or any condition performed by the creature as the *cause* of their election. The rest of mankind he was pleased to pass by and leave to the due punishment of their sins, to the praise of his vindictive justice. In proof of this they allege, among many other Scripture passages, the following: Eph 1:4; Rom 9; 11:1–6; 8:29–30; 2 Thess 2:13; Acts 13:48.

They do not consider predestination, however, as affecting the agency or accountableness of creatures or as being to them the rule of conduct. On the contrary, they suppose men to act as freely, and to be as much the proper subjects of calls, warnings, exhortations, promises and threatenings as if no decree respecting them existed. Calvin's *Institutes*, book iii, chap. xxii, sect. 10; also book ii, chap. V, sect. 4. [This paragraph is not included in Adams's original entry.]

With regard to reprobation, they say, if the question be, "Wherefore did God decree to punish those who are punished?," the answer is, "On account of their sins." But if it be, "Wherefore did he decree to punish them rather than others?," there is no other reason to be assigned but that *so it seemed good in his sight.* Calvin's *Institutes*, book iii, chap. Xxiv, sect. 14. [Again, there is no parallel to this paragraph in Adams.]

2. They maintain that though the death of Christ be a most perfect sacrifice and satisfaction for sin, of infinite value, abundantly sufficient to expiate the sins of the whole world—and though on this ground the gospel is to be preached to all mankind indiscriminately—yet it was the will of God that Christ, by the blood of the cross, should efficaciously redeem those only who were from eternity elected to salvation and given to him by the Father. Acta. Syndodi, Sess 136, p. 250. [Adams had written simply, "That Jesus Christ, by his death and sufferings, made an atonement *only* for the sins of the *elect.*"]

This is called particular redemption, and in proof of the doctrine, among others, the following Scriptures are alleged: John 17:2; 10:11, 15; 11:52; Titus 2:14; Eph 5:25; Rev 5:9.

3. They maintain that mankind are totally depraved in consequence of the fall of the first man, who being their public head, his sin involved the corruption of all his posterity. This corruption extends over the whole soul and renders it unable of itself to turn to God or to do anything truly good; this exposes it to his just displeasure, both in this world and in that which is to come. Calvin's *Institutes*, book ii, chap. 1, sect. 8; Acta. Syndodi. See also the ninth article of the church of England. In confirmation of this doctrine they refer to the following passages: Rom 5:12–19; Psm 51:5; Gen 6:5; Psm 53:2–3; Rom 3; Eph 2:1–3.

4. They maintain that all whom God has predestinated unto life he is pleased in his appointed time effectually to call by his own word and Spirit out of that state of sin and death in which they are by nature, to grace and salvation by Jesus Christ.

They admit that the Holy Spirit, as calling men by the ministry of the gospel, may be resisted. Where this is the case, "the fault is not in the gospel, nor in Christ offered by the gospel, nor in God calling by the gospel and also conferring various gifts upon them; but in the called themselves. They contend, however, that where men come at the divine call, and are converted, it is not to be ascribed to themselves, as though by their own freewill they made themselves to differ; but solely to him, whose regenerating influence is certain and efficacious." Acta. Syndodi, p. 257–8; Calvin's *Institutes*, book iii, chap. Xxiv. In support of this doctrine they allege the following texts: Rom 8:20; Eph 1:19–20; 2:9–10; 2 Cor 4:6; Ezek 36:26. [This paragraph has no parallel in Adams.]

5. Lastly, they maintain that those whom God has effectually called and sanctified by his Spirit shall never *finally* fall from a state of grace. They admit that true believers may fall partially and awfully and would fall totally and finally but for the mercy and faithfulness of God, who keepeth the feet of his saints; also, that he who bestoweth the grace of perseverance bestoweth it by means of reading and hearing the word, meditation, exhortation, threatenings and promises; but that none of these things imply the possibility of a believer's falling from a state of justification into perdition. Calvin's *Institutes*, book ii, chap. V, sects. 3–4. Acta. Syndodi, pp265–68. In proof of this doctrine they refer to these passages: Jer. 32:40; Mark 16:16; John 4:14, 6:40, 17:3; 1 Jn 3:9, 2:19; Jude 24, 25.

Such were the doctrines of the first Calvinists, though not always expressed with sufficient caution and prudence; and such in substance are those of the present Calvinists. In this, however, as in every other denomination, there are considerable shades of difference. Some think Calvin, though right in the main, carried things too far; these are commonly known by the name of *moderate* Calvinists. Others think he did not go far enough; and these are known by the name of *high* Calvinists, by many called *Antinomians*. [This is vintage Fuller; Adams's original entry made no distinctions within the Calvinistic system.] It is proper to add that the Calvinistic system includes in it the doctrines of the Trinity, Atonement, and Justification by faith alone, or by the imputed righteousness of Christ.

# Bibliography

Adams, Hannah. *A Dictionary of all Religions and Religious Denominations: Jewish, Heathen, Mahotmetan, Christian, Ancient and Modern*. 4th ed. Boston: Cummings and Hilliard, 1817; facsimile edition in Classics in Religious Studies. Vol. 8. Edited by Carl A. Raschke. Atlanta: Scholars Press, 1992.

Akin, Daniel L. "The Pastor as Theologian." An address delivered at the Pastors' Conference of the South Carolina Baptist State Convention, Taylors, SC, November 13, 2006.

Anonymous. "Andrew Fuller: A Story of Religious Life Sixty Years Ago." Pages 285–301 in *Men Who Were Earnest: The Springs of Their Action and Influence*. London: Gall & Inglis, n.d.

Ascol, Thomas Kennedy. *The Doctrine of Grace: A Critical Analysis of Federalism in the Theologies of John Gill and Andrew Fuller*. Ph.D. diss., Southwestern Baptist Theological Seminary, 1989.

———. "The Pastor as Theologian." *Founders Journal* 43 (2001): 1–10.

Ban, Joseph D. "Was John Bunyan a Baptist? A Case-Study in Historiography." *Baptist Quarterly* 30 (1984): 367–76.

"The Baptist Missionary Society Archives: 1792–1914." The Angus Library, Regent's Park College, Oxford University. [Available in microfilm.]

Bebbington, D. W. *Evangelicalism in Modern Britain: A History from the 1730s to the 1980s*. N.p.: Unwin Hyman, 1989. Repr., London: Routledge, 2004.

———. "Introduction." Pages 1–9 in *The Gospel in the World: International Baptist Studies*. Edited by D. W. Bebbington. SBHT 1. Carlisle, UK; Waynesboro, GA: Paternoster, 2002.

Belcher, Joseph, ed. *The Last Remains of the Rev. Andrew Fuller: Sermons, Essays, Letters, and Other Miscellaneous Papers, Not Included in His Published Works*. Philadelphia: American Baptist Publication Society, 1856.

Benedict, David. *Fifty Years among the Baptists*. Boston: Gould & Lincoln, 1860. Repr., Glen Rose, TX: Newman & Collins, 1913.

Black, J. William. *Reformation Pastors: Richard Baxter and the Ideal of the Reformed Pastor*. Studies in Christian History and Thought. Edited by Alan P. F. Sell et al. Carlisle, UK; Waynesboro, GA: Paternoster, 2004.

Booth, Abraham. *The Reign of Grace: From Its Rise to Its Consummation*. Leeds, UK: Griffith Wright, 1768.

Boyce, James Petigru. *Abstract of Systematic Theology*. Cape Coral, FL: Founders Press, 2006.

———. "Three Changes in Theological Institutions." Pages 30–59 in *James Petigru Boyce: Selected Writings*. Edited by Timothy George. Nashville: Broadman, 1989.

Brackney, William H., ed. *Baptist Life and Thought: 1600–1980: A Sourcebook*. Valley Forge, PA: Judson, 1983.

———. *A Genetic History of Baptist Thought: With Special Reference to the Baptists in Britain and North America*. Macon, GA: Mercer, 2004.

Brine, John. *The Certain Efficacy of the Death of Christ Asserted . . . in Answer to a Book Called "The Ruin and Recovery of Mankind"* [by Isaac Watts]. London: Aaron Ward, 1743.

Brown, Raymond. *The English Baptists of the Eighteenth Century*. A History of the English Baptists. Vol. 2. Edited by B. R. White. London: The Baptist Historical Society, 1986.

Burch, Jarrett. *Adiel Sherwood: Baptist Antebellum Pioneer in Georgia*. Baptists: History, Literature, Theology, Hymns. Edited by Walter B. Shurden. Macon, GA: Mercer, 2003.

Bush, Russ, L., and Thomas J. Nettles. *Baptists and the Bible*. Rev. and exp. ed. Nashville: B&H, 1999.

Calvin, John. *Institutes of the Christian Religion*. Translated by Henry Beveridge. 2 vols. Grand Rapids: Eerdmans, 1953.

Carey, Samuel Pearce. *William Carey: 1761–1834*. London: Hodder & Stoughton, [1923 publication date according to other sources].

Carey, William. *An Enquiry into the Obligations of Christians to Use Means for the Conversion of the Heathens*. Leicester: Ann Ireland, 1792; facsimile edition, London: Baptist Missionary Society, 1942.

Chute, Anthony L. *A Piety above the Common Standard: Jesse Mercer and the Defense of Evangelical Calvinism*. Baptists: History, Literature, Theology, Hymns. Edited by Walter B. Shurden. Macon, GA: Mercer, 2004.

Clipsham, E. F. "Andrew Fuller and Fullerism: A Study in Evangelical Calvinism." *Baptist Quarterly* 20 (1963–64): 99–114, 146–54, 214–25, 268–76.

Cox, F. A., and J. Hoby. *The Baptists in America: A Narrative of the Deputation of the Baptist Union in England to the United States and Canada*. New York: Leavitt, Lord and Co., 1836.

Daniel, Curt. "Andrew Fuller and Antinomianism." Pages 74–82 in *"At the Pure Fountain of Thy Word": Andrew Fuller as an Apologist*. Edited by Michael A. G. Haykin. SBHT 6. Carlisle, UK; Waynesboro, GA: Paternoster, 2004.

———. *Hyper-Calvinism and John Gill*. Ph.D. diss., Edinburgh University, 1983.

Duncan, Pope Alexander. *Influence of Andrew Fuller on Calvinism*. Th.D. diss., The Southern Baptist Theological Seminary, 1917.

Eddins, John W., Jr. *Andrew Fuller's Theology of Grace*. Th.D. diss., The Southern Baptist Theological Seminary, 1957.

Edwards, Jonathan. *An Humble Attempt to Promote Explicit Agreement and Visible Union of God's People for the Revival of Religion and Advancement of Christ's Kingdom on Earth*. n.p., 1747.

Ella, George M. "The Evangelical Liberalism of Andrew Fuller." Unpublished article. Online: http://www.evangelica.de/The_Evangelical_Liberalism_of_Andrew_Fuller.htm.

———. *John Gill and the Cause of God and Truth*. Durham, UK: Go Publications, 1995.

———. *Law and Gospel in the Theology of Andrew Fuller*. Durham, UK: Go Publications, 1996.

———. "Why I Am Not a Follower of Andrew Fuller." Unpublished article. Online: http://wwww.evangelica.de/Why%20I%20Am%20Not%20a%20Follower%20of%20Andrew%20Fuller.htm.

———. *William Huntington, Pastor of Providence*. Darlington, UK: Evangelical Press, 1994.

Ellis, William, T. *"Billy" Sunday: The Man and His Message*. Philadelphia: Universal Book & Bible House, 1914.

Everts, W. W. "Andrew Fuller." *The Review and Expositor* 17 (1920): 408–30.

Fisher, George Park. *History of Christian Doctrine*. Edited by Charles A. Briggs and D. F. Salmond. The International Theological Library. Vol. 4. New York: Charles Scribner's Sons, 1906.

Fuller, Andrew. *The Complete Works of the Rev. Andrew Fuller with a Memoir of His Life by Andrew Gunton Fuller*. 3 vols. Edited by Joseph Belcher. Philadelphia: American Baptist Publication Society, 1845. Repr., Harrisonburg, VA: Sprinkle, 1988.

———. *The Gospel of Christ Worthy of All Acceptation: or the Obligations of Men Fully to Credit, and Cordially to Approve, Whatever God Makes Known. Wherein is Considered the Nature of Faith in Christ, and the Duty of Those Where the Gospel Comes in That Matter*. Northampton, UK: T. Dicey & Co., [1785 publication date according to other sources].

———. *The Last Remains of the Rev. Andrew Fuller: Sermons, Essays, Letters, and Other Miscellaneous Papers, Not Included in His Published Works*. Edited by J. Belcher. Philadelphia: American Baptist Publication Society, 1856.

————. *The Letters of Andrew Fuller*. Transcribed by Ernest Payne and scanned to disc by Nigel Wheeler. Originals and transcriptions in the Angus Library, Regent's Park College, Oxford, England.

Fuller, Andrew Gunton. *Andrew Fuller*. London: Hodder & Stoughton, 1882.

Fuller, Thomas Ekins. *A Memoir of the Life and Writings of Andrew Fuller: By His Grandson, Thomas Ekins Fuller*. London: J. Heaton & Son, 1863.

George, Timothy. "John Gill." Pages 11–33 in *Theologians of the Baptist Tradition*. Edited by Timothy George and David S. Dockery. Nashville: B&H, 2001.

————. "Southern Baptist Theology: Whence and Whither?" *Founders Journal* 19/20 (1995): 29–30.

George, Timothy, and Denise George, eds. *Baptist Confessions, Covenants, and Catechisms*. Library of Baptist Classics 11. Nashville: B&H, 1999.

Gerstner, J. H. *The Rational Biblical Theology of Jonathan Edwards*. 3 vols. Orlando, FL: Ligonier Ministries, 1991–93.

Gill, John. *A Body of Doctrinal Divinity: or, A System of Evangelical Truths, Deduced from the Scriptures*. 2 vols. London: n.p., 1769.

Hall, Robert, Sr. *Help to Zion's Travellers*. London: The Book Society, 1781.

Hansen, Colin. "Young, Restless, Reformed: Calvinism Is Making a Comeback—and Shaking up the Church." *Christianity Today* 50 (September 2006): 32–38.

Harris, Gerald. "Martinez Pastor [William Harrell] on National Stage Representing Georgia Baptists." *The Christian Index* 185 (October 26, 2006): 9.

Hayden, Roger. *Continuity and Change: Evangelical Calvinism among Eighteenth-Century Baptist Ministers Trained at Bristol Academy, 1690–1791*. Milton under Wychwood, Chipping Norton, Oxfordshire, UK: Nigel Lynn Publishing for the Baptist Historical Society, 2006.

————. *Evangelical Calvinism among Eighteenth-Century British Baptists, with Particular Reference to Bernard Foskett, Hugh and Caleb Evans and the Bristol Baptist Academy, 1690–1791*. Ph.D. diss., University of Keele, 1991.

Haykin, Michael A. G. "Andrew Fuller." In *Biographical Dictionary of Evangelicals*. Edited by Timothy Larsen. Leicester, England; Downers Grove, IL: Inter-Varsity, 2003.

————. *The Armies of the Lamb: The Spirituality of Andrew Fuller*. Dundas, Ontario: Joshua Press, 2001.

————, ed. *"At the Pure Fountain of Thy Word": Andrew Fuller as an Apologist*. SBHT 6. Carlisle, UK; Waynesboro, GA: Paternoster, 2004.

————. *One Heart and One Soul: John Sutcliff of Olney, His Friends and His Times*. Durham, UK: Evangelical Press, 1994.

————. "'The Oracles of God': Andrew Fuller and the Scriptures." *Churchman* 103 (1989): 60–76.

———. "Particular Redemption in the Writings of Andrew Fuller." Pages 107–28 in *The Gospel in the World: International Baptist Studies*. Edited by D. W. Bebbington. SBHT 1. Carlisle, UK; Waynesboro, GA: Paternoster, 2002.

Howson, Barry. "Andrew Fuller and Universalism." Pages 174–202 in *"At the Pure Fountain of Thy Word": Andrew Fuller as an Apologist*. Edited by Michael A. G. Haykin. SBHT 6. Carlisle, UK; Waynesboro, GA: Paternoster, 2004.

———. "The Eschatology of the Calvinistic Baptist John Gill (1697–1771) Examined and Compared." *Eusebeia: The Bulletin of the Jonathan Edwards Centre for Reformed Spirituality* 5 (2005): 33–66.

Ivimey, Joseph. *A History of the English Baptists*. 4 vols. London: Isaac Taylor Hinton, 1830.

Jarvis, Clive. "The Myth of High-Calvinism?" Pages 231–64 in *Recycling the Past or Researching History?* Edited by Philip E. Thompson and Anthony R. Cross. SBHT 11. Carlisle, UK; Waynesboro, GA: Paternoster, 2005.

Kevan, Ernest F. *The Grace of the Law: A Study of Puritan Theology*. London: Carey Kingsgate Press, 1976. Repr., Morgan, PA: Soli Deo Gloria Publications, 1993.

Laws, Gilbert. *Andrew Fuller: Pastor, Theologian, Ropeholder*. London: Carey Press, 1942.

Lemke, Steve W. "The Future of Southern Baptists as Evangelicals." Paper presented to the "Maintaining Baptist Distinctives Conference." Mid-America Baptist Theological Seminary, April 2005. Online: http://www.nobts.edu/Faculty/ItoRLemkeSW/Personal/SBCfuture.

Lloyd-Jones, David Martyn. "Sandemanianism." Pages 170–90 in *The Puritans: Their Origins and Successors, Addresses Delivered at the Puritan and Westminster Conferences, 1959–1978*. Edinburgh, UK; Carlisle, PA: Banner of Truth, 1987.

Lovegrove, Deryck W. *Established Church, Sectarian People: Itinerancy and the Transformation of English Dissent, 1780–1830*. Cambridge, UK: University Press, 1988.

———. "Particular Baptist Itinerant Preachers during the 18th and 19th Centuries." *Baptist Quarterly* 28 (1979): 127–41.

Lovelace, Libby. "10 Percent of SBC Pastors Call Themselves 5-Point Calvinists." Unpublished Baptist Press article. Online: http://www.bpnews.net/printerfriendly.asp?ID=23993.

Lumpkin, W. L. *Baptist Confessions of Faith*. Rev. ed. Valley Forge, PA: Judson, 1969.

Manley, Ken R. *"Redeeming Love Proclaim": John Rippon and the Baptists*. SBHT 12. Carlisle, UK; Waynesboro, GA: Paternoster, 2004.

McBeth, Harry Leon. *The Baptist Heritage: Four Centuries of Baptist Witness*. Nashville: Broadman, 1987.

McGlothlin, W. J. *Baptist Confessions of Faith*. Philadelphia: American Baptist Publication Society, 1911.

McMullen, Michael, ed. *The Diary of Andrew Fuller*. In *The Complete Works of Andrew Fuller*. Vol. 1. Edited by Michael A. G. Haykin. Carlisle, UK; Waynesboro, GA: Paternoster, forthcoming.

Mercer, Jesse. *Letters Addressed to the Rev. Cyrus White; In Reference to His Scriptural View of the Atonement. By His Friend and Fellow Labourer in the Gospel of Christ*. Washington, GA: Printed at the News Office, 1830.

Meyers, John Brown, ed. *The Centenary Volume of the Baptist Missionary Society, 1792–1892*. London: Baptist Missionary Society, 1892.

Mohler, R. Albert, Jr. "The Call for Theological Triage and Christian Maturity." *The Tie* 74 (2006): 2–3.

———. "The Pastor as Theologian." *The Tie* 74 (2006): i.

Morden, Peter J. "Andrew Fuller (1754–1815) and the Revival of Eighteenth-Century Particular Baptist Life." M.Phil. thesis, Spurgeon's College, University of Wales, 2000.

———. "Andrew Fuller as an Apologist for Missions." Pages 237–55 in *'At the Pure Fountain of Thy Word': Andrew Fuller as an Apologist*. Ed. Michael A. G. Haykin. SBHT 6. Carlisle, UK; Waynesboro, GA: Paternoster, 2004.

———. *Offering Christ to the World: Andrew Fuller and the Revival of Eighteenth-Century Particular Baptist Life*. SBHT 8. Carlisle, UK; Waynesboro, GA: Paternoster, 2003.

Morris, J. W., ed. *Memoirs of the Life and Writings of the Rev. Andrew Fuller*. 2nd. ed. London: Wightman & Cramp, 1826.

———. *Miscellaneous Pieces on Various Subjects Collected and Arranged by J. W. Morris: Intended as a Supplement to His Memoirs of the Author* [Andrew Fuller]. London: Wightman & Cramp, 1826.

———. *Periodical Accounts Relative to a Society, Formed among the Particular Baptists, for Propagating the Gospel among the Heathen*. 3 vols. London: J. W. Morris, 1800.

Murray, Iain H. *Revival and Revivalism: The Making and Marring of American Evangelicalism: 1750–1858*. Edinburgh, UK; Carlisle, PA: Banner of Truth, 1994.

Nettles, Thomas J. "Andrew Fuller (1754–1815)." Pages 97–141 in *The British Particular Baptists 1638–1910*. Vol. 2. Edited by Michael A. G. Haykin. Springfield, MO: Particular Baptist Press, 2000.

———. *By His Grace and for His Glory: A Historical, Theological, and Practical Study of the Doctrines of Grace in Baptist Life*. 2nd. ed. Lake Charles, LA: Cor Meum Tibi, 2002. Rev. and exp. 20th anniv. ed., Cape Coral, FL: Founders Press, 2006.

——. "Christianity Pure and Simple: Andrew Fuller's Contest with Socinianism." Pages 138–73 in *"At the Pure Fountain of Thy Word": Andrew Fuller as an Apologist*. Edited by Michael A. G. Haykin. SBHT 6. Carlisle, UK; Waynesboro, GA: Paternoster, 2004.

Noll, Mark. "Jonathan Edwards." Pages 366–68 in *Evangelical Dictionary of Theology*. Edited by Walter A. Elwell. 2nd ed. Grand Rapids: Baker; Carlisle: Paternoster, 2001.

——. "New England Theology." In *Evangelical Dictionary of Theology*. 2nd ed. Edited by. Walter A. Elwell. Grand Rapids; Carlisle, UK: Paternoster, 2001.

Nuttall, G. F. "Northamptonshire and *The Modern Question*: A Turning-Point in Eighteenth-Century Dissent." *Journal of Theological Studies* 16 (1965): 101–23.

——. "'The State of Religion in Northamptonshire (1793)' By Andrew Fuller." *Baptist Quarterly* 29 (1980): 177–79.

Oliver, Robert W. "Andrew Fuller and Abraham Booth." Pages 203–22 in *"At the Pure Fountain of Thy Word": Andrew Fuller as an Apologist*. Edited by Michael A. G. Haykin. SBHT 6. Carlisle, UK; Waynesboro, GA: Paternoster, 2004.

——. "The Emergence of a Strict and Particular Baptist Community among the English Calvinistic Baptists, 1770–1850." D.Phil. thesis, London Bible College, 1986.

——. *History of the English Calvinistic Baptists 1771–1892: From John Gill to C. H. Spurgeon*. Edinburgh, UK; Carlisle, PA: Banner of Truth, 2006.

Osborne, Grant R. *The Hermeneutical Spiral: A Comprehensive Introduction to Biblical Interpretation*. Downers Grove, IL: InterVarsity, 1991.

Owen, John. *The Death of Death in the Death of Christ: A Treatise in Which the Whole Controversy about Universal Redemption Is Fully Discussed*. London: Banner of Truth, 1959.

Packer, J. I. *The Redemption and Restoration of Man in the Thought of Richard Baxter: A Study in Puritan Theology*. Studies in Evangelical History and Thought. Carlisle, UK: Paternoster, 2003.

Paine, Thomas. *The Age of Reason: Being an Investigation of True and Fabulous Theology*. Chicago: Belfords, Clarke & Co., 1897.

Payne, Ernest A. *The Baptist Union: A Short History*. London: Kingsgate, 1959.

Piper, John. "Holy Faith, Worthy Gospel, World Vision: Andrew Fuller's Broadsides against Sandemanianism, Hyper-Calvinism, and Global Unbelief." An address delivered at the Desiring God 2007 Conference for Pastors, Bethlehem Baptist Church, Minneapolis, MN, February 6, 2007.

Price, Nelson. "Evangelical Calvinism Is an Oxymoron." *The Christian Index* 185 (November 23, 2006): 8–9.

Priest, Gerald L. "Andrew Fuller, Hyper-Calvinism, and the 'Modern Question.'" Pages 43–73 in *"At the Pure Fountain of Thy Word": Andrew Fuller as an Apologist*.

Edited by Michael A. G. Haykin. SBHT 6. Carlisle: UK; Waynesboro, GA: Paternoster, 2004.

——. "Andrew Fuller's Response to the 'Modern Question'—a Reappraisal of *The Gospel Worthy of all Acceptation.*" *Detroit Baptist Seminary Journal* 6 (2001): 45–73.

Prochaska, Franklyn K. "Thomas Paine's *The Age of Reason* Revisited." *Journal of the History of Ideas* 22 (1972): 561–76.

Richards, Wiley W. *The Winds of Doctrine: The Origin and Development of Southern Baptist Theology*. Lanham, MD: University Press of America, 1991.

Rinaldi, Frank. *"The Tribe of Dan": A Study of the New Connexion of General Baptists, 1770–1891*. SBHT 10. Carlisle, UK; Waynesboro, GA: Paternoster, 2005.

Roberts, Philip R. "Andrew Fuller." Pages 34–51 in *Theologians of the Baptist Tradition*. Rev. ed. Edited by Timothy George and David S. Dockery. Nashville: B&H, 2001.

——. *Continuity and Change: London Calvinistic Baptists and the Evangelical Revival: 1760–1820*. Wheaton: Richard Owen Roberts, 1989.

Robison, O. C. "The Particular Baptists in England: 1760–1820." D.Phil. diss., Regent's Park College, Oxford, 1986.

Ryland, John, Jr. *The Work of Faith, the Labour of Love, and the Patience of Hope, Illustrated; in the Life and Death of the Rev. Andrew Fuller*. 2nd ed. Charleston: Samuel Etheridge, 1818.

Sandeman, Robert. *Letters on Theron and Aspasio. Addressed to the Author* [James Hervey]. 2 vols. Edinburgh: Sands, Donaldson, Murray, and Cochran, 1757.

Schaff, Philip. *The Creeds of Christendom with a History and Critical Notes*. 4th rev. ed. New York: Harper & Bros., 1877. Repr., Grand Rapids: Baker, 1950.

Sell, Alan P. F. "Andrew Fuller and the Socinians." *Enlightenment and Dissent* 19 (2000): 91–115. [Festschrift issue for D. O. Thomas]

——. *"The Gospel Its Own Witness*: Deism, Thomas Paine, and Andrew Fuller." Pages 111–43 in *Enlightenment, Ecumenism, Evangel: Theological Themes and Thinkers 1550–2000*. Studies in Christian History and Thought. Carlisle, UK; Waynesboro, GA: Paternoster, 2005.

——. *The Great Debate: Calvinism, Arminianism, and Salvation*. Eugene, OR: Wipf & Stock, 1998.

Smith, A. C. "The Spirit and the Letter of Carey's Catalytic Watchword." *Baptist Quarterly* 33 (1989–90): 226–37.

South, Thomas Jacob. "The Response of Andrew Fuller to the Sandemanian View of Saving Faith." Th.D. diss., Mid-America Baptist Theological Seminary, 1993.

Spurgeon, C. H. *The Metropolitan Tabernacle: Its History and Work*. London: n.p., 1876.

Stanley, Brian. *The History of the Baptist Missionary Society: 1792–1992*. Edinburgh, UK: T&T Clark, 1992.

Stetzer, Ed. "Disturbing Trends in Baptisms." Unpublished paper. Online: http://www.namb.net/site/apps/nl/contents3.asp?c=9qKILUOzEpH&b=1594357&ct=31984.

Strong, Augustus H. *Systematic Theology: A Compendium*. One-vol. ed. Old Tappan, NJ: Revell, 1907.

Strong, Thomas L., III. "Mentoring in a Seminary Community." Paper presented at the Ola Farmer Lenaz Faculty Lectures, New Orleans Baptist Theological Seminary, New Orleans, Louisiana, May 20, 1999. Online: http://www.baptistcenter.com/Church-Resources.html.

Sweeney, Douglas A., and Allen C. Guelzo, eds. *The New England Theology: from Jonathan Edwards to Edwards Amasa Park*. Grand Rapids: Baker, 2006.

Taylor, Abraham. *The Modern Question Concerning Repentance and Faith, Examined with Candour in Four Dialogues*. London: James Blackstone, 1742.

Thompson, Philip E. "Baptists and 'Calvinism': Discerning the Shape of the Question." *Baptist History and Heritage* 39 (2004): 61–76.

Toon, Peter. "Hyper-Calvinism." Pages 324–25 in *New Dictionary of Theology*. Edited by Sinclair B. Ferguson, David F. Wright, and J. I. Packer. Leicester, UK; Downers Grove, IL: InterVarsity, 1988.

Tull, James, E. *Shapers of Baptist Thought*. Valley Forge, PA: Judson, 1972. Repr., Macon, GA: Mercer Press, 1984.

Underwood, A. C. *A History of the English Baptists*. London: Kingsgate, 1947.

Watson, John H. "Baptists and the Bible: As Seen in Three Eminent Baptists." *Foundations* 16 (1973): 237–54.

Watts, M. R. *The Dissenters: From the Reformation to the French Revolution*. Oxford: University Press, 1978.

———. *The Dissenters: The Expansion of Evangelical Nonconformity 1791–1859*. Oxford: University Press, 1995.

Wayland, Francis. *Notes on the Principles and Practices of Baptist Churches*. New York: Sheldon, Blakeman & Co.; Boston: Gould & Lincoln; Chicago: S. C. Griggs & Co., 1857.

Weaver, C. Douglas, and Nathan A. Finn. "Youth for Calvin: Reformed Theology and Baptist Collegians." *Baptist History and Heritage* 39 (2004): 19–41.

Wells, David F. *No Place for Truth, or Whatever Happened to Evangelical Theology?* Grand Rapids: Eerdmans, 1993.

White, B. R. *The English Baptists of the Seventeenth Century*. Rev. ed. A History of the English Baptists. Vol. 1. Edited by Roger Hayden. Oxford, UK: The Baptist Historical Society, 1996.

Whitely, W. T. *Calvinism and Evangelism in England, Especially in Baptist Circles*. London: Kingsgate, n.d.

———. *A History of British Baptists*. London: Charles Griffin & Co., 1923.

Williams, William R. *Lectures on Baptist History*. Philadelphia: American Baptist Publication Society, 1877.

Yarnell, Malcolm B. III. "The TULIP of Calvinism: In Light of History and the Baptist Faith and Message." *SBC Life* 15 (April 2006): 9.

Young, Doyle. "The Place of Andrew Fuller in the Developing Modern Missions Movement." Ph.D. diss., Southwestern Baptist Theological Seminary, 1981.

———. "Andrew Fuller and the Modern Mission Movement." *Baptist History and Heritage* 17 (1982): 17–27.

# Name Index

Adams, Hannah   82, 189, 192
Akin, Daniel   172

Baxter, Richard   39, 120
Benedict, David   102–3, 107
Booth, Abraham   11, 88–89, 95
Boyce, James Petigru   4, 33, 105, 107
Brewster, Paul   xv, xvi
Brine, John   23–24, 41–42, 68, 71, 73,
    84, 98, 100, 105
Buck, Charles   189
Bunyan, John   12, 24–25, 42–43, 65,
    71, 96

Calvin, John   45, 80–81, 83, 90, 98,
    167, 175, 190–92
Carey, William   xv, 9, 27, 33–34,
    87–88, 91, 101, 119, 130–35, 137,
    140, 142–43, 155, 162
Chute, Anthony L.   103, 161, 175
Clipsham, E. F.   6, 45, 53, 66, 76, 98,
    179
Collett, John   98, 130, 181
Cox, F. A.   101–2, 106
Crisp, Tobias   90–91

Diver, Joseph   17–21

Edwards, Jonathan   xv, 17, 27, 34, 43,
    44, 48, 61–62, 78–79, 87, 95, 117,
    122, 161, 165
Eliot, John   25

Ella, George M.   69, 79, 91, 95, 100,
    163
Erskine, Ralph   12, 14
Eve, John   10–12, 16–18, 20, 24
Everts, W. W.   145, 147

Fountain, John   140, 142–44, 147,
    149, 151, 155
Fuller, Andrew   xv, xvi, 6–12, 14–35,
    37–73, 75–157, 159–70, 172–75,
    178–79, 181, 189–90, 192
Fuller, Andrew Gunton   6, 9, 23, 77
Fuller, Joseph   173
Fuller, Robert, Sr.   9
Fuller, Sarah   21

Gadsby, William   100
Gardner, Sarah   21–22, 55
George, Timothy   4, 6, 9, 65, 69, 74,
    163
Gill, John   9, 23–24, 41–43, 67–71, 73,
    76, 90, 98, 100, 105, 155, 161, 175
Glas, John   152
Grigg, Jacob   142

Haddon, Charles   33
Hall, Robert, Sr.   26–27, 29, 61, 72,
    102, 160
Haroutunian, Joseph   xv
Haykin, M. A. G.   xvi, 5, 7, 10, 17, 24,
    28–29, 33, 37, 45, 48, 62, 87, 89, 92,
    94, 131, 136, 142, 144, 147, 149, 151,
    155, 163–64

Hervey, James    98, 152
Howson, Barry    149, 160
Huntington, William    91

Johnson, P. E.    177–78
Judson, Adoniram    101

Kinghorn, Joseph    99, 160

Leland, John    107
Lemke, Steve W.    2, 174, 176–78
Lloyd–Jones, D. M.    151–54

McLean, Archibald    152
Mercer, Jesse    103–4, 175, 176
Miles, John    75
Miller, Perry    xv
Mohler, R. Albert, Jr.    2, 8, 166, 171–72
Morden, Peter J.    9, 28, 55, 65, 67, 76,
    99, 107–8, 121–22, 144, 165
Morris, Brother J. W.    6, 30–31, 48, 50,
    71–72, 109–10, 113–14, 125, 131,
    133–34, 137, 140, 144, 148, 150, 155,
    162, 169–70
Murray, I. H.    106

Nettles, T. J.    23, 51, 67, 69, 73, 95,
    105, 107, 147–48, 163–64
Newton, John    xvi

Oliver, R. W.    9, 89, 91, 95, 100–101,
    155–56
Owen, John    24, 84–85, 87

Paine, Thomas    48–49, 75, 87–88,
    145–46, 164, 167–68
Payne, Ernest A.    11, 99
Pearce, Samuel    27, 137–38

Pounds, Thomas    75
Priestly, Joseph    50, 147–48

Rice, Luther    101
Roberts, P. R.    xvi, 9, 37, 105, 166, 168
Ryland, John    6, 8, 16–18, 20, 23,
    27–28, 30–35, 46–47, 55–56, 60, 65,
    70, 73, 88–92, 98, 109–10, 114–16,
    118, 120, 123, 129–32, 141, 143, 150,
    161–62, 165, 173

Sandeman, Robert    152, 154
Sell, A. P. F.    24, 48, 120, 147
Sellers, Ian    108
Spurgeon, Charles    9, 33, 66–67, 105
Strong, L. T.    5, 61
Sunday, Billy    1, 20, 35, 46, 115–17,
    120, 123
Sutcliff, John    5, 26–28, 34, 57, 61, 76,
    88, 117–19, 132, 136–37, 139

Taylor, Abraham    24–25, 31–32, 43,
    77–78, 81–82, 95, 99, 144
Taylor, Daniel    31, 32, 81, 95, 99, 144
Thornton, Henry    143

Underwood, A. C.    37, 66, 75

Vidler, William    149–51

Wallis, Beeby    134
Wayland, Francis    105
Wells, David F.    2, 4, 168–71
William, Wilberforce    143
Williams, W. R.    144–45
Winchester, Elhanan    149
White, Cyrus    103–4
Whitley, W. T.    67

# Subject Index

accountability, theological
  method 58–63
Act of Toleration 66, 69, 75, 143
*Age of Reason* (Paine) 48–49, 87–88,
  145–46, 167
Akin, Daniel 172
American Baptists 4, 101–5, 161, 175
antinomianism 69, 91, 100, 155–56,
  183
apologist 144–56
Arminianism 45, 103, 107–8
atonement 87–89
  governmental view 163–65
  limited 85–95
  nature of 75–76
  Particular Baptist view 73–76

balance 161–62
baptism, Fuller 16–17
*Baptist Annual Register, The* 1
Baptist churches
  decline 1–6
  mentoring in 5
Baptist Missionary Society (BMS) 7,
  33, 60, 89, 110, 115, 129–30, 129–44,
  134–37, 142, 144, 152, 157, 160–62
Baptists
  interdependence 61–63
  legacy of Fuller on 97–108
  reaction against Fuller 100–101
Baxter, Richard 120
Bible 17, 39–40, 43, 45–51, 77, 81, 84,
  167–68

biblical theology 167–68
birth, Fuller 9–11
*Body of Doctrinal Divinity, A* (Gill) 41
Boyce, James Petigru 4
Brine, John 23–24, 41–42, 68, 71, 73,
  84, 98, 100, 105
British Particular Baptists 8, 65–66,
  97–99. *See also* English Particular
  Baptists
Brown, R. 71, 99, 129

Calvinism 7, 24
  evangelical 175–78
  High 10, 68
  hyper-Calvinism 18, 175
  theological dictionary entry
    on 189–92
*Calvinistic and Socinian Systems Exam-
  ined and Compared, The* 50
Carey, William 33–34, 119, 130–34
centrality, gospel 178–79
children, Fuller 21–22
Chillenden, E. 74
Christ, offering to world 76–78
Clipsham, E. F. 6, 45, 53, 98, 179
confession of faith 181–87
conservative innovator 44–45
conversion, Fuller 11–16
creeds 60–61
Crisp, Tobias 90–91
cure 111, 120–29

death, Fuller 34–35

*Defence of a Treatise Entitled The Gospel Worthy of All Acceptation, A* (Fuller)   85
defense, mission   141–44
degrees   37
deism   145–47
diary   118–20
discipleship, Fuller   16–21
Diver, Joseph   17–21
divine assistance in evangelism   128–29
doctrine to practice   109–57

Edwards, Jonathan   43
Emerging Church movement   3
English Dissenters   12, 16, 24, 58
English Particular Baptists   38, 41, 66, 85, 100, 110, 130, 155, 159. *See also* British Particular Baptists
evangelical Calvinism   175–78
evangelism, divine assistance in   128–29
Eve, John   10–11
experience, role of, in theological method   53–58
experimental religion   53–56
extravagant vagaries of enthusiasm   58

friendships, Fuller   26–28
Fuller, Andrew
  baptism   16–17
  biography   8–35
  birth   9–11
  bishopric   29–30
  call to ministry   16–21
  children   21–22
  conversion   11–16
  death   34–35
  discipleship   16–21
  early life   9–11
  friendships   26–28
  Kettering Baptist Church   28–35
  publications   32–33
  secretary to Baptist Missionary Society (BMS)   33–34

Soham Pastorate   21–28
  statement of faith   30–33
  why   6–8
  wife   21–22
Fuller, Robert, Jr.   122–24
Fuller, Robert, Sr.   9, 121
Fullerism   45, 69, 76, 99–100, 103, 107–8, 129, 163
funding for missionaries   135–37

George, Timothy   65
Gill, John   23
  hyper-Calvinist   69
God   40
gospel   168–69
  centrality   178–79
  offers to unconverted   72–73
*Gospel Worthy of All Acceptation, The* (Fuller)   32–33, 44, 62–63
governmental view of atonement   163–65

Hall, Robert, Sr.   26, 29, 72
High Calvinism   10
  widespread   68
high view of Scripture   47–51
hyper-Calvinism   18, 175

imputation   89–92
*Inquiry into the Modern Prevailing Notions . . .* (Edwards)   43
integrity in ministry   169–70
interdependence, Baptists   61–63
inward call, outward call of gospel versus   96–97
irresistible
  grace and perserverance of saints   95–97
  spirit's work   95–96
Ivimey, J.   66

Jude   165

Kettering Baptist Church   8, 28–35, 46, 49, 56, 60, 62, 105, 111, 114–19, 162, 181

legacy of Fuller on Baptists   97–108
limited atonement   85–95
local church ministry pace   173–74
*London Confession*   74, 155
Lord's Supper   55, 160, 186

Manley, K.   70
McBeth, Harry Leon   75
McKnight, S.,   3
McLean, Archibald   152
mentoring in Baptist churches   5
ministry
    call, Fuller   16–21
    integrity in   169–70
    and theology   169
missions
    defense   141–44
    funding for   135–37
*Modern Question, The* (Taylor)   31, 43
Mohler, R. Albert, Jr.   8, 166, 171–72
moral abilities, natural abilities
    versus   78–79
Morden, Peter   9, 28, 76, 121, 144, 165
Morris, J. W.   71, 113–14, 133

natural abilities versus moral
    abilities   78–79
New Testament   2, 43–44, 50, 111, 124–26, 182
Northamptonshire Baptist Associa-
    tion   26–27, 56, 61–63, 96, 120, 125, 128, 130, 132, 134

Old Testament   23
Oliver, R., 89
outward call of gospel versus inward
    call   96–97
Owen, John   24, 84, 87

Paine, Thomas   48–49, 87–88, 145–46, 167
Particular Baptists   10, 30–33. *See also*
    American Particular Baptists; British
    Particular Baptists; English Particular
    Baptists
    decline   68–69
    view of atonement   73–76
pastor   2, 110–29
pastor-theologian   159–79
    strengths as   165–70
    weakness as   161–65
Pauline Epistles   2
Pearce, Samuel   137–38
perserverance of saints   97
postmillennialism   160
prayer place   56–57
preaching
    matter and manner   112–13
    priority   110–20
    village   116–20, 143
Priestly, Joseph   50, 147–48
priority of Scripture   45–53
private judgment   58–59
pulpit work   113–16

reading Scripture   56–57
reason, role in theological
    reflection   51–53
regeneration in order of
    salvation   80–81
resistible Spirit's work   95–96
Ryland, John, Jr.   23, 27–28, 30, 34, 47, 55, 70, 88–92, 109, 114–15, 120, 130, 132

salvation order   80–81
Sandeman, Robert   152
Sandemanianism   151–56, 168
Scriptures
    high view of   47–51
    priority   45–53
    reading   56–57

secretary to Baptist Missionary Society
(BMS)   33–34
Socinianism   50, 147–49, 159, 183
Soham   10–11, 13, 16–30, 21–28, 82,
96, 114, 116
*sola Scriptura*   63
soteriology   65–108
American Baptists   101–5
British Particular Baptists   97–99
Fuller's impact   105–8
gospel offers to unconverted   72–73
high Calvinism challenge   76–97
irresistible grace and perserverance of
saints   95–97
legacy of Fuller on Baptists   97–108
limited atonement   85–95
offering Christ to world   76–78
older historical consensus   66–67
Particular Baptist view of
atonement   73–76
qualifications to historical
consensus   68–69
strict Baptist reaction against
Fuller   100–101
total depravity   78–81
unconditional election   81–85
souls, cure of   120–29
Southern Baptist Convention
(SBC)   171
Spirit's work   95–96
spiritual friendships   17
Spurgeon, Charles Haddon   33
statement of faith, Fuller's   30–33
strengths as pastor-theologian   165–70
Strong, L. T.   5
substitution   92–95
Sunday, Billy   1
Sutcliff, John   27–28, 34, 117–19, 132,
137
system   40–41
importance, theological
method   38–45

systematic theology   3

Taylor, Abraham   24–25, 43, 77
Taylor, Daniel   32, 81–82, 95, 99
theologians   2
retrieving value of   170–72
theological triage   8
theology
accountability   58–63
dictionary entry on
Calvinism   189–92
method   37–64
ministry and   169
pace of local church
ministry   173–74
priority of Scripture   45–53
reflection and reason's role   51–53
role of experience   53–58
system importance   38–45
total depravity   78–81
traditionalism pitfalls   45–47
truth
discovery   41–44
withholding   165–67

unconditional election   81–85, 84–85
unconverted, offers to   72–73
Underwood, A. C.   37
universalism   149–51
unknown identity of elect   84–85

Vidler, William   149
village preaching   116–20, 143

weakness, as pastor-theologian   161–65
Wells, David   2
Whitley, W. T.   67
wife, Fuller   21–22
Williams, W.   144